AESTHETICS AND LITERATURE

Continuum Aesthetics series editor:
Derek Matravers, Open University

Aesthetics and Architecture, Edward Winters
Aesthetics and Film, Katherine Thomson
Aesthetics and Morality, Elisabeth Schellekens
Aesthetics and Music, Andy Hamilton
Aesthetics and Nature, Glenn Parsons
Aesthetics and Painting, Jason Gaiger

AESTHETICS AND LITERATURE

DAVID DAVIES

continuum

Continuum International Publishing Group

The Tower Building
11 York Road
London SE1 7NX

80 Maiden Lane
Suite 704
New York NY 10038

www.continuumbooks.com

British Library Cataloguing-in-Publication Data
A catalogue record for this book is available from the British Library.

ISBN:
HB: 0-8264-9611-3
978-0-8264-9611-9
PB: 0-8264-9612-1
978-0-8264-9612-6

Library of Congress Cataloguing-in-Publication Data
A catalog record for this book is available from the Library of Congress.

Typeset by Kenneth Burnley, Wirral, Cheshire

CONTENTS

CONTENTS

PREFACE

In this book, I examine a range of philosophical questions that are posed by the literary arts. The philosopher's interest in literature is similar to her interest in other human practices like visual art, science, and law. In each case, she seeks to help us better understand the nature of those practices – their goals, the entities with which they deal, the standards that govern our participation in them, and the broadly ethical questions to which they give rise. In some cases, the puzzles and problems with which the philosopher wrestles are ones of which reflective participants in a practice are already aware. In other cases, she tries to bring out hitherto unremarked features of a practice which may help us better to understand its significance and the conditions for its flourishing.

This book examines four kinds of questions that philosophers have pursued with respect to literary art.

First there are 'ontological' or classificatory questions about the entities that enter into our literary practices. What kind of thing is a literary artwork? To what extent does the context in which the text of a literary artwork was composed enter into the very identity of the work? If, as is clearly the case, the majority of literary artworks are classified as works of fiction, in what does their fictionality consist? And is there a sense in which fictional characters must exist in order for us to be able to understand, and discuss, stories 'about' them?

Second, there are broadly epistemological questions that examine the sorts of rational grounds that can be provided for those claims to understand literary works that seem so central to our critical and interpretive practice. One such question concerns our understanding of fictional narratives – the grounds for claims about what is 'true in a story' – while another concerns the significance to be accorded to an author's intentions in the understanding and appreciation of her works. Should we assume that there is, at least in principle, a single 'right' interpretation of a given literary work – perhaps the interpretation intended by the author – or should we expect such works to admit of a plurality of equally 'right' but otherwise very different interpretations?

Third, a number of puzzling questions relate to our capacity, and desire, to be moved in certain ways by literary fictions. Can we feel genuine emotions for characters in a story, and, if so, does that mean that, in our imaginative engagement with a fiction, we believe it to be real? And why do we seek out fictions that seem to produce in us painful feelings of a kind that we seek to avoid in real life, such as pity and fear?

Finally, we can ask about the values offered to readers through their engagement with literary works, and the sorts of moral and legal constraints that should apply to the creation and distribution of such works. Can works of fiction give us knowledge that bears upon the extra-fictional world, and if so, how? Does literature have moral value, and if so, does the moral worth of a literary work make it better as literature? And are we justified in censoring literary works that may disturb or upset certain members of the public, either directly or indirectly?

In writing this book, I have drawn upon or extended ideas developed in other publications. The general framework for thinking about artworks introduced in Chapter 1 is more fully elaborated in chapter 3 of *Art as Performance*. Chapter 2 draws upon some themes in 'Works, Texts, and Contexts'. In both Chapters 3 and 4, I develop some points in 'Fictional Truth and Fictional Authors'. Chapter 5 contains arguments presented in 'Semantic Intentions, Utterance Meaning, and Work Meaning', forthcoming in David Davies and Carl Matheson (eds), *Contemporary Readings in the Philosophy of Literature* (Peterborough, Ont.: Broadview), and in 'Interpretive Pluralism and the Ontology of Art', *Revue internationale de philosophie* 198 (1996), 577–92. In Chapter 8, I draw upon my 'Learning through Fictional Narratives in Art and Science', under review.

CHAPTER I

THE NATURE OF LITERATURE

What is literature? As with many philosophical questions, it may seem at first glance easy to provide an answer. Literature, after all, is something a lot of us claim to enjoy and to spend our time reading, and upon whose virtues we are prepared to expound at length at parties if given half the chance. Literature is the plays of Shakespeare and Molière, the novels and short stories of Tolstoy, Dostoevsky, and Jane Austen, the poetry of T. S. Eliot, Coleridge, and Rilke . . . We could go on, but someone interrupts us by adding some of their own favourite examples: '– the Bible, Gibbon's *Decline and Fall*, Hume's *History of England*, Boswell's *Life of Johnson* –' And another voice pipes in: '– and the James Bond novels, and Harlequin Romances, and Superman comics –' And then one more voice seeking to put an end to all of this nonsense: '– and the manual for my computer, and gardening books, and the Highway Code – they're all literature!'

We want to object that these things are *not* all literature in the sense we had in mind when we introduced the topic. Our conversational partners, we protest, are wrong to classify all of the things they mention as literature. But we are soon forced to withdraw the accusation of misuse of the term 'literature', for all of the things they have cited *are* correctly described as literature in certain linguistic contexts. So now we must try to distinguish different senses in which something can rightly be said to be literature, corresponding to the different kinds of discursive contexts to which our partners have appealed. Were we able to prevail upon them to remain as Socratic interlocutors in a further examination of these issues, how should we proceed?

We should begin by granting that the term 'literature' has at least three different senses. In what we might term the *broad* sense, 'literature' refers to any body of writing that has a shared topic. It is in this sense that we talk of the literature on shampooing carpets, or indeed, of the literature on the nature of literature! Perhaps (though this is less clear) we can in this sense refer to Superman comics as 'the Superman literature', although this is more naturally read as referring to (scholarly?) books *about* the comic-book hero, rather than to the comics themselves. A related use of the term refers to any piece of writing that has a generally informative role – for example, the 'promotional literature' for a new software program, or the 'instructional literature' for installing the new program on your computer. Since, in the right context, almost any piece of writing can count as literature in the broad sense, it is unlikely that anything more illuminating than the preceding remarks will be forthcoming if we ask how literature differs from non-literature understood in this way. Nor should we expect there to be interesting philosophical questions about literature so construed.

Literature, in the sense that interests us, picks out a narrower class of writings that possess, or are presented as possessing, some qualities that we value over and above their being useful to us in a particular practical context. In this sense, writings on shampooing carpets are most unlikely to qualify as *literature*, while *Hamlet*, *War and Peace*, and *The Decline and Fall of the Roman Empire* might be offered as paradigm cases that do so qualify. But here again we need to distinguish different senses in which certain writings can count as literature in this narrower sense. Often, when questions are raised about the nature of literature, our interest is in delimiting those writings that might be studied in courses on literature taught in Arts faculties at colleges and universities, analogous to the task of delimiting those daubed canvasses that might be studied in college courses on visual art. To be literature, in this sense, is to be a literary artwork. We may term this the *artistic* sense of the term. To ask about the nature of literature in the artistic sense is to ask what makes a piece of writing a literary artwork. What we are now seeking is a principled distinction between novels, poems, and plays, for example, and scientific articles, biographies, essays, comics, and advertising material. This is indeed a distinction that has interested many writers, and it is literature in the artistic sense that we tried to define 'extensionally' by offering examples.

But the term 'literature' is also often used evaluatively in what we may term the *extended* sense, to include not only literary artworks but also writings in non-artistic genres – travel writing, essays, some works of philosophy and history – that are taken to share with literary artworks some of the qualities for which the latter are valued. It is in this sense that Terry Eagleton cites, as examples of seventeenth-century English literature, not just the works of Shakespeare, Webster, Marvel, and Milton, but also 'the essays of Francis Bacon, the sermons of John Donne, Bunyan's spiritual autobiography', and even philosophical and historical works such as Hobbes' *Leviathan* and Clarendon's *History of the Rebellion*.[1] Eagleton's own conclusion is that literature in the extended sense is just 'a highly valued kind of writing',[2] where this, in turn, will reflect the things that are valued in a given culture. All other proposed criteria of literariness, he maintains, fail to capture what falls in the extension of the term.

It is important, however, not to conflate the question Eagleton answers negatively – is there an objective criterion of literariness in the extended sense? – with the question, are there any distinguishing characteristics of the literary artwork? This is particularly important if, as suggested above, we see the extended sense of the term 'literature' as an extension of its artistic sense, so that certain pieces of writing that are not literary art qualify as literature in the extended sense in virtue of possessing qualities valued in literary artworks. It is also important because it is with literature in the artistic sense that this study will be principally concerned.

Some would argue that the notion of literary art is as culturally inflected as the notion of literature in the extended sense, and that the distinction between literary artworks and other works of literature in the extended sense is a matter of convenience and convention rather than principle. Consider, for example, the difficulty we experience in classifying much recent writing that employs many of the distinctive characteristics of literary art for more standardly non-artistic purposes. A couple of examples may help here. Truman Capote's *In Cold Blood* is often heralded as initiating a new kind of writing, journalistic in purpose yet employing the distinctive linguistic figures and structures of literary art. The opening lines of *In Cold Blood* could easily be drawn from a twentieth century American novel:

> Until one morning in mid-November, few Americans – in fact few Kansans – had ever heard of Holcomb. Like the waters of the river, like the motorists on the highway, and like the yellow trains streaking down the Santa Fe tracks, drama, in the shape of exceptional happenings, had never stopped there.[3]

Similarly, in his book *The New Journalism*, Tom Wolfe discusses the use of an autobiographical approach in Norman Mailer's *Armies of the Night*, whereby Mailer turns himself into a character in the story.

The same device is found in the writings of one of the most notorious 'new journalists', Hunter S. Thompson, whose *Fear and Loathing in Las Vegas* begins with the sentence: 'We were somewhere around Barstow on the edge of the desert when the drugs began to take hold.'[4]

With these examples in mind, we can consider possible answers to the question, what makes a piece of writing a literary artwork – what makes something literature in the artistic sense? As we noted earlier, this seems analogous to questions we can ask of works in the other arts – what makes some paint-daubed canvasses, photographs, and assemblages of objects works of painting, photography, and sculpture, while other superficially similar entities are not? We might think that, in each case, we can explain what makes certain things works of art by, first, identifying a particular *medium* – pigment on a surface, language, bronze, sound structures, for example – and then saying what makes a particular entity that results from the manipulation of that medium *art*. Of course, we may have to explain how certain works of contemporary visual art fail to count as literary works even though they utilize language. For example, a famous painting by Magritte depicts a pipe beneath which are inscribed the words 'Ceci n'est pas un pipe'. Is it only the sheer volume of words in a novel by Dickens, with illustrations by Boz, that makes this a work of literature rather than a work of visual art? More troubling still are some late-modern and 'conceptual' works. Fiona Banner's *Break Point*, for example, short-listed for the Turner Prize in 2002, is a large canvas, 2.7 × 4.25 metres, upon which a lengthy text, expressive of an erotic stream of consciousness, is inscribed, line by line, in red marker pen and acrylic.

We might say that language can be *used* by a visual artist in her paintings without being, in the relevant sense, the medium of her works. This, however, requires that we explain what it is for something to be the medium of an artwork. An answer might be that the medium of a work is the means whereby the salient, contentful artistic properties are realized in the work – the means whereby certain things are represented or expressed, for example. As may be clear, however, a lot more will need to be said if this kind of explanation is to be persuasive. Fortunately, we can postpone further investigation of these questions until later in this chapter. As we shall see, answers to these questions require the same sorts of resources as are needed to answer our original question: what is it that makes the product of certain kinds of manipulations of the linguistic medium a literary artwork?

One suggestion is that literary works differ in their *content*, being pieces of fictional writing. (We shall look at what makes something *fictional* in Chapter 3.) But this clearly isn't sufficient. Jokes ('A panda goes into a restaurant and orders a meal . . .'), philosophical thought experiments ('Suppose that a demented scientist removed your brain while you slept and placed it in a vat . . .'), scientific thought experiments (see Chapter 8) and comic strips are usually viewed as fictions, but not as literary artworks. Also, some literary works, such as works of lyric poetry, seem to be non-fictional in their subject-matter. So being fictional doesn't seem to be necessary either.

This suggests an alternative criterion of literary art, namely, the *style* of a piece of writing. This answer was favoured by the Russian Formalists, one of whom, Roman Jakobson, defined literature as 'organised violence committed on ordinary speech'.[5] Literary writing in the artistic sense, they claimed, deliberately departs from ordinary speech, and relies for its effects on this disruption, which forces us to read it differently and to reflect on our ordinary comprehension of language and of the world. While this seems to be an implausible characterization of most literary prose, it is not difficult to find examples of poetic art that lend themselves to such a description. The first stanza of Gerard Manley Hopkins' 'The Sea and the Skylark', for example, runs as follows:

> On ear and ear two noises too old to end
> > Trench—right, the tide that ramps against the shore;
> > With a flood or a fall, low lull-off or all roar,
> Frequenting there while moon shall wear and wend.[6]

And the opening stanza of Dylan Thomas' 'Fern Hill' is similarly impenetrable to normal reading:

> Now as I was young and easy under the apple boughs
> About the lilting house and happy as the grass was green,
> > The night above the dingle starry,
> > Time let me hail and climb
> > Golden in the heydays of his eyes,
> And honoured among wagons I was prince of the apple towns
> And once below a time I lordly had the trees and leaves
> > Trail with daisies and barley
> Down the rivers of the windfall light.[7]

A related view was defended by the American 'New Critics', who took as their focus the 'literary use' of language – the use of distinctive rhythms, syntax, sound patterns, imagery, metaphor, tropes, ambiguity, and irony. Literary artworks are to be distinguished in terms of their possession of these features, in virtue of which they lend themselves to a particular kind of close reading that focuses on relationships within the text.[8]

A first difficulty with such a view is that, even if we restrict ourselves to the field of poetry, we can find parts of poems, and even entire poems, that do not seem to commit any violence on ordinary speech, but merely to reflect it, and that are not distinctive in their use of 'literary language'. T. S. Eliot's *The Waste Land*, for example, contains over thirty lines of uninterrupted 'ordinary conversation' set, it seems, in a pub. The opening lines will convey the overall flavour of the passage:

When Lil's husband got demobbed, I said –
I didn't mince my words, I said to her myself,
HURRY UP PLEASE IT'S TIME
Now Albert's coming back, make yourself a bit smart,
He'll want to know what you've done with the money he gave you
To get yourself some teeth. He did, I was there.
You have them all out, Lil, and get a nice set,
He said, I swear, I can't bear to look at you,
And no more can't I, I said . . .[9]

Of course, this passage occurs in the context of a poem with many other lines that do display semantic and syntactic features we wouldn't encounter in ordinary uses of language, but this doesn't explain what the lines in question are doing in Eliot's poem. Furthermore, there are contemporary 'prose poems' that not only are composed entirely of what might pass as ordinary prose, but also eschew standard poetic conventions. Consider, for example, Michael Palmer's 'A Mistake':

I mistakenly killed a man some years ago. I do not mean that I killed him by mistake, since I killed him intentionally. I mean that it was a mistake to kill him. I slit his throat with a serrated hunting knife I then always carried. It was in front of a Chinese laundry on Manhattan's Lower East Side. I thought he had called me 'little dago boy,' though in fact, as others later attested, he had called out,

'Hey, little day-glo boy,' in playful reference to the bright colour of my shirt.[10]

This testifies to a more fundamental problem with any attempt to characterize literary art – even for an art form like poetry – in terms of stylistic features of the writing. In literature, as in the other arts, accepted features of artistic style are always open to challenge by artists who produce artworks that deliberately depart from the received style. We see this, for example, in the intentionally flat and 'objective' writing of French 'new novelists' such as Alain Robbe-Grillet and Nathalie Sarraute. We also see it in the short stories of Jorge Luis Borges which deliberately adopt for fictional purposes the academic style found in professional journals, complete with scholarly footnotes and erudite references. Furthermore, it seems that writers in fields that we would not naturally classify as artistic can employ stylistic devices of the sort celebrated by the formalists. This applies to 'new journalists' like Capote, Mailer, Wolfe, and Thompson, as noted above. Perhaps some works of 'new journalism' are properly viewed as works of literary art, but it is questionable whether this conclusion should be forced upon us by the kinds of linguistic resources upon which they draw. Nor would we say that I can turn this sentence into poetry by breaking it up into four separate lines placed one after another, nor indeed, that, in virtue of being presented in such a fashion, my shopping list is a poem.

Some have concluded that there is no distinctive class of 'literary artworks', but only distinctive 'literary' ways of *reading* texts – for example, attending to the very features of 'writing' to which the formalists and the New Critics drew our attention. The suggestion, then, is that a text is a literary artwork just in case we choose to read it in a certain way. For some theorists, this way of reading is institutionalized and historically contingent, a set of operations and procedures to which texts are subjected by those who belong to a particular tradition of literary criticism. Michel Foucault associates the kinds of critical practices celebrated by the New Critics with the contemporary conception of an author. Certain classes of texts, Foucault maintains, become associated with what he terms the 'author function',[11] something he feels we should overcome in order to allow greater freedom to readers and a corresponding proliferation of interpretations of works. We shall return to some of these issues in Chapter 5. But, in the present context, we may note that, if something is a literary work purely because of cultural conventions as to how texts are to be read, this seems to elide an important distinction between something's *being* a literary artwork, and its *being treated as* a literary artwork. And, it might also be noted, the decision to adopt a particular strategy in reading a particular text seems to reflect a prior expectation that the text in question is profitably approached through such a strategy, an expectation which seems to reflect, in turn, a prior classification of certain texts as literary artworks.

This suggests that we might try to distinguish literary artworks from other texts not in terms of how they are or might be read, but in terms of how their authors *intended* them to be read. Suppose that, as was just suggested, there exist, in given cultural contexts, established ways of treating certain classes of texts, corresponding to the sorts of reading strategies described by the New Critics. We could further elaborate this story by talking about the sorts of values made possible by engaging in such readings, perhaps also explaining, in this way, why such practices have evolved. We might point, for example, to certain 'aesthetic' values whose realization is furthered by the reader's attention to formal properties of texts and the use of various figures of speech; to moral values to be pursued through a broadly 'humanistic' approach to texts; to certain kinds of pleasure that attend the sort of imaginative engagement with a text promoted by the reading strategies informally 'institutionalized' in a culture; or to certain cognitive values furthered by such strategies. It could then be argued that works of literary art are texts that are intended by their authors to furnish such values to readers who adopt the relevant kinds of reading strategies. This allows both for something's being treated as a literary artwork when it is not (because the required general intentions were not instrumental in its history of making), and also for flawed or downright bad works of literary art (where an author fails to produce something that readers find valuable in the relevant ways when they adopt the intended reading strategies).

But, even if we bring authorial intentions into the picture in this way, the challenge is to say what is distinctive about the ways in which literary artworks are intended to be read, especially given the broad disagreement in the scholarly community as to how such works *should* be read. Is there any common core to the reading strategies that have been proposed by literary theorists, and is this core sufficiently distinctive to allow us to distinguish an intention that a work be read in line with one such strategy from the intention that a text be read as a work of literature in the extended sense – as a work of history or of philosophy, for example? What is it, if anything, about the way in which a text is intended to function that could make that text a literary artwork?

In trying to get to grips with this question, it will be helpful to begin by looking at how we might answer analogous questions which present themselves in relation to other art forms. If asked to say what makes a sequence of bodily movements a performance of a work of dance, for example, the natural response is to maintain that the sequence is composed of more specific movements or routines for which we can, if we are aficionados of the art of dance, provide labels such as – in the case of the ballet – 'plié', 'glissade', 'battement', 'pas de chat', etc. This suggests that the arthood of a dance consists in the distinctive nature of the elementary movements of which it is composed and the manner in which those elementary movements are organized. This is the analogue of the claim, criticized above, that the arthood of a piece of writing consists in its distinctive semantic and/or syntactic properties. But, analogous to our examples of literary artworks indistinguishable in such terms from non-works, we find in the modern dance repertoire works consisting of sequences of movements indistinguishable, *as such sequences*, from sequences of movements that are not enactments of a work of dance. Consider Yvonne Rainer's *Room Service*, where the dancers work in three teams performing a series of ordinary movements that involve, among other things, the moving, arranging, and rearranging of objects such as mattresses and ladders. In a paper that cites Rainer's work, Noel Carroll and Sally Banes, who attended a performance of the piece, remark that one of the central elements in the performance is 'the activity of two dancers carrying a mattress up an aisle in the theatre, out one exit, and back in through another'.[12] Crucially, the movements of the dancers were in no visible way intensified so as to differentiate them from ordinary activities such as moving a mattress around in a sequence of rooms.

What, then, makes the sequence of movements prescribed by Rainer a work of dance, such that the execution of that sequence of movements by the members of her troupe is properly viewed as a performance of the work? To say that the sequence is a dance because it is prescribed by a choreographer, or that the performance is a performance of a work of dance because of its institutional setting, is to beg all of the interesting questions. What is it, for example, to prescribe a sequence of movements as a dance, if the movements prescribed can be the kinds of movements that we execute in our ordinary daily lives? And what is the significance, for the audience, of watching the given sequence of movements being presented in a theatre rather than in, say, a furniture showroom or a gymnasium? And if Rainer were to have given an aerobics class in which she prescribed the same sequence of movements, would this have been a work of dance just in virtue of her other work as a choreographer? Carroll and Banes comment on the piece as follows:

> The point of the dance is to make ordinary movement qua ordinary movement perceptible. The audience observes the performers navigating a cumbersome object, noting how the working bodies adjust their muscles, weights, and angles . . . The *raison d'être* of the piece is to display the practical intelligence of the body in pursuit of a mundane goal-oriented type of action – moving a mattress.[13]

They also note that one can find many other examples of dances of this sort – they term them 'task-dances' – produced by choreographers in the late 1960s and the following decades.

This suggests that, put in simple terms, the sequence of movements prescribed by Rainer is a work of dance because of how she wanted her intended audience – people familiar with the more general traditions of the dance – to respond to an execution of that sequence. She wanted the audience to attend to the movements with the same sort of care and intensity, and the same kind of 'artistic' interest in grasping the *point* of the movements, as they would do if they were watching a performance of a more traditional work of dance composed of the kinds of distinctive elements described above. Of course, for viewers familiar with other 'avant-garde' works of modern dance, there will be aspects of the movements prescribed by Rainer that will have a resonance, with reference to those works, that would not be there in a performance of a more traditional work of ballet or modern dance. But the general structure of the attention desired and anticipated by Rainer will be the same.

We can note a couple of features of this attention. First, there are many details of the movements to which we would pay no attention if observing two people moving a mattress in a furniture showroom, but which are significant if we attend to those movements as a work of dance. In fact, every visible inflection of the body through which the act of moving the mattress is executed is significant in this way.

We are therefore required to attend much more closely to the nuances of the movements than if we were observing the same movements executed in an ordinary setting. Second, as Carroll and Banes make clear, we are expected to look for a 'point' to the sequence of movements performed that is not merely the practical point of moving a mattress, but the point of presenting such a sequence of movements to us in a context where we are required to attend to them in the close and discriminating way just described. The actions of the dancers stand as *examples* of how the human body serves us as an instrument of our desires and purposes. By being presented to us as such examples, they also serve as a comment on our embodiment as described by Carroll and Banes.

Before drawing some general lessons from this example and bringing them to bear on our immediate topic – the nature of literary artworks – another example, this time drawn from the visual arts, may be helpful. Damien Hirst, the contemporary British visual artist, is perhaps best known for a piece whose visual manifestation in the gallery where it is exhibited is a large rectangular tank filled with formaldehyde and containing a suspended (dead) 12-foot-long tiger shark. An object looking exactly the same might be found in a natural history museum. Our question, once again, is how, in the one case, we have an art object that belongs in an art gallery, whereas in the other case we have a scientific exhibit that belongs in a natural history museum. What if we swapped them overnight? Would it matter? We should again reject any attempt to explain this in crude institutional terms, such as saying that the tank in the gallery is art because Hirst is an artist, or that it is art because it is being presented in an art gallery. Nor is it sufficient to point to the fact that, like the Rainer piece, Hirst's piece has a title – *The Physical Impossibility of Death in the Mind of Someone Living*. For what we want to know is how giving it this title somehow makes it an art object, whereas giving an indistinguishable object the title *Australian Tiger Shark* only admits it to a natural history museum.

As with the Rainer piece, the answer seems to lie in how the intended audience is supposed to respond to the object on display. Again, this is partly a matter of the attention to be paid to the visible properties of the object. When the tank is displayed in the natural history museum, our interest is directed solely to the shark, its physical properties, how it is presented as moving, etc. The tank is merely a receptacle for our object of interest. When it is displayed in the art gallery, however, Hirst presumably intends that we attend to it in the way we respond to works of visual art. When we walk around the tank, we are aware not only of the shark but also of the way in which its visual appearance is influenced by the optical properties of the transparent material of which the tank is made. The shark always appears to be pressing up against the surface closest to us, and, as we pass a corner of the tank, it appears first in duplicate and then in a position quite different from the one it appeared to occupy before we reached the corner. In other words, the shark is presented in the gallery as a physically impossible physical object, capable of occupying two spatial locations at the same time and of moving from one location to another without passing through the points in between. Given the title, we can then reflect on the *point* of the piece, the physical impossibility of the shark in the tank standing, perhaps, as a metaphor for the physical impossibility characterized in the title.

In both the Rainer and Hirst examples, we have seen how the difference between something that serves as an art object and something, indistinguishable in terms of its manifest properties, that does not so serve is to be explained in terms of how the first entity is intended to function. In the case of the art object, it is intended to function as a means of representing, expressing, or exemplifying certain things. Suppose, in order to have a general expression in terms of which we can relate different art forms to one another, we call the entity which serves as the means whereby such functions are performed the *artistic vehicle*. In Rainer's piece the artistic vehicle is a certain type of sequence of movements, tokens of which are performances of the piece. In Hirst's piece the vehicle is the tiger shark displayed in its transparent container. We can then characterize the representational, expressive, and exemplificational functions performed by the artistic vehicle as the *artistic content* which it serves to articulate. We have seen that the artist presents the artistic vehicle with the intention that it articulate a particular artistic content. (When the artist can be said to have realized her intention is one of the topics of Chapter 5.) We have also seen that, in so doing, the artist relies upon certain understandings shared with her intended audience. She assumes that the audience will know that it is supposed to treat the object in particular kinds of ways. This involves a certain degree of attention to the artistic vehicle, an interest in which properties it exemplifies, an assumption that there is a more general 'point' behind the vehicle's manifest properties, and that this point is being made by means of the piece's more obvious representational, expressive, and exemplificational properties. Finally, we have seen that the shared understandings upon which the artist relies may include knowledge of other artworks either by the same artist or by other artists whose work has related goals.

We have, in other words, not only the idea that art-making involves the articulation of a content by means of a vehicle, but also the idea that it involves certain kinds of shared understandings that enable content to be articulated in distinctive ways. These distinctive ways of articulating content were described by the philosopher Nelson Goodman as 'symptoms of the aesthetic'.[14] We have seen that close attention to the details of the artistic vehicle is necessary if we are correctly to determine the content articulated, that artistic vehicles serve to exemplify some of their properties, that many of the different properties of the vehicle contribute to the articulation of content, and finally that the vehicle not only serves a number of distinct articulatory functions, but does so in a 'hierarchical' manner, where 'higher-level' content is articulated through lower-level content. These features are characterized in more technical terms by Goodman as the 'syntactic' and 'semantic' density of the symbol system to which the artistic vehicle belongs, the use of exemplification, the relative 'repleteness' of the artistic symbol, and the serving of multiple and complexly inter-related referential functions.

The suggestion, then, is that what makes something an artwork is not, per se, the elements of which it is composed or the way in which those elements are put together, but how the assemblage of elements that make up the artistic vehicle is intended to function in the articulation of content. Cases where the artistic vehicle is not visually discriminable from something that does not serve as an artistic vehicle serve to clarify this point. But, of course, most artistic vehicles do have distinctive features that distinguish them from other entities, and artists presumably confer these features on their vehicles because they are particularly apposite for the articulation of content in an 'aesthetic' way, given the shared understandings within the relevant artistic community as to how one should 'take' an artistic vehicle. It doesn't follow from this, however, that we have art wherever we have the articulation of content in an 'aesthetic' way, as measured by Goodman's 'symptoms'. First, as I suggested above, we should restrict the term 'artwork' to those entities that are intended by their creators to articulate their content in an 'aesthetic' manner. Second, I have suggested that artists articulate the content of their pieces by drawing upon shared understandings as to how the artistic vehicle is to be apprehended. These shared understandings, which might be termed an *artistic medium*, provide a basis for the articulation of content in a distinctively 'aesthetic' way. But (1) one may draw on these understandings yet fail, either deliberately or by incompetence, to articulate a content in an 'aesthetic' way. In the first case, we have avant-garde art, and in the second bad art, but in both cases, we have works of art. Further, (2) one may use something as a vehicle to articulate content in an 'aesthetic' way without drawing upon an artistic medium, in which case one has an object that functions as an aesthetic symbol, but not a work of art. Goodman did not grant this point, but I think it is important if our sense of what makes something an artwork is not to depart in unnecessary ways from our ordinary understanding of the term.

Let us now return to our immediate subject of investigation. Can we answer our question about what makes something a literary artwork in the way we have answered parallel questions for works of visual art and for works of dance? I think we can, and I shall illustrate this with reference to the poetic examples that were introduced earlier in our discussion. Consider, first, the passage from Eliot. The string of words that we might have encountered on a night out at the pub in the early 1920s is intended to function in certain distinctive ways. We assume that the choice of words is to be taken as deliberate, and that we are not to overlook grammatical infelicities as we might do in ordinary conversation. More significantly, the string of words is used to exemplify its banality, its crudity, its conversational vacuity, and its lack of broader cultural relevance. In this sense, the specific words employed are not important – other words would have served these exemplificational functions just as well. But, in exemplifying these properties, the passage expresses the broader thematic meaning of the poem reflected in its title – the falling away from culture and tradition which Eliot finds in contemporary life, the lack of cultural and spiritual values, etc. While the words of the conversation are not crucial to its exemplificationary role, we still read them with a close attention that they would not receive if overheard in a pub, for they occur as part of a larger text that we read in this way. In this respect, our reading has the capacity to enrich the conversation serving as the textual vehicle, for our reading brings out relationships between the words, resonances with words used elsewhere in the poem, etc., all of which we, as readers, take to be relevant to our appreciation of the poem.

In the case of the passage from Eliot, the writer's intention that such reading strategies should be employed is clear to the reader because the textual fragment occurs in the context of the larger poem, and because, like the rest of the poem, it is presented as verse rather than as prose. This mobilizes such reading strategies in the reader who is familiar with the 'artistic medium' of poetry. In the case of the extracts from the poems by Hopkins and Thomas, on the other hand, the 'violence' done to the language through the unusual syntax and unfamiliar semantic couplings not only serves as an additional cue as to how the text is to be read, but also generates the kinds of qualities celebrated as 'literary' by the New Critics. We may note, for example, the ambiguity of Hopkins' constructions. The uncertain grammatical status of 'trench' in the second line – is it a verb or a noun? – and the uncertainty as to how 'right' relates to 'trench', allow different meanings to play off one another. Also, the sounds of the words become relevant to the content articulated through the text, as artistic vehicle – the homophonies of 'two', 'too', and 'to' in the first line, for example, or the assonance and alliteration in the third line, with its talk of 'a flood or a fall, low lull-off or all roar' also sonically representing the sounds of the sea verbally represented elsewhere in the stanza. Or again, in the Thomas poem, the knotting together of unassociated expressions, as in 'windfall light', which pick up on the earlier talk of apple orchards.

What should be clear even from these few examples is the ways in which poetic texts demand, for their appreciation, techniques of reading which allow the texts to function as 'aesthetic symbols' in the sense introduced in our discussion of dance and visual art. We take account of a much fuller range of properties of the words used – their cultural resonance, their associations, their sounds, for example – and we take account of what a given string of words can be taken to exemplify, qua string, and not merely of what the words 'mean'. We also take the content articulated at more immediate levels to contribute towards the higher-order thematic content of the piece, the 'point' of the piece that we expect to uncover in our reading. Furthermore, the higher-level content is not articulated explicitly, as might be the case if we were simply giving examples in support of a general conclusion, but has to be determined by the reader through close attention to the lower-level articulatory functions performed by the artistic vehicle. As with dance and visual art, then, it is our understanding, in encountering a poem, that we are supposed to attend to it in these sorts of ways – that, in Goodman's terms, we are supposed to treat the text as replete, semantically and syntactically dense, exemplificational, and complexly referential – which explains the different kinds of functions that a given text performs if taken to be the vehicle of a poetic artwork. As before, I suggest that it is in virtue of the creator's intention that the text be approached through such reading strategies that the text serves as the vehicle of a poetic artwork.

Of course, poems are only one kind of literary artwork, and most of us are more familiar with prose works such as novels and performed works such as plays. How can the proposed account of what it is to be a literary artwork be applied to these other examples? I shall not answer this question here. But the issue will be addressed, albeit indirectly, in later chapters. First, in Chapter 4, we shall see how our attempts to understand the narratives in fictional works of literary art require that we take account of the more thematic content of the work. Second, in Chapter 8, in looking at the claims of the literary cognitivist, we shall examine the distinctive ways in which literary fictions contribute to our understandings of the world.

In summary, then, I have suggested that literary artworks are to be distinguished not in terms of their distinctive contents, nor in terms of their distinctive style or syntax, but in terms of how, in virtue of their linguistic composition, they are intended to function as vehicles for the articulation of content. The more manifest features of literary artworks – the prosodic structures of poems, the syntactic dislocation of certain works of which the formalists spoke, the use of certain 'figures' of speech, of metaphor, and of ambiguity – are means whereby content is articulated, but can serve as such means only given shared understandings as to how the linguistic text is to be read. These understandings are assumed by the writer, and must be grasped by the reader if she is to 'get' the work.

CHAPTER 2

WHAT IS A LITERARY WORK?

THE ONTOLOGICAL ISSUE

Literary artworks, we have seen, are to be distinguished from works of literature in the extended or broad sense by the ways in which their makers seek to articulate content through a linguistic vehicle. The linguistic vehicle, we have been assuming, is some kind of text. Thus, it seems, we might summarize the conclusions of Chapter 1 as follows: literary works in general are entities that articulate some content or other through a text, and literary artworks are distinguished by the *means* of articulation employed and strategies of reading intended by the author of the text. But this way of putting things, as we shall now see, leaves unaddressed some important questions about the nature of literary works, artistic and otherwise, and (as we shall see in subsequent chapters) about what is involved in the appreciation of such works. To use the philosophical terminology often employed in discussing such things, what concerns us in this chapter is the 'ontological status' of the literary work. What kind of thing, in a very general sense, is a literary work?

A helpful way to get to grips with what is at issue here is to follow the philosopher Quine who, in advancing the slogan 'no entity without identity', insisted that, if we are to have a clear idea of what a particular kind of thing is, we need to know when we have *two occurrences of the same thing* of that kind, and when we have *occurrences of two different things* of that kind. What changes in the properties of an entity are consistent with that entity's continuing to exist, and what changes are not? Some extremely difficult issues in philosophy turn upon how we should answer these questions for particular kinds of entities. For example, the problem of 'personal identity' concerns the conditions under which a given person could survive certain kinds of changes in her properties. Would I still exist if all of my memories were irreversibly erased, or if, as in some science fiction scenarios, my entire body was scanned and then copied at another location, while the body that was scanned was destroyed? A more ancient puzzle is that of Theseus' ship, which we suppose to have been rebuilt plank by plank until none of the original planks remain. If someone preserves all of the original planks and puts them together to make up a ship, which ship is Theseus' ship? Another puzzle challenges the idea that a statue is to be identified with a particularly shaped lump of clay, or of some other material. For, it might seem, we no longer have the same lump of clay if a piece breaks off and we replace it with another, identically shaped piece of clay, but, it might be argued, this change doesn't mean that we have a different statue. After all, when we 'restore' paintings that have become cracked or otherwise damaged, we assume that this *preserves* the original painting rather than leading to its replacement by a different one. So the continued existence, or 'persistence', of the statue and that of the piece of clay seem to involve different kinds of continuities in properties, and this calls into question the original claim that the statue just is the lump of clay.

It might be thought that the last of these examples challenges one of our most confident intuitions about the 'ontological status' of particular kinds of artworks. Isn't it obvious that a painting or a statue is a physical object, given such undeniable facts as that paintings hang on the walls of galleries, can be damaged by deranged individuals wielding knives or bottles of acid, can be stolen by thieves who break into galleries, etc., and that statues can be damaged, weigh a certain amount, etc.? Perhaps we can say that a painting or a statue is indeed a physical object, but that it is a kind of physical object that can preserve its identity even though there are changes in the physical elements of which it is composed. After all, don't we want to say the same thing about Theseus' ship, or, indeed, about our computers if we decide to add some memory? Paintings, we might say, are physical *artefacts*, and artefacts preserve their identity across such changes in their physical composition.

Fortunately, we don't need to dwell further on these questions in order to see that, were it to be suggested that *literary* works are physical objects, no such subtle strategems would avail. For it is obvious upon even the briefest reflection that there is no physical object which has anything like the identity and persistence conditions of a literary work. Any individual copy of a literary work – including the original manuscript – can perish without threatening the work's existence. Nor can we identify a literary work with the entire collection of physical copies of a book. For one thing, this would mean that the work was still coming into existence as long as new copies were being printed. And we surely want to insist that, even if all physical copies of a literary work were destroyed, and no new copies were ever printed, the work itself could still persist as long as it was preserved in the memory of either its author or those who had read it. For similar reasons, when we spoke, in the previous chapter, of the artistic vehicle of a literary work as a text, we cannot have meant by that a particular physical object or collection of physical objects. But what, then, did we mean?

TEXTUALISM

Philosophers who ask themselves this question often appeal to a distinction between 'types' and 'tokens' of those types. This is a distinction with which we are very familiar from our everyday dealings with the world. If I ask how many letters there are in the word 'three', there are two correct answers, corresponding to two distinct questions I might be asking. If I am asking for the number of occurrences of some letter or other in the word, the correct answer is five: 't', 'h', 'r', 'e', 'e'. If, on the other hand, I am asking how many of the 26 letters in the alphabet occur in 'three', the correct answer is four: 't', 'h', 'r', 'e'. In the second case, I am asking how many letter-*types* occur – or are 'tokened' – in the word, while in the first case I am asking how many letter-*tokens* – instances of some letter or other – occur. Furthermore, the word 'three' contains two tokens of the letter-type 'e'. Indeed, the word 'three' is itself a type, three tokens of which I might inscribe on a blackboard. Types, as generic entities that have particular entities falling under them, are not physical objects, if an entity's being a (macroscopic) physical object requires that it have, at each moment of its existence, a determinate spatial location. But the tokens of a type may be physical entities of some kind. Each inscription of the word 'three' on the blackboard, for example, is a physical state of affairs. If we think of the word 'three' as a very simple *type* of text – a very simple type of linguistic structure – then each inscription of the word 'three' will count as a token of that text-type.

It might be suggested, then, that a literary work, or at least the artistic vehicle of a literary work, is not a token of a text but a text-type, and that individual copies of the work are tokens of that text-type. What, then, is the relationship between a type and its tokens?

19

We need to note that types are not the only kinds of 'generic entities' that can have other entities fall under them. Consider a property like 'being an "e"', which has among its *instances* the last two letters of the word 'three'. Is the relationship between this property and its instances the same as the relationship between the letter-type 'e' and its tokens? Richard Wollheim, in discussing the idea that literary works are text-types,[1] answered this question in the following way. Consider which properties a generic entity can share with the entities that are its instances or tokens. In the case of types and their tokens, it seems that most of the properties that an entity must have to be a token of a type T are also properties of the type T itself. For example, to be a token of the word 'three', an inscription must contain five letters in a particular order, must have 'r' as its third letter, must end with two occurrences of the letter 'e', etc. And, it seems, the word-type 'three' has each of these properties that must be possessed by its tokens. Similarly, the Union Jack is a type of flag individuated in terms of certain design properties, the very properties a particular design token must have to be a token of the Union Jack. It might be acknowledged that not *all* of the properties required in a token of a given type are also properties of the type, since some of the properties are properties the token must have to be a *token* of some kind or other. For example, every token of the Union Jack occupies a certain region of space, even if the token is an image on a computer screen, but the type Union Jack has no spatial location. But, if we could somehow rule out these kinds of properties, then we could say, following Wollheim, that the properties a token must have *to be a token of a particular type T as opposed to a related type S* (say, a token of the Union Jack rather than a token of the Stars and Stripes) are also properties of the type T itself. In Wollheim's terminology, such properties are *transmitted* between the token and the type. But this doesn't hold in the case of properties and their instances. The property 'being red', for example, does not itself possess the chromatic or appearance properties required in an instance of that property. At best, some properties of a property can be contingently shared with instances of that property. For example, the property of 'being exhilarating' might be rightly attributable both to the property 'being red' and to instances of that property.

Nicholas Wolterstorff, however, has argued that Wollheim is mistaken in thinking that properties are shared and transmitted between types and their tokens.[2] He suggests, as a useful comparison, the relationship between the following two claims: 'The grizzly bear

WHAT IS A LITERARY WORK?

growls', as a claim about the grizzly as a *kind* of animal, and the same sentence used to describe a particular instance of that kind. The first of these claims cannot be a generalization about all instances of the kind, since there surely can be grizzlies that are born mute. Nor does it make sense to read this as ascribing to the *kind* the same property as we are ascribing to a given instance of that kind, since kinds, as generic entities, do not possess the physical attributes necessary to make sounds. What such a claim about a kind is actually saying, according to Wolterstorff, is that *properly formed instances* of the kind have the property of growling. The same analysis would apply to such claims as 'The grizzly bear has four paws', 'The grizzly bear grows to a certain height', etc. Where our conception of a kind or type of thing brings with it such a conception of what properties a *properly formed* instance or token should possess, we have what Wolterstorff calls a 'norm kind'. Norm kinds and their instances or tokens can share *predicates*, like 'growls' or 'has four paws', but the predicate picks out different, although closely related, properties when predicated of the kind, on the one hand, and the instances or tokens of the kind, on the other.

Wolterstorff argues that what holds for norm kinds like 'grizzly bear' also holds for types like 'word', 'text', 'poem', 'Union Jack', etc. To say that the word-type 'three' has a letter 'r' as its third letter is to say that each *properly formed token* of the word has a token of the letter 'r' as its third letter. This allows for *improperly formed* tokens of the word, where that very word is misspelled. Similarly, there can be flawed tokens of the Union Jack, or faulty copies of poems. To say that the poem(-type) *The Waste Land* begins with the words, 'April is the cruellest month', is to say that each properly formed token of the poem begins in this way.

Suppose therefore that we follow Wolterstorff in thinking of a literary text-type as a norm kind that prescribes certain properties for correct tokens of that type. Authors seek to articulate a content by identifying such a text-type – usually by producing a token of that type – which is intended to serve as the vehicle for their work. We can now return to our original question: what kind of thing is the literary work itself, under what conditions do we have the same work, and under what conditions does a given work persist?

The simplest answer is to say that a literary work just is a text-type. Any version of such a view is a form of *textualism*. Textualists may differ as to what they build into the notion of a text, and thus what they take to be the identity conditions for texts. They agree, however, that, given an appropriate understanding of what a text is, if two writers working independently of one another generate tokens of the same text-type, only one literary work can result from their activity. One of the most sophisticated formulations and defences of textualism can be found in the work of Nelson Goodman and Catherine Elgin.[3] According to Goodman and Elgin, texts are linguistic strings that are individuated in terms of the language to which they belong, and the syntax of that language, where the latter is a matter of 'the permissible configurations of letters, spaces, and punctuation marks'.[4] They further maintain that the *interpretation* of a word is not one of the factors individuating texts. Take the word 'cape', as a simple example of a text. Different English occurrences of the word 'cape', they hold, are different tokens of the same text-type, even if some refer to an article of clothing and others to a body of land. The word 'chat', however, as a type of inscription in English, is a different text from the identically spelled string as a type of inscription in French.[5]

As we noted, Goodman and Elgin maintain that the interpretations of linguistic expressions – semantic properties such as reference – do not play a part in the individuation of texts. In so doing, they reject a more restricted conception of sameness of text which *would* take account of such semantic properties. On this more restricted conception, 'cape' as used to refer to an article of clothing would be a different text-type from 'cape' as used to refer to a body of land. They reject this for reasons closely related to their reason for identifying a literary work with a text as they conceive the latter. Their conception of a text permits us to determine whether two separately occurring text-tokens are tokens of the same text-type without having to address matters of interpretation. And textualism, as a view about literary works, allows us to talk unproblematically about different or even incompatible interpretations of *the same work*. The alternative to the textualist claim that a literary work is a text, they maintain, is the 'interpretationist' claim that a literary work is to be identified with a (right) *interpretation* of a text. If there were only one right interpretation of a literary text, then the two construals would agree as to when we have the same literary work and when we do not. But, they argue, the only argument for there being a unique right interpretation of every literary work would require that we define a right interpretation as one which is faithful to the intentions of the author, and no such 'intentionalist' view of interpretation is tenable.

We shall consider 'intentionalist' views of interpretation in Chapter 5, but, for the sake of argument, we may grant that appeal to the artist's intentions cannot yield a single right interpretation of every literary work. We must therefore acknowledge that literary works of any substance admit of a plurality of right interpretations, something which, according to Goodman and Elgin, is clearly true if we take critical literary practice as our guide. Thus we require a distinction between (1) different (right) interpretations of the *same* work, and (2) (right) interpretations of *different* works. But such a distinction cannot be drawn if works are identified with (right) interpretations of texts. So, it is concluded, we must identify works with texts, and textualism is the correct view of the ontological status of literary works.

CONTEXTUALIST CRITIQUES OF TEXTUALISM

Opponents of textualism have insisted, to the contrary, that we can clearly imagine cases where distinct works have identical texts as their vehicles. In spelling out how this could be so, they have proposed a third alternative, apart from textualism and interpretationism. In coming up with imagined cases that would demonstrate the failings of textualism, many have relied on a remarkable short story by the Argentinian writer Jorge Luis Borges. Borges' story, 'Pierre Menard, Author of the *Quixote*', purports to be a critical discussion, of the sort one might find in a scholarly journal, of the literary works of one Pierre Menard, a Frenchman writing in the first third of the twentieth century. Menard's most singular achievement is a work which is textually identical to two chapters of Cervantes' *Don Quixote*. This work was not the result of an act of mechanical transcription of the original. Rather, '[Menard's] admirable ambition was to produce pages which would coincide – word for word and line for line – with those of Miguel de Cervantes'.[6]

We need not dwell upon how this feat is supposedly accomplished. What is significant is that the narrator of Borges' story proceeds to *contrast* Menard's *Quixote* with Cervantes' *Quixote* by citing features of, or passages in, the text which are common to both, and taking those features or passages to have a radically different import in the two cases. The differences in question relate to properties ascribable to the features or passages in virtue of the literary-historical contexts in which tokens of their common text-type were inscribed. Consider the following three examples:

(B1) Menard's *Quixote* is more subtle than Cervantes'. The latter, in a clumsy fashion, opposes to the fictions of chivalry the tawdry provincial reality of his country. Menard selects as his 'reality' the land of Carmen during the century of Lepanto and Lope de Vega. What a series of *espagnolades* that selection would have suggested to Maurice Barres or Dr. Rodriguez Larreta! Menard eludes them with complete naturalness. In his work there are no gypsy flourishes or conquistadors or mystics or Philip the Seconds or *autos da fe*. He neglects or eliminates local colour. This disdain points to a new conception of the historical novel.[7]

(B2) The contrast in style is also vivid. The archaic style of Menard – quite foreign, after all – suffers from a certain affectation. Not so that of his forerunner, who handles with ease the current Spanish of his time.[8]

(B3) It is a revelation to compare Menard's *Don Quixote* with Cervantes'. The latter, for example, wrote (part one, chapter nine):

> . . . Truth, whose mother is history, rival of time, depository of deeds, exemplar and advisor to the present, and the future's counsellor.

Written in the seventeenth century, written by the 'lay genius' Cervantes, this enumeration is a mere rhetorical praise of history. Menard, on the other hand, writes:

> . . . Truth, whose mother is history, rival of time, depository of deeds, exemplar and advisor to the present, and the future's counsellor.

History, the *mother* of truth: the idea is astounding. Menard, a contemporary of William James, does not define history as an inquiry into reality, but as its origin. Historical truth, for him, is not what has happened; it is what we judge to have happened. The final phrases – *exemplar and advisor to the present, and the future's counsellor* – are brazenly pragmatic.[9]

Critics of textualism have cited Borges' provocative fictional example in arguing that interpretationism is not the *only* alternative to textualism.[10] In the Cervantes/Menard case, so it is claimed, the generation of tokens of the same text-type by authors working in very different cultural and/or historical contexts results in different and sometimes incompatible properties bearing on the appreciation of the work which is the product of those generations. This, it is further claimed, demonstrates that generations of tokens of a given text-type in different contexts result in different *works*, and supports a *contextualist* construal of literary works.[11] The contextualist identifies a literary work with a text-type as tokened in a particular art-historical context, or offers another account of the literary work that makes both text-type and generative context constitutive elements of a work.

Rich and ingenious as Borges' story is, it is open to certain objections if presented as an argument against textualism and for contextualism. In the first place, as noted, the text-type tokened by Menard is identical, as text, with a *fragment* of the text-type that serves as the vehicle for Cervantes' work. Thus, as it stands, even if the textualist admits that there are differences in appreciable properties of the sort described by Borges' narrator, and that such differences support the idea that we have different works, we do not have different works *that share a text*. Contextualists who have tried to use Borges' story in arguing against textualism have suggested that we can amend Borges' story so that Menard produces, by the specified methods, not merely something textually identical to a fragment of Cervantes' text, but something textually identical to the whole of Cervantes' text.

There is a second problem, however, if the textualist opponent is someone whose views resemble those of Goodman and Elgin. For such a textualist, as we have seen, we have two occurrences of the same text-type only if two identically spelled inscriptions belong to the same language, and are syntactically equivalent. But it is questionable whether the seventeenth-century Spanish in which Cervantes wrote and the early twentieth-century Spanish in which Menard presumably wrote are indeed the same language. The archaism of Menard's text, for example, is presumably a matter, inter alia, of its using linguistic constructions not current in the Spanish of Menard's day, while failing to employ functionally similar linguistic constructions that were so current. This seems to demonstrate that the linguistic resources of Cervantes' Spanish and Menard's Spanish are significantly different, in which case, the textualist might argue, they are different languages for the purposes of individuating texts.

For these reasons, Gregory Currie formulates an argument against textualism by appealing to another hypothetical example that has the same sorts of positive 'contextualist' features as Borges' story without engendering these kinds of difficulties.[12] In Currie's thought experiment, we imagine that we discover a previously unknown manuscript by Anne Radcliffe, the writer of Gothic fictions, that is textually identical to Jane Austen's *Northanger Abbey* but written some ten years earlier. Assuming that Austen had no knowledge of Radcliffe's manuscript, we have generations of tokens of identical linguistic strings by two authors who are presumably employing the same language. But, as Currie persuasively argues, the resulting works possess strikingly different and apparently incompatible properties. Austen's novel, which has the text-type in question as its artistic vehicle, is valued for the ways in which it satirizes the Gothic tradition, a tradition upon which it comments and to elements of which it frequently refers. Radcliffe's hypothetical text, however, seems incapable of serving as the vehicle for a work having these kinds of properties. Indeed, it would be anachronistic to see it as ironically commenting upon other texts, including other texts by Radcliffe herself, that had not been written at the time when Radcliffe hypothetically composed her text. If, then, we think that these kinds of differences in the artistic content articulated through an artistic vehicle are relevant to the individuation of literary works, we must resist the identification of works with texts. Rather, we must identify them with entities that somehow incorporate both a text, as artistic vehicle, and a context of making, in virtue of which the vehicle serves to articulate a particular artistic content.

Currie considers a number of possible textualist counters to his argument. One option is to reject the assumption – crucial to the argument – that the works resulting from the text-generative activities of Radcliffe and Austen differ in their artistic content – Austen's work being ironic and alluding to other works by Radcliffe, for example, when Radcliffe's work has neither of these properties. Textualists can challenge this assumption by finding other ways to represent those properties that depend upon the context of generation of a token of a text-type. The preferred strategy is to *relativize* such properties in some way or another so that there are no properties that one work possesses and the other lacks. One option is to relativize contextually based properties to an *interpretation* of a work. The literary work *Northanger Abbey*, it might be said, has the property of being interpretable-as-a-satirical-comment-on-Radcliffe's-Gothic-novels, but, given the existence of other equally acceptable interpretations that treat the work as non-satirical, it also possesses the property of being interpretable-as-a-'straight'-Gothic-novel. The work, identified with the text-type, can possess both of these properties without contradiction. So Radcliffe and Austen, in independently tokening the same text-type, author the same work.

As Currie points out, however, this entails that Radcliffe's work possesses both of these properties, even though it seems anachronistic, not to say bizarre, to see her work as interpretable in the first way, as a satirical comment on works she has not yet written. An anachronistic interpretation of this kind, Currie maintains, is unacceptable because it entails an anachronistic *evaluation* of Radcliffe's work, crediting it with possessing this property. But, he argues, our sense of a work's value should reflect our sense of what the artist achieved. Textualists, however, might reject such a conception of artistic value, in which case there is nothing inconsistent in their position. But it may be difficult to reconcile that position with central features of our critical and interpretative practice.

Another relativizing option would be to relativize the context-based properties we ascribe to works to particular acts of *generating* a token of a text-type. Then we can say that *Northanger Abbey*, which is to be identified with a particular text-type, is satirical-or-ironic-as-generated-by-Austen, but a-ripping-Gothic-yarn-as-generated-by-Radcliffe. Again, there is nothing inconsistent in ascribing both of these properties to a given text. But again, it is difficult to reconcile this idea with our ordinary practices of ascribing properties to works as part of their appreciation. *Animal Farm*, we want to say, is a biting commentary on the development of Russian socialism, not merely such-a-thing-as-composed-by-Orwell.

The same kind of difficulty attends a different textualist response to Currie's argument. The textualist might deny that any of the contextually grounded properties to which the argument appeals are genuine properties of literary works at all. Rather, it might be said, they are properly viewed as properties either of authors or of the activities of authors. But to hold such a view seems radically to impoverish works, by denying them any properties that relate them to other works or current events in the artist's milieu. *Animal Farm* becomes a tale about life in the farmyard, while we cannot view Austen's work, or indeed any work, as a satire on other contemporary literary developments.

There is however another kind of strategy open to the textualist, and it is this strategy that Goodman and Elgin adopt. They challenge a different assumption underlying the argument, namely that, in the hypothesized circumstances, we have two acts whose products are works. Only given this assumption does the question arise whether the two acts produce separate instances of the *same* work or instances of *different* works. In the case of Menard's generation of the text of *Don Quixote*, so Goodman and Elgin maintain, the most that Menard can be credited with producing is a novel *interpretation* of Cervantes' work *Don Quixote*, but not with producing a *work*. The author of a literary work is the first individual to produce a token of its text,[13] and, once a work has been so authored, no future generation of a token of that text-type can count as the authoring of a work. We may term this the claim of 'exclusive authorship'. This leads Goodman and Elgin to affirm that 'all and only right interpretations of Cervantes' text are right interpretations of Menard's. If it is incorrect for a contemporary reader to interpret Cervantes' text as archaic, it is equally incorrect so to interpret Menard's.'[14] Thus, whether Menard can at least be credited with offering a novel, right interpretation of *Don Quixote* depends on the constraints we place upon the right interpretation of works. Do we require that right interpretations respect the context of generation of the first token of a text-type, or do we allow as right any interpretation that can be reconciled with the text-type per se?[15] Even if we do allow for right interpretations of *Don Quixote* that treat the text as archaic, we cannot generate the problem for textualism posed by Currie's argument, since we only have inconsistent properties ascribed in right interpretations, not inconsistent properties directly ascribable to the work itself.

In fact, Goodman and Elgin are most plausibly read as holding that the context of generation of the first token of a text-type *does* constrain right interpretation of the resulting work. For one of the properties of a work that they rightly hold to be important for its proper appreciation is its *style*. Style, as Goodman argues elsewhere,[16] is crucial for appreciation because style properties play a vital role in classifying works, and inform how we look at works and the sorts of differences and similarities we seek to discover. Further, style properties are *projectible*, and allow our judgements to be tested against other cases. But, if style properties are to function in these ways in appreciation, works must be located in their generative contexts – the oeuvre of the artist or the more general tradition upon which he draws – in order to detect and ascribe such properties.

We can now see why the 'exclusive authorship' claim – that only the first individual to generate a token of a given literary text-type authors a work having that text-type as artistic vehicle – is crucial to

Goodman and Elgin's defence of textualism. For otherwise, there would seem to be a compelling argument against textualism based on the admitted importance of stylistic properties to the appreciation of works. It seems obvious that, among the different contextual properties it is plausible to ascribe to the products of Cervantes' and Menard's generative activity, or to the products of Radcliffe's and Austen's generative activity, are *stylistic* properties which relate the resulting texts to other texts generated by a given author. Given that we have seen reasons to question the 'relativization' strategy that textualists might employ in response to Currie's argument, the possibility of incompatible style properties ascribable to the *same text* as generated in different contexts would seem to provide a compelling reason to think that, in such cases, we are dealing with different *works*, rather than different interpretations of the same work. What we have in such cases, it might be said, is not different and sometimes incompatible interpretations of the *same* work, but different classes of interpretations that are 'right' in virtue of satisfying different *constraints*. These constraints stem from the contexts in which distinct tokens of a given text-type are generated, contexts which also account for the different sets of stylistic properties ascribable in virtue of each act of generation. Should we not say that, in such circumstances, we are dealing with different *works*?

Goodman and Elgin's 'exclusive authorship' claim would block this reformulation of the anti-textualist argument. The claim allows them to say that only those stylistic properties consequent upon the initial tokening of the relevant text-type are stylistic properties of the work having that text-type as its vehicle, and that only those interpretations consistent with the contextual features of that initial tokening are correct interpretations of that work. But the 'exclusive authorship' claim is itself in need of justification, given the contextualist's contrary contention that different tokenings of a given text-type can result in different works. Is there not something suspiciously ad hoc about the 'exclusive authorship' claim? Once we acknowledge the importance of contextually based properties to the proper appreciation of works, as Goodman seems to do in laying such significance on stylistic properties, what principle rules out the use of a given text-type as the artistic vehicle of quite different works, where that vehicle is used to articulate quite different artistic contents?

What is ad hoc for one philosopher is perhaps an appeal to an obvious truth for another. But it is significant here that Goodman and Elgin's claim about authorship does not, in fact, save textualism from the argument from stylistic properties just outlined. For there is nothing in principle to rule out two *simultaneous* tokenings of a given text-type by authors whose different oeuvres and creative contexts would confer different stylistic properties on the products of their generative activity. In this case, it would appear, the textualist has no remaining resources to block the claim that, in such a circumstance, we would have two different works that share a common text-type as their artistic vehicles. To maintain that, in the envisaged circumstances, *neither* of the authors produces a work seems absurd. It would entail, for example, that had another author tokened the text-type *Kubla Khan* at precisely the same time as Coleridge, then not only would Coleridge's activity have failed to produce a work, but also there could be no poem in the English language having that text-type as its artistic vehicle. As there is no principled reason to uphold the 'exclusive authorship' claim, and it cannot do the job it is intended to do, we should reject that claim. And, once we reject it, we can reiterate Currie's argument, or the closely related argument from stylistic properties, against textualist conceptions of the literary work.

If we grant the force of the arguments against textualism, then we will presumably look favourably on some version of contextualism.[17] But contextualism itself admits of different formulations, given the broad characterization of that view given above. Contextualist accounts of the nature of the literary work insist that we must factor into the identity of a work not only a text-type, as the artistic vehicle employed by the author, but also certain elements of the context in which the author employed that text-type with the intention of articulating a particular artistic content. The simplest form of contextualism, so construed, identifies the literary work not with the text-type that serves as its artistic vehicle, but with that text-type as used as an artistic vehicle in a particular generative context. If we reject the 'exclusive authorship' thesis, then different literary works can share a given text-type as their respective artistic vehicles. But some philosophers have argued that such a simple contextualist account does not fully take account of the artistic significance of what the author does in employing a particular text-type as an artistic vehicle in order to articulate a particular content. The generative process whereby an author came to employ a particular text-type as vehicle is also, it might be argued, a crucial part of the artistic achievement that we seek to understand in appreciating a literary work. It matters, for example, to our appreciation of Eliot's *The Waste Land* or of Austen's *Northanger Abbey* that we grasp the nature of the artistic process in virtue of which the artistic vehicles of those works take the form that they do. Those philosophers moved by such a sentiment have argued that artworks in general, including literary artworks, must be thought of as 'action-types' or 'performances' whereby a structure is discovered or an artistic vehicle is elaborated in the interests of articulating an artistic content.[18]

Having noted this divergence in the contextualist camp, we will leave it up to the interested reader to pursue further the arguments that have been offered on either side. For our purposes, we shall simply assume, in what follows, that there are persuasive reasons to adopt some form of contextualism if we wish our 'ontology' of the literary work to take account of the rich array of contextually based properties that seem to play a part in our critical and appreciative engagement with literary works. We shall return to these issues in Chapter 5, when we reconsider the constraints that govern right interpretation of literary works.

CHAPTER 3

THE NATURE OF FICTION

In 1998, a controversy erupted in British literary circles when it was announced that *Reading in the Dark*, by the Irish author and poet Seamus Deane, had won the prize awarded annually by the British newspaper the *Guardian* to the best work of fiction published in the preceding year. The award was controversial because the book had originally been commissioned by the publishers, Granta, as a work of autobiography, but was then published on Deane's insistence as a work of fiction. Interestingly, the narrative of the prize-winning book, which recounts the story of a boy growing up in Ireland in the 1940s and 1950s, corresponds in all significant details to Deane's own childhood. Deane's book is just one of a number of recent publications that call into question our intuitive understanding of fiction as something which is 'made up' and therefore not a narrative recounting of actual events. For example, in the year prior to Deane's award, the Waterstones non-fiction prize was awarded to Blake Morrison's *And When Did You Last See Your Father?*, a work officially described as a memoir of his father, but in which Morrison changed not only the name of one of the protagonists but also the order in which some of the narrated events occur, justifying these changes as being true to the 'form' of the book as a whole.[1] Another interesting case is Philip Roth, perhaps best known as the author of *Portnoy's Complaint*. In spite of the natural assumption that this book was 'made up' by Roth, some critics maintained that it was in significant respects autobiographical, and that the characters were closely based on his family. Partly in response, Roth published, under the label 'autobiography', a work called *The Facts* supposedly showing that his family was nothing like the one portrayed in *Portnoy's Complaint*. However, in the 1980s and 1990s, Roth also published, as 'novels', a number of works in which the principal character was named Philip Roth!

The recent profusion of 'confessional' writing, where literary techniques are used in the telling of 'real' stories about people's lives, extends a tradition dating back to Truman Capote's *In Cold Blood* and, as noted in Chapter 1, further developed by writers such as

Norman Mailer, Tom Wolfe, and Hunter S. Thompson. Such examples, taken together with the works by Deane, Morrison, and Roth,
give new resonance to a more abiding philosophical concern with the
nature of fiction. If booksellers still seem able to separate fiction
from non-fiction, the principles that should underlie any such
separation are less than clear. In this chapter, we shall try to clarify
what these principles should be and how, given those principles, we
should respond to the kinds of examples just cited.

STYLISTIC AND SEMANTIC CONCEPTIONS OF FICTION

In looking, in Chapter 1, at what is distinctive of literary artworks, we
found a number of reasons to reject the idea that the latter are to be
distinguished in terms of 'intrinsic' properties of the text, such as the
style of writing or the linguistic resources employed. For very similar
reasons, we should reject the idea that it is 'intrinsic' features of a
narrative that make it the vehicle for a work of fiction. This is not to
deny that there are certain stylistic features that are *typical* of
fictional narratives and that might be thought to distinguish them
from non-fictional narratives. On reading the opening pages of
Treasure Island and *The Voyage of the Beagle*, for example, we will
probably correctly classify the first as fiction and the second as non-
fiction.

But these features are neither necessary nor sufficient for fictionality, if we start from our pre-theoretical intuitions as to *clear cases* of
fiction and non-fiction. That they are not necessary is demonstrated
by uncontroversially fictional narratives that employ the style and
generic conventions of a standard form of 'non-fictional' writing,
such as the diary and the autobiography. More strikingly, we noted in
Chapter 1, authors have presented their fictions in the form of
academic articles (such as the short story by Borges discussed in
Chapter 2), or as works of literary scholarship (Nabokov's *Pale Fire*,
for example). And they are not sufficient because, as we have seen,
the works of literary journalists such as Capote, Mailer, and
Thompson employ the standard stylistic devices of literary fiction,
but are presumably not, in virtue of this, works of fiction, whether or
not they are judged to be works of literary art.

Furthermore, to echo again a point made in our discussion of the
nature of the literary artwork, even if it were to turn out that all
existing fictional works share some particular structural or generic

property that no existing work of non-fiction possesses, it would seem that nothing prevents a suitably creative novelist from authoring a work of fiction that lacks this property. And, conversely, if we were to take a standard historical narrative and change its linguistic structure or generic structure to conform to that of, for example, Aristotelian tragedy, this surely would not, in and of itself, produce a work of *fiction*.

An alternative proposal which has enjoyed some currency amongst literary theorists is that fictionality resides not in the intrinsic *stylistic* properties of a narrative, but in the relations that obtain between the narrative and the world. The linguistic expressions employed in non-fictional narratives are properly read as referring, or at least as purporting to refer, to those things in the world that the narrative is rightly taken to be about. In virtue of so referring, the sentences that make up the narrative can be assessed as true or false, and such an assessment may bear upon the value we accord to the narrative. In a work of fiction, it might be claimed, expressions in the narrative refer only inwardly, as elements in a self-enclosed linguistic universe. Northrop Frye, for example, claimed that in all literary verbal structures, 'final direction of meaning is inward', because 'questions of fact or truth are subordinated to the primary literary aim of producing a structure of words for its own sake, and the sign values of symbols are subordinated to their value as a structure of interconnecting motifs'.[2]

There are compelling reasons to resist such a view, however, since it renders mysterious our ability to comprehend many fictional works. When, in reading Conan Doyle's 'Sherlock Holmes' stories, we encounter sentences describing the movements of Holmes through a city identified as 'London', with locations identified as 'Baker Street', 'Paddington Station', and 'Leicester Square', we make sense of the described movements by plotting them onto a mental map of the city of London as we presume it to have been in Victorian times. We make sense of what is going on in Graham Greene's *Our Man in Havana* by locating the fictional narrative in the capital of Cuba during the corruption that preceded Castro's revolution. In both cases, we make sense of what is narrated by supplementing the text with our knowledge of the real-world cities of London or Havana at certain times in their history. Our assumption that this is a legitimate strategy is implicit in our description of such fictions as 'set in' Victorian London or pre-Castro Havana.

It might be responded, at least in defence of Frye, that he is not denying that terms in fiction preserve their normal reference, but only saying that our concern in reading a literary text is not with the factual truth or falsity of the sentences making up the narrative. We will return to these issues in later chapters when we ask about the relationship between truth in a story and the cognitive claims which some have made on behalf of fictions. However, if in at least some cases the 'real' truth or falsity of what is narrated in a fiction is a proper concern for readers who wish properly to appreciate that fiction as such, then the attempt to distinguish fiction from non-fiction in terms of either the referential functions of terms or the relevance of the truth of what is narrated fails.[3]

Suppose we grant that language employed in fictional narratives performs the same referential functions as language in non-fiction, and that, in virtue of this, sentences in fictional works are, or may be, true or false *of the world*. It might still be suggested that the distinguishing feature of fictional works is that the sentences that make up the narrative are *false*. It might be objected, of course, that at least those sentences that serve to establish a real setting for a fictional narrative will generally be true. Suppose, therefore, that we exclude these sentences from our proposal, or modify it to the claim that the *majority* of sentences in a work of fiction are false. There are two conclusive reasons to reject even such a modified proposal. First, there are many undeniably non-fictional works that contain a preponderance of false claims – for example, medieval texts on alchemy or the detection of witchcraft. Second, even if we set aside the Deane case, there seems to be no principled objection to a work of fiction that is entirely *true*. Consider the following example. An author, Smith, composes what she takes to be a short fictional narrative about a family named Brown living in Montreal, Canada, whose apartment catches fire in mid-January and who are forced to move into a shelter. As a matter of fact, it turns out that, entirely unbeknownst to Smith, there is a real family named Brown of whom all of the things narrated in the story are true. Intuitively, this state of affairs of which Smith was unaware does not affect the fictional status of her story because the story wasn't *about* the family in question, even though, if we grant that the terms in the story can refer to entities in the real world, all of the sentences in the story might be true of that family. We shall return to this kind of example, however, later in the chapter, when we examine more closely the conditions under which there can be fictions which correspond in their totality to real states of affairs.

FUNCTIONAL THEORIES OF FICTION

Considerations like the ones advanced thus far have led many to conclude that the fictionality of a narrative depends upon *how it functions*, or *how it was designed to function*. (Again, questions about the nature of fiction seem to parallel questions about the nature of the literary artwork.) For those defending the first of these alternatives, fictionality is conferred on a narrative by the ways in which it is treated by its users. A naive version of this view would maintain that something is fiction if someone *reads it as fiction*, but this is inadequate for at least two reasons. First, it presupposes an understanding of what it is to read something as fiction. Second, it would follow from this view that no-one could ever be *mistaken* in reading something as fiction, whereas someone who took Darwin's *The Voyage of the Beagle* to be fiction and Stevenson's *Treasure Island* to be non-fiction is surely making some kind of mistake. A much more sophisticated account of this kind has been developed by Kendall Walton.[4] He claims that a narrative is fictional when its socially recognized function is to serve as a certain kind of resource in games of make-believe. Just as children employ 'props' in their imaginative play, so readers may use a text as the basis for an exercise of the imagination. Where this use is socially sanctioned for texts of a given kind, those texts are fictions. Fictionality so conceived is independent of the intentions of a narrator. It is a matter of the accepted ways of using a thing, rather than the uses for which it was designed.

It might be thought that this still deprives us of the intuitive distinction between a narrative which *is* fictional and a narrative which a community of readers *treats as or believes to be* fictional, and that we need to take account of how the author of a narrative intended it to be used in order to preserve this distinction. Walton, however, maintains that to make the fictionality of a narrative depend upon the activity of its maker is to treat the narrative as merely a vehicle of the latter's fiction-making. This, he argues, seriously distorts the nature of our interest in fictions, which is focused primarily on the stories themselves rather than on how they came into existence. If we found the text of a story etched into a rock by natural forces, we could read and enjoy it as fiction just as much as if it were a product of human agency. Indeed, he maintains, we could imagine a culture in which fictions were enjoyed but no one made them: all fictions in such a culture would be naturally occurring entities. Similarly, a culture that lacked any activity of visual-image making could still enjoy finding images in clouds. Fictions, for Walton, are first and foremost props in our games of make-believe. How these props came into existence is secondary.

How are we to assess Walton's claims? Is it perhaps just a matter of conflicting intuitions as to whether a naturally occurring string of sentences is properly viewed as a fiction? In Chapter 4, we will see some reasons for calling into question the fictionality of such a string, or, at least, some considerations that may weaken the appeal of Walton's argument. For, as we shall see, to take part in a game of make-believe using a written text as a prop seems to require that we *treat* that text as if it were the product of a particular act of making. To treat the text in this way seems to be a requirement if our make-believe is to be satisfactorily constrained, so that what we are enjoined to make-believe is not simply up to us as individual readers. While we may be happy to see very different things in clouds – you see a dragon and I see a teapot, for example – our shared engagement with fictional texts seems to require some external standard against which our readings of those texts can be measured. Such a standard is most obviously obtained by providing the text with a context of making which constrains our reading. While it might be responded that it is the practices of a community of users that furnishes us with a standard of right imagining, the point remains that these practices treat fictions as narratives with a history of making – as products of acts of fiction-making – even if we allow that such a history is posited rather than discovered. Being the product of a certain kind of generative act does seem to be part of our concept of a fiction, contrary to what Walton maintains.

For these reasons, and also because of the intrinsic interest of such a view, I shall spend the rest of this chapter examining the idea that the fictionality of a text is to be explained in terms of the function its maker(s) intended it to have. Those who have defended this idea view fictionality as the result of a particular kind of action that language users can perform by drawing upon properties of that language that also enable the performance of other kinds of actions. The technical term used for the latter kind of actions is 'speech acts'. There are two prominent 'speech act' theories of fiction. According to an influential theory developed by John Searle, fictions result from authors *pretending* to perform regular speech acts of certain kinds.[5] According to an alternative theory developed by Gregory Currie, fictions result from authors performing a *distinct kind of speech act*, that of 'fiction-making'.[6] I shall examine each of these views in turn.

To understand Searle's position, we need to say a few things of a more general nature about speech act theory as he conceives it.[7] Consider a situation in which Jane utters the words 'The door is shut' in ordinary conversation. We can plausibly take her to have performed a number of different actions in so doing. She has (1) deliberately moved her mouth, tongue, and lips in a particular way, (2) uttered a string of words with certain phonetic properties, a certain way of sounding, (3) uttered a string of words which have various semantic properties in virtue of which she refers to a particular door and predicates being shut of it, and (4) asserted that a particular door is shut. (4) is something she has done in doing (3) – uttering a given meaningful string of words – and (3) in turn is something accomplished by doing (2) and ultimately (1). A *speech act* is then conceived as something a speaker can perform by enacting a meaningful utterance, as in (3). When, as in the case of (4), the action performed is something accomplished in making a particular utterance – the utterance characterized in (3) – we can talk of an 'illocutionary' act.

Different speech acts can trade upon the same meanings of the words that enter into the sentences used to perform those speech acts. Drawing on the meanings of the words that make up the sentence 'the door is shut', for example, I can not only perform the illocutionary act of assertion, but also that of interrogation ('Is the door shut?'), issuing an imperative ('Shut the door!'), expressing a wish ('Would that the door were shut!'), and making a promise ('I promise to shut the door'). These illocutionary acts can be said to have a common *propositional content*, but to involve the application of different *illocutionary forces* to that content to produce different speech acts. To apply a given illocutionary force to a content, according to Searle, involves the use of 'function-indicating devices', such as word order, punctuation, the mood of the verb, and 'performative' verbs such as 'promise' and 'warn' (or, in the case of spoken utterances, stress and intonational contour). This allows us to say that the performance of a speech act draws upon two distinct components in the sentence uttered – one which identifies the propositional content, and one which indicates the illocutionary force applied to that content. In considering how this might relate to the generation of fictions, Searle further claims that the meaning of the sentence as a whole, given the content-component and the function-indicating device, determines the speech act performed. This can be termed the 'functionality principle'.

Searle believes that, given the functionality principle, we face a problem when we try to understand what is going on in fictional discourse. For, so he maintains, there are certain constitutive and regulative rules associated with different speech acts. In the case of assertion, it is constitutive of such an act that the speaker commits herself to the truth of what is asserted. This grounds a number of regulative principles which enable speakers to be held responsible for making such a commitment in inappropriate circumstances. These principles enjoin speakers not to assert things that they have no reason to believe are true, or that they don't themselves believe to be true, or that are obvious. Speakers who make assertions can then rightly be criticized if their assertive practice fails to respect these rules.

The puzzle posed by fictional discourse can now be expressed as follows. Suppose Arthur sets out to write a fictional narrative, and begins by writing the following sentence: 'On a windy day in the summer of 1897, England's most renowned detective set out from his residence on Baker Street to travel by train to visit his cousin in Suffolk.' Given the propositional content of this sentence, and given the function-indicating devices that it contains, it seems to follow from the functionality principle that Arthur is performing the speech act of assertion. Given the rules that govern such a speech act, it follows that Arthur is committed to the truth of this sentence, and is open to criticism if he lacks good reasons to believe that it is true or does not himself believe it to be true. But, given that we take Arthur to be involved in the act of composing a fiction, we do not in fact hold him so responsible. How can that be so? If we explain our failure to hold Arthur responsible by denying that he is actually asserting the standard propositional content of the sentence in question, then, by the functionality principle, it seems to follow that either the propositional content of a sentence used in a fiction differs from its standard propositional content, or that function-indicating devices change their meaning in fictional contexts. But if words used in fiction differ in their meanings from words in their standard use, then our ability to understand fictions will require that we grasp not only the standard meanings of words but also their special 'fictional' meanings, and this seems absurd.

Searle proposes to resolve this dilemma by holding that there is a further set of rules, known to receivers of literary works, that allow words to be used with their normal meanings but which serve to *suspend* the customary rules attending the utterance of sentences that, by the functionality principle, enact particular speech acts. To invoke this further set of rules is to utter an assertive sentence while only *pretending* to perform the relevant speech act, and this is what Arthur and other composers of fiction are doing. Since the meaning of the sentence is unchanged, receivers can understand the resulting fiction. But, since the rules attending the performance of the speech act of assertion are suspended, we do not hold Arthur and other composers of fictions responsible for their failure to conform to those rules.

Searle's account of fictionality can be summarized in terms of four claims:[8]

1. The author of a work of fiction pretends to perform a series of illocutionary acts, although the pretence does not involve any attempt to deceive the audience.
2. What determines whether or not a text is a work of fiction are *the (complex) illocutionary intentions of the author*, on the assumption that one cannot pretend without intending to pretend.
3. This form of pretence is possible because an author can invoke a set of conventions which suspends the normal operations of the rules that relate illocutionary acts to the world.
4. The author produces a work of fiction by actually performing the utterance act of speaking or writing sentences, while having the intention to invoke the relevant conventions.

This account faces a number of difficulties, however. First, it might be thought that, in at least some works of fiction, the author is genuinely asserting at least some of the things expressed by the sentences she uses.[9] This applies, for example, to many of those sentences used to elaborate the 'real' setting in which the fictional narrative takes place. If Arthur continues his narrative by writing 'The train to Suffolk departed, as it had done for some years, from platform 3 at Liverpool Street Station', it seems odd to say that he is only pretending to assert the propositional content of that sentence. Furthermore, traditional novelists have often interpolated into their fictions sentences expressing general propositions about the world, such as the famous opening lines of Tolstoy's *Anna Karenina* about happy and unhappy families. Again, it seems strange to say that Tolstoy is only pretending to assert the proposition that this sentence expresses. But, if we grant that at least some of the sentences that authors incorporate into their fictions are genuinely asserted, we face a problem. For it is questionable whether, at one and the same time, I can both do *X*, for some action *X*, and pretend to do *X*. And it is implausible to respond that the author asserts some sentences – as in the examples proposed – and pretends to assert others, but never does both to the same sentence. For, even if Arthur asserts what is expressed by the above sentence about British Victorian train schedules, he surely also wants what it expresses to be part of the fiction, which seems to require that he also pretends to assert it.

A further difficulty is that Searle's proposed analysis of fictionality seems too broad. There are situations, it can be argued, in which a speaker pretends to assert what is expressed by a sentence that she utters, but where this does not result in anything fictional.[10] Suppose that a student puts on a verbal performance for the benefit of his classmates in which he imitates the professor, uttering a highly jargonized sentence that the professor has used with the same kind of intonation that the latter employed. Suppose, for example, that the sentence is 'The fictionality of a text must be viewed as a matter of function rather than of its intrinsic properties.' The student is clearly pretending to assert the sentence, but the sentence as uttered by the student is not thereby a piece of fiction. It is, of course, fictional, in some sense, that the student is the professor, but that is a different matter.

A second kind of 'speech act' theory of fiction, proposed by Gregory Currie, is intended to overcome these difficulties. Currie proposes that fictions are the products of intentional acts of fiction-making. Fiction-making is a kind of illocutionary act similar in some significant respects to assertion. Authors produce fictions not by pretending to perform the illocutionary act of assertion, but by performing the distinct illocutionary act of fiction-making. To understand how these kinds of speech acts differ, we need to draw upon a different strand of speech act theory most fully explored by Paul Grice.[11] While Searle seeks to distinguish between speech acts in terms of the *implications of performing such acts* – what a speaker commits herself to, and how she can be held accountable for failing to meet certain requirements – Grice treats speech acts as modes of linguistic communication, and enquires as to the particular framework of intentions that a speaker must have in order to engage in a particular kind of speech act for communicative purposes. Communicative acts, for Grice, are acts of 'openly telling someone something' and are possible only through a complex nest of related intentions on the part of the speaker. It is in virtue of such intentions, and of their being recognizable by competent interlocutors, that communicative acts take place. Currie claims that fiction-making is itself a kind of communicative act that is to be grasped by contrasting its intentional structure with that of assertion.

Grice's analysis of the intentional structure of assertion becomes increasingly Byzantine as it is adjusted to deal with various potential counter-examples, but fortunately we need only consider a simpler version of his analysis in order to understand and assess Currie's account of fiction. The first point to grasp is that, for the utterance of a sentence S expressing a proposition p – say, that it is snowing outside – to qualify as a communicative act of 'openly telling someone' that it is snowing outside, the utterer U must intend that her interlocutor I comes to believe that p. Thus a parrot trained to squawk 'it's snowing outside' whenever appropriately visually stimulated would not be performing a communicative act. Furthermore, for U to be *openly* telling I that p, she must intend that I comes to believe that p by grasping (1) that that is U's intention in uttering S, and (2) that U is uttering S with the intention that it be understood to mean that p. So, for example, there would not be an act of 'openly telling' in Grice's sense if U merely pointed to the window. Even though this may lead to the intended result of I's coming to believe that it is snowing outside, I's belief is caused by what he observes, not by the prior recognition that U intends him to believe this. It is through I's recognition that U is using S to express the proposition that it is snowing outside, and is doing so with the intention of bringing about the corresponding belief in I, that U must intend to generate I's change of belief if U's utterance is to count as an act of 'openly telling'. It is *not* necessary, however, that I actually comes to believe that p as a result of U's utterance, nor even, necessarily, that I twigs to U's intentions, as long as, given the circumstances of utterance, I *should* have twigged.

On Grice's analysis of the intentional structure of the communicative act of assertion, therefore, assertion requires acting with the overriding intention that one's interlocutor come to believe something, and with the further intention that this belief be brought about through a process of recognition of the sort just described. Currie's claim is that the same complex structure of intentions is required for an act of fiction-making, with one crucial difference: the utterer's overriding intention is that the audience *make-believe* what is expressed by her utterance, rather than believe it, and it is *this* result that the utterer intends to bring about through the process of recognition in question. This evades at least one of the difficulties confronted by Searle's account. For, while it may be impossible both to assert that *p* and pretend to assert that *p* at one and the same time, it is perfectly possible to intend, in uttering *S*, that one's audience both believes and make-believes the proposition that *S* expresses.

The claim, then, is that fiction-making involves what Currie terms 'fictive utterance', for which he offers the following preliminary definition:

U's utterance of *S* is fictive if and only if . . . *U* utters *S* intending that the audience will:

1. recognize that *S* means *P*;
2. recognize that *S* is intended by *U* to mean *P*;
3. recognize that *U* intends them (the audience) to make-believe that *P*;
4. make-believe that *P*.

And further intending that:

5. (2) will be a reason for (3);
6. (3) will be a reason for (4).[12]

This definition is preliminary because, as Currie acknowledges, we need to allow for a number of things: speakers who intend their sentence to be understood non-literally, speakers who use non-linguistic methods to make a fictive utterance, and speakers who do not have a particular audience in mind. Currie modifies his definition of fictive utterance to take account of these kinds of cases, but we can work with the original definition since nothing in what follows turns on such nuances.

TRUE FICTIONS

Given this account of what it is to engage in a fictive utterance, can we then take a work to be fictional just in case it is the product of a fictive utterance? We need to consider two kinds of objection to such a proposal. First, it might be said that being the product of a fictive utterance is not *necessary* for being a work of fiction. This is what Walton is claiming when he maintains that a naturally occurring string of words would be a fiction as long as we treated it in a certain way. We have already seen reasons to question this assumption, however, so we can ignore it in the present context. A more serious consideration is that being the product of a fictive utterance may not be *sufficient* for being a work of fiction. Currie offers a number of hypothetical examples that seem to demonstrate that this is indeed the case, and then offers a further necessary condition for fictionality to supplement the requirement that a fiction be the product of a fictive utterance.

We need to stress, initially, that Currie's proposal is that a *work* is fictional if it is the product of an act of fictive utterance. There can be fictive utterances that do not produce works, and therefore do not produce works of fiction, as, for example, when a parent reads a bedtime story to a child. The interesting cases, however, are ones in which we have a fictive utterance productive of a work, yet where there is some reluctance to treat that work as fictional. Currie considers a number of different kinds of hypothetical situations. In one example, *U* performs a fictive utterance – with the necessary overriding intention that the audience make-believe what is uttered and with the requisite set of nested intentions – and produces a work by retelling in her own words a true story she has discovered in an old newspaper. Another example differs from this in that the source of the narrative uttered by *U* is *U*'s own remarkable life. In a further case that doesn't involve this kind of deception, *U*'s fictive utterance reworks in his own words and in his own style a narrative he discovers in an old manuscript and takes to be a lost work of fiction, but which in fact is a work of non-fiction. In a final example, *U* has repressed certain terrible real-life experiences and then fictively utters a narrative relating exactly these events, where we assume that this is to be explained in terms of certain subconscious processes in *U*. Currie maintains that, in each of these cases, we are unwilling to classify the resulting work as a work of fiction.

What these hypothetical cases seem to have in common is that the events narrated through *U*'s fictive utterance are *true*. But, as we have already seen (the 'Brown family' example), we must allow for the possibility of true works of fiction. What distinguishes the current hypothetical cases from the 'Brown family' type of case, according to Currie, is that in the latter the story is only *accidentally* true whereas in the former it is *non-accidentally* true. We are to understand the latter notion in terms of the relationship of 'counterfactual dependence' that can obtain between what actually occurs and what is included in a narrative. A narrative is 'counterfactually dependent' on certain actual events just in case: (1) if different events had occurred, the narrative would have differed in corresponding respects, and (2) if the same events had occurred in a different setting, the narrative would not have differed in its account of those events. A narrative is non-accidentally true of a given sequence of events, then, if it is counterfactually dependent on that sequence of events. In each of the hypothetical examples, it is claimed, the narrative fictively uttered by *U* is not merely true but non-accidentally true in this sense. We can classify the resulting works as non-fiction by requiring, for a work of fiction, not merely that it be the product of a fictive utterance but also that, if it is true, it be only accidentally true. We can term this second requirement the 'counterfactual independence' requirement.

Currie's proposal does, indeed, correctly distinguish between those instances where we should say that the work produced by a fictive utterance is a work of fiction, and those cases where we should not say this. But this reflects a more fundamental requirement for fiction-making whose failure to obtain in Currie's hypothetical cases, as he elaborates them, accounts for the failure to meet the 'counterfactual independence' requirement. To put this another way, in accepting that the hypothetical cases are indeed cases where the narrative is coun-terfactually dependent on the facts, we are supplementing what we were told about those cases with a further assumption about the generation of the fictively uttered narratives. In each of these cases, as originally presented, the problem with saying that *U* produces a work of fiction seems to be that the narrative is not merely true but is *known to be true* by the person responsible for generating the narrative. In the first two cases, this is quite explicit, in the third case we assume that the person who produced the discovered manuscript knew it to be true, and in the final case *U* subconsciously knows the narrative to be true. But if the truth of the narrated events does not, by itself, prevent a narrative from being fictional, why should the author's *knowledge* of their truth make a difference as long as the appropriate fictional intention is present? The answer, perhaps, is that it *doesn't* matter, unless this knowledge plays a particular kind of role in the construction of the narrative, a role we are ascribing to such knowledge in acquiescing in the claim that, in each of the hypothetical cases, the 'counterfactual independence' condition is not met.

If what primarily matters for fiction is the intention that the audience make-believe, rather than believe, the narrated events, then what is also crucial is that, whether or not the narrated events are true or known to be true, *their having occurred is not relevant to what the author is trying to achieve in writing the narrative.* In other words, what U wishes to achieve in having readers make-believe that p does not depend upon p's being true. That proposition's being true is not the *reason* for its inclusion in the narrative. Consider the constraints under which narrative construction takes place in acts of fiction-making. We can shed light on the nature of these constraints by asking how *reading* a text as fiction differs from reading it as non-fiction. As a reader of a narrative, I posit a writing process in which certain events are chosen and ordered by an author for some purpose. As a critical reader, I always ask, 'Why am I being told about *those* events in *that* order?' To read a narrative as non-fiction is to assume that the selection and temporal ordering of *all* the events making up the narrative was constrained by a desire, on the narrator's part, to be faithful to the manner in which actual events transpired. We assume that the author has included only events she believes to have occurred, narrated as occurring in the order in which she believes them to have occurred.[13] We may term this the 'fidelity constraint'. To read a narrative as fiction, on the other hand, is to assume that the choices made in generating the narrative were not governed in the first instance by this constraint, but by some more general purpose in story-telling. If considerations of fidelity are taken to enter into the construction of a fictional narrative – where, for example, an author wants to set the narrative in London during the Blitz – this is assumed to be subordinate to this more general purpose.

This enables us to look at Currie's hypothetical cases in a new light. When we acquiesce in the claim that these cases fail to satisfy the 'counterfactual independence' requirement, we are assuming that, in each case, what U utters is determined by what actually occurred, so that, if different events had occurred, the narrative would have differed accordingly. But this is to assume that U's construction of the narrative is governed by the fidelity constraint. There is no reason, however, why this has to be the case in the kinds of situations described. Take the example of the person whose fictive utterance corresponds, in its narrative content, to the facts of his incredible life. We can ask, *why* has he chosen to utter fictively such a narrative? One answer might be: because these are the things that actually happened. In that case, we might expect the narrative to have differed in any circumstance where his life differed. Here we have narrative construction governed by the fidelity constraint, and a work of non-fiction. But another answer might be: because he is interested in constructing a narrative that expresses certain more general thematic meanings, and because the events that actually happened to him furnish just such a narrative. In this case, we can assume that, had his life been different, he would not have incorporated such differences into his narrative, for, so amended, the narrative might no longer express the thematic meanings of interest to him. In this case, if his utterance is a fictive one, then we should say that the product is indeed a work of fiction. And the difference between the two cases is reflected in Currie's 'counterfactual independence' requirement. The first case fails to satisfy the requirement whereas the second case satisfies it.

Currie's other hypothetical examples lend themselves to similar analyses. In the case of the man who discovers what he takes to be a fictional manuscript, the question is whether it interests him as an expression of some more general thematic or literary interest, or whether he is simply moved to plagiarize what he takes to be a fictional work by another author. If the former is the case, then, had the narrative in the manuscript been different, he might not have fictively uttered it as his own work. If the latter, then presumably he still would have. The first scenario satisfies the 'counterfactual independence' requirement whereas the second does not. And, in the case of the man who has repressed his knowledge of the events that provide the substance for his act of fictive utterance, the key question is yet again whether, had the repressed events been different, he would have still been satisfied with the content of the narrative they would have suggested, or whether, had that narrative come to mind, he would have rejected it as failing to speak to his more general literary or thematic concerns. In fact, in this case, the former reading – which is required if we are to have a failure to satisfy the 'counterfactual independence' condition – seems very unlikely. It is only by leaving out of account the motivations driving the process of narrative construction in this case that Currie's analysis is plausible. Even if the narrative that U is moved to utter fictively is a product of subconscious knowledge, U's acceptance of that narrative still depends upon his more general purposes in narrative construction. If he is disposed to reject it if it doesn't speak to these more general concerns, then I think we should treat his work as a work of fiction. Note that, in the latter two cases, none of the posited acts of composition is governed by the fidelity constraint. The crucial difference in these cases is between an act of narrative construction governed by some more general interest in story-telling and an act not so governed.

Suppose we conjoin the idea that fiction-making involves narrative choices governed by certain kinds of constraints with the idea that something is a work of fiction insofar as it is the product of an act of fiction-making, as the latter notion is understood by 'speech act' theorists such as Currie. On the resulting view, the fictionality of a text generated with the intention that receivers make-believe the narrated events depends neither on (1) whether the narrated events correspond to some actual sequence of events, nor on (2) whether the author of the text knows of, or is unconsciously guided by, the actual sequence of events in question. It depends, rather, on (3) what constraints were taken, by the author, as the ones that the ordering of events in the narrative must satisfy. This allows an author to select, as the narrative content of a fiction, a sequence of events she knows or believes to have actually occurred, as long as it is the satisfaction of some other constraint by this sequence of events that governs her choice.

What, then, should we say about the examples with which we began? Were the members of the jury for the *Guardian* fiction prize in error in awarding the prize to Seamus Deane? The answer depends upon the constraints that guided Deane in constructing the narrative of his work. If the overriding constraint was the fidelity constraint, then his fictive intent is not sufficient to make his work fictional, and the jury was mistaken. If, on the other hand, fidelity was always subordinated to some more general interest in story-telling – thematic or otherwise – then they were not. As for works like those of Mailer, Capote, and Morrison, they are non-fictional because they are not the products of fictive utterance. But they differ from other works of non-fiction in that, while the overarching constraint on narrative construction was presumably the 'fidelity constraint', the author held that this could occasionally be relaxed to achieve other narrative ends, such as producing an overall effect on the reader, or communicating some 'higher-order' truth about the world.

CHAPTER 4

READING FICTION (I):
TRUTH IN A STORY

When William Blake, in his poem 'Jerusalem', writes of 'dark satanic mills', it is natural to see a reference to the textile mills of nineteenth-century England, and to interpret the poem accordingly. But neither Blake nor contemporary readers could have understood the poem in this way, since the textile mills were not built until more than half a century after the poem was written. In such a case, it seems reasonable to say that someone who reads Blake's poem as commenting on industrialism in nineteenth-century England is making a mistake. Or consider Jonathan Swift's *A Modest Proposal*. There is, it might be said, nothing explicit in the text of this work to inform the reader that Swift is being satirical when he suggests that the two largest contemporary social problems in Ireland – poverty and a high birth rate – may be solved by encouraging the Irish to raise their babies as food for the wealthy. Again, however, it seems reasonable to say that one who interprets Swift as making a serious suggestion is misreading the work in question.

Similar issues arise in our understanding of fictional narratives. In so-called 'magic realist' novels, such as Gabriel García Márquez's *One Hundred Years of Solitude*, the narrator recounts certain occurrences which clearly violate the natural laws that we take to obtain in the actual world. No such violations of natural law are required by the sequence of events described by Dr Kinbote, the narrator of Vladimir Nabokov's *Pale Fire*. Yet readers characteristically assume that the supernatural events described by Márquez's narrator 'really occur' in the story, whereas they dismiss some of the things narrated by Dr Kinbote as the products of radical self-deception on his part. Nothing explicitly contained in the texts of these novels seems to require that they be read in this way, yet many would view as simply mistaken a reader who took everything narrated by Kinbote to be 'true in the story' *Pale Fire*, or who took the narrator of *One Hundred Years of Solitude* to be naive or deceived in affirming the occurrence of 'supernatural' events.

Consider, finally, some more prosaic examples. Nowhere in the

Sherlock Holmes stories is there any explicit indication as to how many toes Dr Watson has. Nor, in the novels of Jane Austen, are we usually informed that the characters perform such everyday acts as washing, having their hair cut, or eating on a regular basis. But, as readers, we assume that, in the story, Watson has the usual complement of digits, and members of the Bennett family engage in normal human activities and exercise normal biological functions.

Epistemology, as a domain of philosophical enquiry, examines the grounds for claims to knowledge or understanding of various matters. The 'epistemology of literature', then, asks what rational grounds can be provided for the sorts of claims to knowledge or understanding of literary works that seem to underpin our critical and interpretative practice. If certain readings of literary works that appear compatible with what is to be found in the written texts of those works are generally viewed as mistaken, as the foregoing examples suggest, what constraints on right reading do they violate? Can there be legitimate readings of a literary work that *do* violate the sorts of constraints to which we seem to be appealing in these interpretative judgements?

In this and the following chapter, we shall examine three closely related issues in the epistemology of fiction. First, to what principles can we justifiably appeal to determine what is 'true' in a fictional narrative? Second, and more generally, what are the constraints on the ascription of different kinds of 'meanings', including story meanings, to fictional works? In particular, what role, if any, do ascriptions of intentions to authors play in determining the meanings of works? Third, do fictional works admit of a plurality of different right interpretations, where there is no possibility of combining these interpretations into a single unified reading of a work?

CONSTRAINTS ON A THEORY OF TRUTH IN FICTION

In this chapter, we shall address the first of these questions. In the previous chapter, we concluded that a crucial distinction between fiction and non-fiction is the requirement, for proper appreciation of the former, that we make-believe the content of the narrative. We also saw that this requirement is best understood as grounded in the intention of the author of the narrative that we respond in this way. Presumably, what we are invited to make-believe is what occurs in the tale narrated. But then we may ask, what *does* occur in that tale?

What is true in the story being told to us? Answering this question is answering one kind of interpretative question about a work of fiction: given this text, what is rightly said about the story narrated in it? This is distinct from other, more abstract interpretative questions about the story – for example, what does Dostoevsky's *Notes from Underground* or Kafka's *The Trial* say about 'the human condition'? or is Peter Brook's *King Lear*, which takes Lear's speech about 'poor naked wretches' as the 'message' of the play, a misreading? It is generally assumed that the issue of 'truth in a fiction', or 'story-meaning', is more tractable than issues about such 'higher-order' thematic meanings of literary works.[1] The idea is that we can give an account of story-meaning without having to consider how we would answer these higher-order questions, and, furthermore, that it is only when we have worked out what is 'true in the story' that we can sensibly raise questions about the thematic meanings explored through that story. We shall reassess these assumptions later.

In the opening paragraphs of this chapter, we surveyed some of the kinds of judgements that we make in reading stories. This helps to clarify what is required if an account of 'truth in fiction' is to make sense of our reading practice. First, as we have seen, we do not assume that everything explicitly affirmed by the narrator of a story, whether first or third person, is true in the story. The narrator may be self-deceived, as in the case of Dr Kinbote, or the narrator of Istvan Svevo's *Confessions of Zeno*. Or the narrator may be intending to deceive the reader, as is arguably the case with Humbert Humbert, the narrator of Nabokov's *Lolita*,[2] or may, in places, be speaking ironically, or using language metaphorically rather than literally.

Even if we take the narrator of a story to be trustworthy, we do not restrict what is true in a story to what is explicitly affirmed by the narrator. For sometimes, as in ordinary discourse, we take a narrator to be communicating more by her words than is strictly stated. Narrators of stories, like ordinary speakers, sometimes *imply* things by their words. Paul Grice, whose views on the communicative use of language we encountered in the previous chapter, has provided perhaps the most comprehensive treatment of what are termed *conversational implicatures*.[3] In ordinary conversation, he maintains, contributions to the talk exchange are regulated by certain principles which are grasped by all competent conversational partners. The most fundamental of these is what he terms the Cooperative Principle: 'Make your conversational contribution such as is required, at the stage at which it occurs, by the accepted purpose or direction of the talk exchange in which you are engaged.' Other, more specific principles such as 'be as informative as is required', 'try to speak only what is true', 'be relevant', and 'be perspicuous', are properly viewed as conversational maxims that spell out how one should act in order to comply with the Cooperative Principle.

He claims that speakers are able to convey one thing by using words that, taken literally and at face value, say something else – that is, to conversationally imply something by their words – because they correctly assume that their audience will be able to work out what they mean. The audience assumes that the speaker intends to comply with the Cooperative Principle. If, then, the speaker says something that, taken at face value, would violate one or more of the conversational maxims, the audience can work out what the speaker must be trying to convey if the latter is not in fact guilty of violating those maxims. In one of Grice's most famous examples, a tutor, asked to provide a letter of reference for one of her students who is applying for a philosophy position, writes that the student is a neat writer and attends class punctually. The tutor will be taken to be communicating that the student is not a promising candidate for the position. The audience can infer this because, taken at face value, the tutor's letter fails to convey the relevant information that she must possess about the student's philosophical ability, and thus violates the maxim to 'be (appropriately) informative'. Grice's analysis can also help us to understand how we grasp when a speaker is being ironic or is speaking metaphorically.

Our ability to grasp conversational implicatures used by the narrators of fictions does not seem to pose any difficulties not already posed by our ability to grasp such implicatures in ordinary conversational contexts, save, perhaps, that in our reading, we lack some of the visual clues on which we sometimes rely in conversation. Even in the case of trusted interlocutors, we don't always believe what people literally assert, and we don't always make-believe what they (literally) fictively utter. In both cases, we sometimes come to believe or make-believe what is not explicitly asserted or fictively uttered, because we take it that this is what the assertion/fictive utterance is intended to convey to us. It is reasonable to expect, therefore, that we can appeal to more general work in the philosophy of language to explain how readers are able to work out what to make-believe given what is explicitly fictively uttered, where this is simply a matter of the trustworthiness of narrators and the use of conversational implicature.

The narrator of a fictional narrative makes certain explicit assertions. By working out when, if at all, a narrator is being deceptive or self-deceptive, or is speaking ironically or metaphorically, or is using some other kind of conversational implicature, we can determine what is true in the story *in virtue of* what is explicitly asserted. We may speak here of what is *explicitly true* in a fiction, noting that this will rarely be identical, as a whole, to what is explicitly (literally) asserted by a narrator. But we also assume, in our reading, that many things are true in a story even though they are not explicitly true. We assume, for example, that it is true in the relevant stories that Sherlock Holmes is a human being rather than an extraterrestrial; that when we are informed that James Bond met with M in London and then with an agent in Paris, he has employed some means of transport that required going through various intermediate points, rather than being teleported; and that Mr Jarndyce wore footwear of some kind when he attended the Courts of Chancery to hear the final resolution of *Jarndyce* v. *Jarndyce*. But none of these things is explicitly true. In such cases, certain things are taken to be true in the story in virtue of being part of the *unstated background* to the narrative, something that the author is assuming that the competent reader herself will provide.

Suppose, for example, that it is explicitly true in a novel *N* that a character *C* took a flu powder. The author generally assumes that the reader will bring to her reading of the novel the background knowledge that flu powders dissolve in water and will assume, unless told to the contrary, that this is not only true in the real world but also true in the story. This allows us to identify a third way in which something can be true in a story. It can be true in virtue of what is explicitly true in the story when taken together with unstated background. If it is explicitly true in *N* that *C* poured a flu powder into a glass of water and a few seconds later drank the contents of the glass, and true in *N* as unstated background that flu powders dissolve in water, then we can say that it is *derivatively true* in *N* that the contents of the glass drunk by *C* are liquid, rather than granular.

Our ability to grasp what is explicitly true in a story can, as we have seen, be explained in terms of interpretative mechanisms that we employ in non-fictional contexts. For similar reasons, there seem to be no problems specific to fictional narratives in understanding how we can grasp what is derivatively true in a story, given that we know what is explicitly true and what is true as unstated background. The same does not hold, however, for our capacity to grasp what is true as unstated background in a story. To see why this is the case, consider how we go about making sense of non-fictional narratives. Suppose you write to a friend narrating various things that occurred during your vacation in St Petersburg. You go into details about the dates of your visit, how you got there, how the city struck you on first impression, your hotel, your visit to the Hermitage, the restaurants where you dined, and some local residents with whom you were able to strike up some kind of a conversation in your rudimentary Russian. As with the writer of fiction, you assume certain background understandings on the part of your reader – perhaps about the history of the Hermitage, or the history of St Petersburg, or about the kinds of things you do on an everyday basis. You expect your reader to 'fill in' gaps in your narrative with relevant facts about the world, drawing upon her knowledge of you as a person and her more general knowledge of the things you mention.

As a result of reading your letter, supplementing it with unstated background knowledge of the world, and drawing conclusions about what is derivatively true in your narrative, your friend will come to certain beliefs as to what is true – true in the actual world – as a result of reading what you say. This will include truths about what occurred during your trip to St Petersburg, truths about the city and its museums, etc. Of course, as with fictional narratives, your friend, if she is a critical reader, will use various interpretative strategies in order to decide what is explicitly true in your narrative. Perhaps she knows that you are prone to exaggerate in describing new places, or are a bad reader of people's emotions, or are given to irony or to a certain mythologizing of your experiences. And it is possible that, because she is less familiar with the things that you discuss than you suppose, she will find herself unable to supply sufficient unstated background to make sense of everything you say. Even if this is the case, however, it is easy to identify the sorts of background under-standings that would be necessary to grasp what is true of the world, given your narrative. What is required is a grasp of further facts about you and the things that you describe, and a general under-standing of the ways in which the world in general, and people in particular, work.

But we cannot adopt the same strategy to identify the relevant unstated background information when we are attempting to work out what is true in a fictional narrative. There are a number of related reasons why this is so. First, in nearly all fictional narratives, many things that are *explicitly* true in the story are false in the actual world. It is not actually true that a person named Sherlock Holmes practised his detective arts from a domicile at 221B Baker Street in turn-of-the-century London, nor that he fought with a Dr Moriarty at the Reichenbach Falls. Even less so is it true that a person named Gregor Samsa, a resident of a town in central Europe, awoke one morning to find himself turned into a giant beetle. If we were to take everything independently known to be true of the actual world as unspoken background in our reading of fictions, we would usually render the narrative inconsistent, or even incoherent.

It might be objected, however, that we do not call upon everything we know about the actual world in our reading of a *non-fictional* narrative. So perhaps we would not call upon the aforementioned facts in reading the stories of Conan Doyle or Kafka. But the problem goes much deeper, for there are more general assumptions about the fictional world that we must take as unstated background if we are to make sense of many fictional narratives, and these assumptions can, again, conflict with what we know to be true of the actual world. Magic realist novels, for example, are so-called because they contain incidents that violate what we take to be laws of nature – for example, Márquez's *One Hundred Years of Solitude* contains episodes involving levitation, flying carpets, the use of supernatural powers, and the transformation of the human body into other things. Tolkien's *Lord of the Rings* contains similar acts of wizardry, as do the Harry Potter novels. And *Star Trek* narratives require both the instantaneous transportation of the human body ('Beam me up, Scotty!') and the possibility of travel faster than the speed of light, while comic 'superheroes' possess the power to transform themselves (the Incredible Hulk), to fly (Superman) and to scale vertical surfaces (Spiderman). A reader who, in her attempts to determine what is true in such fictions, took as 'unstated background' our best current scientific view of the world could only conclude that much of what is explicitly stated by the narrator is false in the story. The narrator, one would have to conclude, is either deceived or is endeavouring to deceive the reader. But such a conclusion represents a failure to understand the narrative, which requires that we take, as unstated background, general assumptions about nature that fail to conform to our contemporary scientific picture of the world.

Finally, as may be obvious, if we take as unstated background for our understanding of fictional narratives all and only those things we take to be true of the actual world, we will generate unacceptable and sometimes bizarre *derivative* truths in the story. If, for example,

221B Baker Street had actually existed at the time of the Sherlock Holmes stories and had been a bank, then it would follow that Sherlock Holmes lived in a bank.[4] Or consider our example of the letter that you write to your friend recounting your adventures in St Petersburg, where your friend comes to believe that certain things are true of the actual world as a result of reading your narrative. Suppose that your friend knows that another friend of hers, J, was also visiting St Petersburg at the time you were there, and visited the Hermitage on the same day that you recount visiting it in your letter. Then your friend, as a result of reading your letter, will come to believe, derivatively, that it is true that both you and J visited the Hermitage on the same day. But now suppose that you are a novelist searching for a narrative that will articulate certain thematic meanings, and that, having written to your friend recounting your adventures, you realize that the events that occurred when you were in St Petersburg provide the basis for just such a narrative. Guided by your overriding thematic concerns, you incorporate into your broader fictional narrative the very events that you described in your letter to your friend, because those events exactly fit what you are looking for in your novel.[5] Suppose, now, that your friend is reading the resulting novel. If she understands clearly what it is appropriate to make-believe in reading a fictional narrative, she will not take it to be derivatively true *in the fictional story* that the narrator was visiting the Hermitage at the same time as her friend J.

But this is not to say that knowledge of real-world events temporally related to events narrated in a fiction can never bear upon what is derivatively true in the story. Later in this chapter, we shall consider Russell Hoban's novel *Riddley Walker*, our understanding of which, as we shall see, depends crucially upon our knowledge, but the narrator's ignorance, of what *precedes* the events narrated. An adequate account of how the reader supplies the appropriate unstated background in her attempts to determine what is true in a fiction must, therefore, explain why knowledge of real events not contradicted by what is explicitly true in the fiction sometimes is (*Riddley Walker*) and sometimes isn't (the 'St Petersburg novel') included in this unstated background, and thus sometimes is and sometimes isn't a proper basis for determining what is derivatively true in the story.

There is a second constraint on an adequate account of truth in fiction, which again brings out differences between the comprehension of fictional and non-fictional narratives. Suppose you are reading a biography of Conan Doyle. However thorough a particular biography may be, there will be many facts about its subject that will not be mentioned, either because they are trivial or uninteresting or because they are not known by the author. One such fact about Conan Doyle is the number of moles on his left arm when he wrote 'The Hound of the Baskervilles'. Although there is no mention of this in the biography, you can assume, in your reading, that it is true that he had a determinate number of moles on his arm at that time, and, furthermore, that, for some number n, it is true that he had n moles on his arm, even if no one is now able to discover what that number n is. 'The Hound of the Baskervilles' itself makes no mention of the number of moles on Sherlock Holmes' left arm at the time he solved the case in question. However, in our reading of the fictional story, we take it to be true in the story, as a matter of unstated background, that Holmes had a determinate number of moles on his arm at that time. We take this to be true because it is part of a more general unstated background assumption that, for any general detail not specified in the narrative, it is true in the story that there is some fact of the matter. So, for similar reasons, if we are not told where Holmes spent the night during one of his sleuthing expeditions, we assume that it is true in the story that he spent the night *somewhere* in the general geographical location of the story. But, crucially, while we assume that it is true in the story that, for some number n, Holmes had n moles on his arm when solving the crime, we don't assume that, for some determinate number n, it is true in the story that Holmes had n moles on his arm. It makes no sense to think, in the absence of its being explicitly or derivatively true in the story, that Holmes had, say, ten moles, or eight moles, even though we can never discover this fact. Similarly, while we assume that it is true in the story that there is some place P where Holmes spent the night, we don't take it that there is some determinate place P such that it is true in the story that Holmes spent the night at P, unless the location P is determined by what is explicitly or derivatively true in the story. This phenomenon – that there is no determinate answer to some of the questions we might wish to ask about a fiction – can be termed the 'narrative incompleteness' of fictions. An adequate account of truth in fiction must explain when and why fictions are narratively incomplete.

'POSSIBLE WORLDS' ANALYSES OF TRUTH IN FICTION

An adequate account of truth in fiction must, therefore, explain how, consistent with the above constraints, we are to determine, for a given fiction, the unstated background of propositions that are true in the story. As we have seen, only when we know this background are we in a position to tell what further propositions are derivatively true in the story. David Lewis suggests that we seek to explain this feature of our understanding of fictions by considering what would be true in a counterfactual situation in which the text of a story *S* is uttered as known fact. How, in other words, would we assess a counterfactual claim of the form: 'If *S* were to be uttered as known fact, then *p* would be true in *S*'? A counterfactual conditional is a conditional whose antecedent posits some state of affairs contrary to what is assumed actually to be the case, and whose consequent affirms that a particular outcome would occur if that posited state of affairs obtained. For example, I might claim that 'If I had left home five minutes earlier, I would have caught the bus'. In his account of truth in fiction, Lewis draws upon his more general theory of how we evaluate counterfactual claims.[6] We must therefore briefly sketch the latter in order to assess what Lewis says about fictional truth.

Lewis proposes that we assess the truth of counterfactual claims by considering how things are in certain 'possible worlds' – where a 'possible world' is, roughly, a way the world might be or might have been. Lewis offers the following example. Suppose I have a box of matches, from which I take one match and say 'If I had struck this match five minutes ago, it would have lit'. When we try to determine whether such a claim is correct, we need to take account of various facts concerning the situation five minutes ago – for example, the condition of the match at that time, and the presence or absence of oxygen. But, since the match in question *wasn't* struck five minutes ago, we have to consider what *would* have happened five minutes ago if the world had differed in certain ways. We have to consider what would happen in one or more possible worlds in which the match *was* struck five minutes ago.

But there are many such possible worlds. While the match lights in some of them, in many others it does not. For example, in some worlds we have radically different laws of nature such that dry matches do not light when struck upon a suitable surface in the presence of oxygen, and in other worlds, while the laws of nature are generally the same, the match is suddenly showered with water just as it is about to be struck. So we need to determine *which* possible worlds we need to consider to assess the truth of a counterfactual claim. Lewis suggests that we consider the 'nearest' worlds in which the match is struck. We measure the 'nearness' of a possible world by gauging in how many ways it differs from the actual world, taking account also of the significance of these differences: 'We hold fixed the features of actuality that do not have to be changed as part of the least disruptive way of making the supposition true'.[7] Normally the possible worlds we need to consider in assessing a counter-factual claim will resemble the actual world in all essential respects. But sometimes they won't, as when we consider a counterfactual with the antecedent, 'if the dinosaurs hadn't been wiped out by a meteor'. In some cases, the nearest possible worlds will be *physically* impossible, but still logically possible – for example, if we are considering what would happen were we able to travel faster than the speed of light.

Lewis considers a number of ways in which we might try to cash out the notion of 'truth in a story' in terms of possible worlds, whether or not we draw upon the theory of counterfactuals. He suggests that we focus on possible worlds where a given story S is 'told as known fact'.[8] We can term these the 'S-worlds' for the story S. Lewis doesn't address the question, 'What precisely must one tell in order to tell S as known fact?' But we shall assume, in line with our earlier discussion, that one must tell those things that are *explicitly true* in the story. Clearly, we cannot require that, to be true in the story S, a proposition must be true in *every* S-world. S-worlds will vary drastically from one another in all respects save for those that qualify them as S-worlds – the known truth in those worlds of those things that are explicitly true in S. Indeed, only those things that are explicitly true in S, or that are logically entailed by what is explicitly true in S, will be true in every S-world. So, if we required that anything true in S must be true in every S-world, this would not licence *any* unstated background truths or derived truths in the story. Since our practice, as readers, clearly commits us to truths in a story that go beyond explicit truths, we need to place further restrictions on the relevant class of S-worlds. This is where Lewis' treatment of counterfactuals comes into play. What we need is a subset of the S-worlds whose members more closely approximate to – are 'nearer' to – some standard than other S-worlds. The question, then, is what we should take as our standard, closeness to which will single out members of the relevant subset of S-worlds.

One possibility is to follow the recommended practice in dealing with counterfactuals in general and take the actual world as our standard. Then something will be true as unstated background in S just in case it is true in the subset of S-worlds that are closest to the actual world. Notice that, even though we are using the actual world as our standard, this does not entail that S is narratively complete. For, to return to our earlier example, it is reasonable to assume that the subset of S-worlds for 'The Hound of the Baskervilles' that are closest to the actual world differ amongst themselves as to the precise number of moles on Holmes' left arm. Although, in each world, there is a determinate number of moles on his arm, there is no determinate number n such that, in each member of the subset of S-worlds closest to the actual world, Holmes has n moles on his arm. In some such S-worlds he has ten moles, in others eight, etc. Given that what is true in S is what is true in each member of the subset of S-worlds closest to the actual world, this provides just the result that we want if we are to satisfy the 'narrative incompleteness' constraint.

But there are problems with the idea that we should take the actual world as our standard in a 'possible worlds' account of truth in a story. First, there may be facts, unknown to the author, that would obtain in those S-worlds closest to the actual world but would raise problems for the overall coherence of the narrative if taken as unstated background in S. Perhaps the best-known example of this occurs in another Sherlock Holmes story, 'The Speckled Band'. The puzzle, for Holmes, is to solve a murder committed in a closed room to which no one could have gained entry. Holmes' 'solution' is that the perpetrator of the crime had trained a venomous snake, a Russell's Viper, to descend a bell rope over the bed, bite the victim, and then return up the bell rope leaving only a small mark on the victim as evidence of what had occurred. The problem, however, is that, unbeknownst to Conan Doyle, a Russell's Viper could not perform such a feat since, not being a constrictor, it is physically incapable of descending and ascending a bell rope. Since a world in which the Russell's Viper changes its physical capacities is arguably further from the actual world than one in which a detective, however smart, comes to the wrong conclusion about a murder, the current proposal concerning truth in a story seems to entail that it is true, in 'The Speckled Band', that Holmes failed to solve the case and that either the snake reached its victim in another way or the murderer is still unknown.[9]

A second problem concerns things that are true in the actual world, and that would be true in each member of the set of S-worlds closest to the actual world, but that, again, seem inappropriate as unstated background for the story S. They may seem inappropriate either because knowledge of these things could not have been available to either the author or his intended audience, or because it is reasonable to think that the author intended that these things *not* be true in the story, even though nothing that is explicitly true in the story rules them out. A controversial example of the first kind is psychoanalytic theory which, if taken to be true in the actual world, will presumably also be true in each member of the set of *Hamlet*-worlds closest to the actual world.[10] If we take the actual world as our standard in a theory of fictional truth, then psychoanalytic theory is part of the unstated background for the play, and a psycho-analytic explanation of some of Hamlet's more puzzling actions will be derivatively true in the story, even though no such explanation could have been intended by Shakespeare or understood by his intended audience.[11] As for the second kind of case, we have already seen examples of this in 'magical realist' fictions and superhero comics.

We might try to get round these difficulties by taking as our standard not closeness to the actual world but closeness to *the way we, as readers, believe the actual world to be*. Since we, as readers, only have beliefs about certain things, no single possible world will corre-spond to our beliefs. Rather, there will be a set of worlds, differing in other respects, in each of which all of our beliefs are true. The standard against which we measure S-worlds, then, will be the extent to which they preserve our beliefs about the actual world. This approach clearly overcomes some of the problems with the 'actual world' account,[12] but it faces difficulties of its own. First, as Lewis observes, it entails that what is true in a story changes as our beliefs change. Second, as Lewis also notes, both of the accounts of the standard considered thus far cannot explain how certain general propositions can be true as unstated background to a story even though they are neither true in the actual world nor believed by us to be true in the actual world. Lewis cites Brecht's *Threepenny Opera*, in which all but one of the characters are demonstrably treacherous. If we ask whether the remaining, minor, character is also treacher-ous, it is plausible, given the rest of the play, to say that he is, in virtue of its being a truth of human psychology in the story that human beings are, by nature, treacherous. But this 'truth' in the story is not explicitly true, nor – let us assume – is it either true, or believed to be true, in the actual world.

Given the problems seen to attend the views considered thus far, the natural response is to take, as our standard for measuring S-worlds, neither closeness to the actual world nor closeness to our beliefs, as readers, concerning the actual world, but closeness to the beliefs about the actual world of either the author or the members of the intended audience. But the first of these options, which preserves the author's beliefs in so far as they are consistent with what is explicitly true in the story, fails to provide us with either a necessary or a sufficient condition for being true in S. It is not sufficient because an author may have strange and idiosyncratic beliefs that are completely orthogonal to what is explicitly true in the story. For example, in his later life, Conan Doyle held many quite exotic spiritualist beliefs, including belief in fairies. But we surely don't want to say that, in any Sherlock Holmes stories written at that time, it is true in the story, as unstated background, that fairies exist, unless, of course, there is something in what is explicitly true in the stories that would support such an idea. Or, if an author of a story about a child growing up on a farm in the Hebrides happens to believe (falsely) that Madagascar is an island in the West Indies, but there is no mention in the story of geographical matters beyond the immediate location of the narrative, it is again surely not the case that it is true in the story, as unstated background, that Madagascar occupies a different geographical niche from the one it occupies in the actual world.

Nor, for reasons already noted, should we say that *only* things believed to be true by the author can be true in the story as unstated background. For, as in the case of magical realist novels and superhero comics, an author can write a story in which some of the unstated background goes against her own beliefs. The unnatural occurrences narrated in *One Hundred Years of Solitude* are to be understood against an unstated background which allows for such supernatural events to occur, quite independently of whether Márquez himself believed that such events are possible. And, combining this point with the preceding one, determining whether or not Henry James believed in ghosts cannot by itself resolve the long-standing dispute over whether the events narrated in *The Turn of the Screw* are properly read as having a natural or a supernatural explanation.

Lewis suggests that the standard for determining the unstated background of truths in a story should be the extent to which S-worlds are able to preserve the beliefs about the actual world of *the community of readers for whom the author is writing.* What matters is not the author's own beliefs, which may be idiosyncratic as we have seen, but what is widely believed in this community of readers. Since the relevant community is identified by reference to the context in which the text of a literary work was authored, this proposal does not entail that what is true in a story changes as the beliefs of different generations of readers change. In setting out his proposal, Lewis talks of what is common knowledge in the community of origin of a literary work:

> Call a belief *overt* in a community at a time iff more or less everyone shares it, more or less everyone thinks that more or less everyone shares it, and so on . . . What is true in the Sherlock Holmes stories is what would be true, according to the overt beliefs of the community of origin, if those stories were told as known fact rather than fiction.[13]

The proposed standard for measuring *S*-worlds, then, is their ability to preserve those beliefs that are overt in a literary work's community of origin. This proposal clearly circumvents problems arising from idiosyncratic authorial beliefs orthogonal to the text. It also allows us to explain the unstated background in terms of which readers make sense of magical realist novels and superhero stories, if, plausibly, we assume that there are, in the community of origin, overt beliefs about what is to be taken as unstated background in certain special kinds of literary genres.

But, while Lewis' proposed analysis of truth in a story is clearly the best option given a 'possible worlds' approach to such matters, there are still difficulties which suggest that we need to look for another strategy. First, as Gregory Currie points out, the 'possible worlds' strategy faces problems if we confront a story in which *inconsistent* truths obtain.[14] For example, 'time-travel' stories seem to entail that a person could travel back in time and kill his own parents. The problem is that the 'worlds' to which we appeal in our counterfactual analysis of fictional truth must themselves be *consistent*, if they are to be possible. No possible world can be one in which an inconsistent narrative is told as known truth, so we seem to lack an account of how we are able to understand such stories (as we seem to be able to do). A further difficulty emerges given Lewis' claim that the unstated background for a story is to be determined by reference to the beliefs of the culture in which the work originates. How, on this account, can an author write a fiction in which the unstated background is meant to differ from the beliefs of the community in which she finds herself? For example, if an author lives in a country where 'overt belief' includes belief in personal angels and satanic forces, can that author nonetheless write a fiction in which it is unstated background that no such things exist? This, as we shall see, is something that authors do seem able to do, by locating the narrator of their fiction in a cultural context different from their own. If this is possible, then it is no answer to this objection to maintain that the author is able to pick out an *intended* audience whose beliefs differ from those in the culture of origin of her work. For an author may intend, as the unstated background for her fiction, things that she does *not* take her intended audience to believe, as in the case of magical realist novels. Rather, as we shall see, it is the intended audience of what Gregory Currie terms the 'fictional author' that matters.

FICTIONAL TRUTH AND FICTIONAL AUTHORS

Currie offers a promising alternative to Lewis' approach. Rather than try to explicate truth in a story in terms of possible worlds in which a given set of beliefs is true, he proposes that we take, as the basis of our analysis, sets of beliefs themselves. His proposal is that we identify what is true in a story with the set of beliefs reasonably imputed to what he terms the 'fictional author'. The latter, according to Currie, is an essential element in the games of make-believe that we play in our reading of fictional stories:

> When we make believe the story, we make believe that the text is an account of events that have actually occurred. But for this to be our make-believe we have to see the text as related in a certain way to those events; we have to see it as the product of someone who has the knowledge of those events. Our make-believe is not merely that the events described in the text occurred, but that we are being told about those events by someone with knowledge of them. Thus it is part of the make-believe that the reader is in contact, through channels of reliable information, with the characters and their actions, that the reader learns about their activities from a reliable source. To make-believe a fictional story is not merely to make-believe that the story is true, but *that it is told as known fact*.[15]

The 'fictional author', then, is the 'reliable source' from whom the reader learns about the events narrated in the story: 'The fictional author (as I shall call him) is that fictional character constructed within our make-believe whom we take to be telling us the story as known fact. Our reading is thus an exploration of the fictional author's belief structure'.[16]

Currie points out that belief-sets, like some fictional narratives, can be internally inconsistent, even though, as noted above, no possible world can correspond to an inconsistent belief-set.[17] Furthermore, belief-sets exhibit some of the other properties of truth in a story that we have already noticed. Truth in a story, we saw, is 'narratively incomplete' in that, while it may be true in the story that Holmes slept somewhere on a given night, there may be no determinate location such that it is true in the story that Holmes slept there on that night. Similarly, I may believe that Holmes slept somewhere on a given night without believing, of any particular place, that Holmes slept there on that night.

Currie's 'fictional author' of a story cannot be identified with either its *real* author or its explicit narrator(s), if any, if Currie's proposal is to avoid objections already raised against alternative accounts. We have seen that what is true as unstated background in a story may diverge from the beliefs of the actual author, and that the narrator may be deceived as to what is true in the story. But in that case we need to ask how we are supposed to discover what the beliefs of the 'fictional author' are, and thus what is true in *S* in virtue of being among those beliefs. Currie suggests that, in our attempts to determine the beliefs of the fictional author, we are guided by two sorts of considerations: (1) the text of the story, which provides our only direct evidence as to the fictional author's character and mental idiosyncracies; and (2) whatever assumptions we are justified in making as to the cultural and historical location of the fictional author. The first of these seems to be the resource upon which we rely in our attempts to work out what is explicitly true in the story. It is, so Currie claims, the 'overall impression' of the work that guides our judgements as to what is explicitly true in a story, given what is literally stated.[18] It is also our reading of the text that helps us to decide when the narrator is to be trusted:

> What the explicit narrator believes and what is true in the story can always come apart. The reader must decide, as his reading progresses, whether to put his faith in the explicit narrator. When we

decide that the explicit narrator cannot be trusted we move to the level of an unobtrusive narrator who, by putting words in the mouth of the explicit narrator in a certain way, signals his skepticism about what the explicit narrator says.[19]

What, though, of our concerns about determining the unstated background of a story? Currie suggests that our main guide in ascertaining the latter is the historical and cultural location of the *real* author:

> Although the real author and the fictional author are distinct, it is quite likely that the kind of person the fictional author is will depend in some way or other on the kind of person the real author is . . . When we read a work from a certain period and place, we usually assume we are dealing with a fictional author of that period and place.

But, as Currie immediately notes, this isn't always the case:

> A modern author who writes a novel set in the Middle Ages may succeed in placing within the novel a fictional author who has the beliefs that medieval people tended to have. In that case, what will be true in the novel will reflect medieval belief. More likely, his fictional author will display beliefs and attitudes that are distinctly modern. In that case, what is true in the novel will have little to do with the overt beliefs of medieval times.[20]

But how are we, as readers, to distinguish these two types of cases? Faced with a novel whose temporal (or, indeed, cultural) setting differs from that of the real author, how are we to 'historically situate' (or culturally situate) the fictional author? More specifically, how does the fictional author 'display beliefs and attitudes' of a particular kind? Currie responds to these kinds of questions by referring us again to the first kind of evidence cited above: it is properties of the *text* that enable us to situate the fictional author. It is, he maintains, our reading of the text that enables us to locate the fictional author *within* a given community, and identify any beliefs idiosyncratic in the context of that community.[21] The style of a story is the means whereby the personality of the *fictional* author is displayed: 'That personality may be pessimistic or misogynistic, rigidly conventional or sternly moralistic, without the real author being any of these things. But if that is the personality the style suggests, that is the personality the fictional author has'.[22]

To see why such a view is problematic, consider, as exemplifying a more general difficulty, Russell Hoban's novel *Riddley Walker*. This novel is set in England, in the area around Canterbury, in the aftermath of some kind of nuclear disaster or nuclear war. The narrator is a boy belonging to a tribal culture whose members have (mistakenly?) assumed that various recognizable disparate elements of our culture, surviving in more or less damaged form, must have been parts of a unified theoretical framework, a framework they have tried to re-create. The narrator shares these beliefs about the historical relationships between these elements. Nothing in the text undercuts his credibility, or 'displays beliefs and attitudes that are distinctly modern'. Suppose we ask whether it is true in the story that the narrator and his culture misunderstand the significance of the cultural fragments in question. Given Currie's general approach, what we are asking is whether the fictional author shares the cultural perspective of the narrator, or whether he shares with us the ability to recognize, in the narrator's description of uncovered artefacts and relics, a mistaken apprehension of the significance of these elements drawn from late twentieth-century science, technology, religion and popular culture. For reasons to which I shall turn in a moment, I think that, as readers, we will say that it is indeed true in the story that the narrator and his culture are labouring under a misconception. If Currie's account is to accommodate this intuition, he must situate the 'fictional author' *not* in the narrator's culture but in some temporal extension of the culture of the real author.

Compare this example with the case, cited earlier, of *One Hundred Years of Solitude*. In spite of our belief, and (let us assume) Márquez's belief, that natural events proceed according to natural laws, it is surely incorrect to say that the various 'supernatural' events narrated in the story have natural explanations *in the story*. In this case, given Currie's account, we must be locating the 'fictional author' within the culture of the *narrator*, not within the culture of the real author. But is it plausible that the different decisions concerning the historico-cultural situation of the 'fictional author' in the two cases are to be justified by reference to different properties of the two texts? Or is it, rather, *because* we decide, for independent reasons, that it is true in the story *Riddley Walker* that the narrator's culture is deceived, whereas we make no such decision in the case of *One Hundred Years of Solitude*, that we situate the 'fictional author' as we do in the two works? If, as I suggest below, this is the case, then, if there is a place for talk of the 'fictional author' in a theory of fiction, it cannot be the role that Currie allots to this device.

Where, then, should we go from here? One possible avenue is to appeal to the *real* author, not in respect of her general beliefs about the world, but rather, in respect of her *intentions* concerning the context of reception for her story – the unstated background that she intends readers to bring to their imaginative engagement with the narrative. If this approach is to work, however, it will have to allow for the *failure* of the real author to produce a work in which her intention is realized.[23] As with the idea that the author's own beliefs provide a standard for a 'possible worlds' analysis of truth in a story, one option here is to bring in the reasonable inferences that would be made by the intended audience. We might then try to develop the following kind of proposal: a given proposition p is true in a story S just in case it is reasonable for the informed reader to infer that the real author of S intended that the reader make-believe that p.[24] We shall defer to the following chapter an assessment of these kinds of 'intentionalist' strategies.

But I think there is a deeper lesson to be drawn from our consideration of the above examples. It is fundamental to Currie's approach to the question of truth in a story that what he terms 'story meaning' is *basic* to an account of fiction in the sense that it is presupposed by any attempt to 'understand' the 'meaning' of a fictional work in any deeper sense.[25] Our discussion of *Riddley Walker* and *One Hundred Years of Solitude*, however, suggests that this is incorrect, at least for what might be termed 'serious fiction'. In the case of *Riddley Walker*, I would suggest, it is precisely because we see the deceived status of the narrator's culture as crucial to the *point* of the novel – because we recognize, in the situation of the narrator's culture, an analogue of our own relationship to our cultural predecessors – that we take the deception to be true in the story. And, I would also suggest, analogous reasons explain our judgement that the narrator of *One Hundred Years of Solitude* is not deceived concerning the supernatural nature of the events he describes. It is only given these kinds of judgements as to the *thematic meaning* of the work – the 'point' of telling this story rather than a different one – that we can decide where to locate a Curriean 'fictional author'. In other words, working out what is true in the story in 'serious' works of fiction requires not merely a familiarity with generic conventions, but reflection upon the possible thematic meanings that the story may have. It is not that we *first* get clear on 'story meaning' and only then can ask about thematic meaning. Indeed, it may be a feature of those narratives we treat as 'serious fiction' that a reader who has not enquired as to the point of *this* story being told in *this* way can be held to have failed to exercise a properly responsible attitude towards the work. Thus the issues of 'truth in fiction' and what may be termed 'truth *through* fiction' – to be examined in Chapter 8 – are more closely related than many have supposed.[26]

CHAPTER 5

READING FICTION (2): INTERPRETING LITERARY WORKS

INTERPRETATION AND THE 'INTENTIONAL FALLACY'

'Story meaning', or 'truth in a story', discussed in the previous chapter, is one kind of meaning that we ascribe to a work of fiction in our attempts to understand and appreciate it. Determining story meaning is one of the things we do in interpreting fictional works. As was noted at the end of the previous chapter, it might be concluded, in light of the difficulties seen to confront alternative accounts, that determining story meaning requires that we ascribe to the author of the story either certain intentions as to what the reader is to make-believe, or certain intentions to tell a story that articulates a given thematic meaning. Indeed, we may recall from Chapter 3 that ascribed intentions also play a crucial role in our taking a narrative to *be* fictional. A fictional narrative, we argued, is one whose author intends the reader to make-believe what is narrated, and who is guided in her construction of the narrative by some overriding interest in story-telling other than the 'fidelity constraint'.

But any account of story meaning that accords a determining role to the intentions of the author must address a more general, and very influential, argument against what has been termed the 'intentional fallacy'. According to William Wimsatt and Monroe C. Beardsley,[1] authorial intention plays no legitimate role in either the interpretation or the evaluation of a literary work. What matters in both cases, they claim, is what the author actually achieved, not what she intended to achieve, and the former is to be determined without reference to the latter. In the first three sections of this chapter, I shall look in more detail at Wimsatt and Beardsley's argument, and at different ways in which other philosophers have tried to give a role to the ascription of authorial intentions in an account of literary interpretation. I shall defend an 'uptake' theory of interpretation that acknowledges the motivations behind intentionalist accounts while preserving what is right in Wimsatt and Beardsley's account. In the final section, I shall assess the claim that literary works admit of a multiplicity of different interpretations corresponding to the multiplicity of interpretative aims.

Wimsatt and Beardsley make two related claims. First, they maintain that knowledge of what an author intended to do in bringing a particular literary work into existence is irrelevant to the *evaluation* of her work. What matters for evaluative purposes is *what the artist actually achieved*, not what she intended to achieve. Second, they claim that knowledge of the contentful properties that an artist intended her work to possess is irrelevant to the *interpretation* of what the artist produces. What matters for interpretation is, again, the contentful properties that the artistic product actually possesses, not those it was intended to possess.

What is the relationship between these two claims? First, it might be assumed that anti-intentionalism about evaluation presupposes anti-intentionalism about interpretation. For, it might be thought, the only way in which intentions might bear upon evaluation would be by determining the meanings rightly ascribable to the text produced by the author. Those who have responded to Wimsatt and Beardsley have generally endorsed such a view, either tacitly or explicitly. Defenders of 'intentionalism', as the opposing view is usually termed, have sought to establish the relevance of authorial intentions to the appreciation and evaluation of literary artworks by defending an intentionalist view of interpretation. But, second, one might grant the case against an intentionalist view of interpretation while not granting the case against an intentionalist view of evaluation. For one might hold that authorial intention bears in some other way on a work's understanding and appreciation.[2] Some of the contemporary critics cited by Wimsatt and Beardsley held such a view, believing that an artist's ability to execute successfully what she intended is one kind of value ascribable to a work. In their attack on the 'intentional fallacy', Wimsatt and Beardsley do not clearly separate the two intentionalist theses, but for the present we shall assume that the key issue, in assessing their anti-intentionalism, is their claim about interpretation.

Wimsatt and Beardsley describe the author's intentions as 'a design or plan in the author's mind',[3] and offer a number of reasons for excluding them from the enterprise of interpreting and evaluating works of literary art. First, so they claim, while we are clearly right in assuming that a given literary text was caused to be the way it is by a 'designing intellect', it doesn't follow that authorial intention provides a standard for evaluating the work. Second, they argue that the role accorded to the author's intentions by intentionalist critics presents insuperable epistemological difficulties. How are we supposed to know what the author intended? The intentionalist faces a dilemma. Either the author succeeded in realizing her intentions or she didn't. If she succeeded, then what was intended will coincide with what the reader can find in the literary text, and there is no need to appeal to what the author intended. If, on the other hand, she failed, then one can determine what was intended only by appeal to things that are external to the work, such as the author's letters, diaries, etc. But why should such things bear upon the understanding or the value of the work?

The idea that evidence of authorial intention not manifest in the literary text is external to the work rests upon a view of the nature of a literary work, and the ways in which it differs, as a linguistic utterance, from utterances that we encounter in ordinary conversation. The poem, so Wimsatt and Beardsley maintain, is 'detached from the author at birth and goes about the world beyond his power to intend about it or control it . . . The poem belongs to the public. It is embodied in language, the peculiar possession of the public'.[4] Thus only certain kinds of evidence can rightly be brought in support of a given interpretation of a poem. Most significant is what they term 'internal' evidence, which 'is also public: it is discovered through the semantics and syntax of a poem, through our habitual knowledge of the language, through grammars, dictionaries, and all the literature which is the source of dictionaries, in general through all that makes a language and culture'.[5] On the other hand, it is not permissible to appeal to what they term 'external' evidence, which is 'private or idiosyncratic; not a part of the work as a linguistic fact: it consists of revelations (in journals, for example, or letters or reported conversations) about how or why the poet wrote the poem – to what lady, while sitting on what lawn, or at the death of what friend or brother'.[6] However, they do allow the critic to appeal to what they term 'intermediate evidence' concerning 'the character of the author or private or semi-private meanings attached to words or topics by an author or by a coterie of which he is a member'.[7] Such evidence, while it is in a sense external to the poem as text, is admissible because 'the meaning of words is the history of words, and the biography of an author, his use of a word, and the associations which the word had for *him*, are part of the word's history and meaning'.[8]

The admission of 'intermediate evidence' on such grounds is interesting in light of our discussion, in Chapter 2, of the nature of the literary work. While one might initially think that Wimsatt and Beardsley subscribe to a textualist conception of the literary work, it is clear that, in allowing evidence as to the ways in which the author of a text employs language in other contexts, they are taking a literary work to be a particular text as generated by a particular author, and thus as generated in a particular context. Thus their position is a kind of contextualism. A second interesting point is that, according to Wimsatt and Beardsley, 'external' evidence as to the speaker's intentions *is* admissible when we are interpreting what people say in ordinary conversation. In their paper on the 'Intentional Fallacy' this point is made only obliquely, when it is remarked that success in a poem is a matter of the interwoven and non-extraneous meaningful elements to be found within the text, whereas a 'practical message' is successful 'if and only if we correctly infer the intention'.[9] Beardsley develops this point more fully, however, in a later paper.[10] There he contrasts our interpretative interests in practical contexts with our interests as literary interpreters:

> There are many practical occasions on which our task is precisely to try to discover authorial meaning, or intention, what the speaker or writer had in mind and wanted us to understand. When there is a difficulty in reading a will or a love letter, or in grasping an oral promise or instruction, our primary concern is with authorial meaning. If there is ambiguity or the possibility of misspeaking, we want to correct it. To do this, we may avail ourselves of such evidence as fuller explanations by the author himself, if we can find him, and information about his actions . . . But I hold that the case is different when we turn to literary interpretation. The proper task of the literary interpreter is to interpret textual meaning.[11]

Beardsley offers two arguments in support of this claim about literary interpretation. First, as he rightly points out, while we are usually able to consult the author of a remark or letter in practical contexts, this is only possible in literary contexts when we are dealing with works by contemporary authors. Consider two contested issues in literary interpretation. Do the 'ghosts' in James' *Turn of the Screw* really exist in the story? And does the final stanza of Wordsworth's poem, 'A Slumber Did My Spirit Seal',

No motion has she now, no force,
She neither hears nor sees,
Rolled round in earth's diurnal course
With rocks, and stones, and trees –

express the poet's horror at the inertness of the loved one – as Cleanth Brooks maintained[12] – or the pantheistic sentiment that she is now part of the greater life of Nature – as F. W. Bateson maintained?[13] Neither of these issues could be resolved by consulting the poet unless there is some unambiguous expression of intention in a letter or note. But this argument, as Beardsley grants, is hardly conclusive, since the intentionalist can say that, as with our attempts to understand historical events, this may only testify to our ignorance of what a text or an action means, not to its meaning being independent of the intentions of the agent.

The second consideration adduced by Beardsley is that we should take the task of literary interpretation to be to actualize the 'aesthetic goodness' of the work. The critic's task is to help the reader to approach the work from the aesthetic point of view, and to do this is to take an interest in something arising out of the verbal elements that make up the poem. As Beardsley notes yet again, however, this argument will only convince an opponent who shares certain fundamental assumptions about 'the function of literary interpretation, the nature of literature, and the nature of artistic goodness'.[14] However, I have already defended, in Chapter 1, certain assumptions that might be used to reinforce Beardsley's claim. In particular, it was argued in Chapter 1 that a distinctive feature of literary artworks is the way in which the linguistic medium serves to articulate content 'aesthetically' in Goodman's sense. We shall return to this later in the chapter.

Before looking at intentionalist responses to the kinds of arguments advanced by Wimsatt and Beardsley, it is worth considering some practical consequences of their anti-intentionalist position. Of particular interest is the issue of literary allusion and its bearing upon a correct understanding of a work. Taking an author to be making an allusion to someone else's work seems to presuppose biographical knowledge of the author, and to entail that 'we do not know what a poet means unless we have traced him in his reading – a supposition redolent with intentional implications'.[15] A salient example discussed by Wimsatt and Beardsley is the use of allusion in Eliot's *The Waste Land*. They separate two issues arising in connection with this poem. First, there are resemblances that one might find between elements in the poem and elements in the work of other writers. They insist that, in such cases, we are not required to track down such allusions to their sources in order properly to appreciate the poem: 'Eliot's allusions work when we know them – and to a great extent even when we do not know them – through their suggestive power'.[16] Second, there is the question how to treat Eliot's 'notes' attached to the poetic text which, in many cases, identify a source for an allusion in the text. For example, to the lines

> The sound of horns and motors, which shall bring
> Sweeney to Mrs. Porter in the spring

Eliot appends the note

> Cf. Day, *Parliament of Bees*
> When of a sudden, listening, you shall hear,
> A noise of horns and hunting; which shall bring
> Actaeon to Diana in the spring,
> Where all shall see her naked skin . . .

Wimsatt and Beardsley argue that, in this case, the salient question is whether the notes are parts of the poem itself. Once we raise this question, we can account for their contribution to the poem without endorsing an intentionalist view of interpretation:

> Whereas notes tend to seem to justify themselves as external indexes to the author's *intention*, yet they ought to be judged like any other parts of a composition (verbal arrangements special to a particular context), and when so judged their reality as parts of the poem, or their imaginative integration with the rest of the poem, may come into question.[17]

It might still be thought that an intention on the part of the poet to allude to another work is at least *necessary* for the poem to be correctly described as making such an allusion. But Wimsatt and Beardsley resist even this limited concession to the intentionalist. They consider whether the line in Eliot's 'The Love Song of J. Alfred Prufrock', 'I have heard the mermaids singing each to each', should be taken as an allusion to John Donne's 'Song', where the poet writes, 'Teach me to heare Mermaides singing'. There are, they maintain, two ways in which we might resolve this question.[18] One is 'the way of poetic analysis and exegesis', where we ask whether the poem makes *sense* if we grant the allusion. This, they maintain, is 'the true and objective way of criticism'. The alternative is 'the way of biographical and genetic inquiry', which seeks to determine whether the poet intended to make such an allusion. How this question is answered, they maintain, has nothing to do with the *poem* as a literary work.

But it is difficult to see how the latter claim can be sustained. For alluding to the work of another writer is something an *author* does in a poem, rather than something the poem itself can do purely in virtue of its own internal resources. It is, arguably, like being ironic or being sarcastic – it requires that language be intentionally used in a certain way by an author or speaker. Intending to make an allusion, or to be ironic, or to be sarcastic, is not sufficient to succeed in any of these actions – success depends upon properties of the utterance one produces and possible uptake by one's audience. But authorial intention seems to have some part to play in an adequate account of these kinds of linguistic phenomena. Nevertheless, there are many insights in Wimsatt and Beardsley's account that are worth preserving in a theory of literary interpretation. Later in this chapter, we shall see how they might be preserved in a theory that also preserves what is right in intentionalism.

'ACTUAL INTENTIONALIST' THEORIES OF INTERPRETATION

To clarify how one might defend the idea that the artist's intentions play a legitimate role in the interpretation of artworks, we need to distinguish between three kinds of meanings that may be in play in either ordinary conversational contexts or in the interpretation of artworks. First, shared understandings embodied in the making and interpreting of past utterances confer a meaning on the linguistic vehicle employed which can be termed the *conventional meaning* of that vehicle. Conventional meaning is something grasped by competent users of the language. Second there is the *utterer's meaning*, the content that the utterer, in employing a particular linguistic vehicle, intends her audience to ascribe to that vehicle as uttered. Utterer's meaning may be basic or higher-order. A speaker often intends her audience to ascribe a certain basic meaning to what she says but also to draw some kind of conversational implicature to a higher-order meaning she is trying to convey. Finally, there is the *utterance meaning*, the content rightly ascribable to the utterance itself, as the product of the utterer's action. We can distinguish, again, between basic and higher-order utterance meaning.

We can re-express the disagreement between Wimsatt and Beardsley and their intentionalist opponents in terms of these notions. Each offers an account of utterance meaning, of what is said, at both a basic and a higher-order level, by a speaker who employs a particular linguistic vehicle on a particular occasion. For Wimsatt and Beardsley, utterance meaning is identical to conventional meaning, understood in a broad sense that encompasses ordinary linguistic norms, specialized literary conventions, and idiosyncratic senses of words manifest in the history of use by a particular individual or social group. The intentionalist, on the other hand, proposes that utterance meaning be identified with utterer's meaning.

But the intentionalist has to say something about the conditions under which such an identity obtains in order to distinguish his position from the view espoused by Lewis Carroll's Humpty Dumpty.[19] The latter notoriously maintained that, when he employed a linguistic expression, it meant whatever he wanted it to mean. If we construe Humpty Dumpty's talk about his wishes as talk about what he *intends* to say in using a particular linguistic expression, this represents an extreme version of the view that it is utterer's meaning – the speaker's semantic intentions – that determines what she says in a given use of language. Alice was quite properly horrified at such a view of linguistic meaning, and philosophers have generally shared her disquiet, pointing out that such a view would make it impossible to use language as a communicative medium.

Much recent work on interpretation in both the philosophy of language and the philosophy of literature has been broadly intentionalist in flavour. The aim has been to demonstrate that our justifiable qualms about Humpty Dumpty should not blind us to the proper place of utterer's meaning in any adequate theory of utterance meaning. But intentionalism, as we shall see, comes in more than one flavour. Defenders of what is usually termed 'actual intentionalism' argue that, properly understood, the thesis that the semantic intentions of the utterer determine utterance meaning is correct, and have adopted a couple of distinct strategies to counter the charge of Humpty-Dumptyism. A popular strategy for actual intentionalists is to see conventional meaning as imposing *limits* on

AESTHETICS AND LITERATURE

utterance meaning, where utterer's intentions determine utterance meaning within these limits.

This strategy can be traced back to E. D. Hirsch, who defended a form of actual intentionalism in his *Validity in Interpretation* and other publications. Hirsch takes as his target what he terms the thesis of 'semantic autonomy', according to which an author's semantic intentions can play no part in our critical attempts to interpret her literary works. He argues that, if we grant this thesis, the very practice of literary criticism, as an activity that can be held to objective standards, is undermined. For, so he claims, unless we take the author to play a part in determining the meaning of her text, there will be no determinate meaning for critics to discern or disagree about, but only the different readings of different readers who bring their individual concerns to the text. Criticism as a responsible practice, according to Hirsch, can operate only when literary works have a determinate meaning that the critic can reproduce for the enlightenment of readers. But the norms and conventions of language, taken independently of a particular *use* of language to convey some intended meaning, nearly always leave open a plurality of interpretations. This holds, so Hirsch maintains, not only for short texts but also for longer ones. We get *determinate* meanings only if we posit a speaker who is using the words with a particular intention. As Hirsch puts this point, 'a determinate verbal meaning requires a determining will . . . Unless one particular complex of meaning is willed . . . there would be no distinction between what an author does mean by a word sequence and what he could mean by it'.[20] This is not to deny that the practice of critical interpretation requires public norms of language, for without such norms we are back with Humpty Dumpty, with no prospect of shared meanings. But it is only by appeal to the author's 'determining will' that we can select one out of the plurality of meanings that a text might bear, given those public norms.

Gary Iseminger has further elaborated Hirsch's argument,[21] offering, as an example of the sort of 'indeterminacy' that Hirsch had in mind, the poem 'Henry Purcell' by Gerard Manley Hopkins, whose opening lines are as follows:

Have fair fallen, O fair, fair have fallen so dear
To me, so arch-especial a spirit as heaves in Henry Purcell.[22]

These lines, Iseminger argues, are open to two quite different interpretations, given the relevant linguistic norms. In the first, the poem
expresses the wish that Henry Purcell shall have had good fortune,
while in the second, the wish expressed is that Henry Purcell shall
have been a good person and have done good things. We have
evidence, however, in a letter of Hopkins to the poet Robert Bridges,
that Hopkins intended the poem to express the first of these wishes.
The suggestion, then, is that, in light of this knowledge, we should
ascribe a determinate meaning to the poem, rather than hold it to be
an ambiguous work. Iseminger, like Hirsch, maintains that linguistic
norms make available, for any given linguistic vehicle, a range of
possible meanings. The author's intention 'activates' one of those
meanings as the determinate meaning of the work.

In the paper cited earlier, Beardsley responded to Hirsch, arguing
that, in general, public linguistic norms *do* render meaning determinate once we place a bit of text in its broader linguistic context.
Iseminger's example seems to provide an instance of an admittedly
fairly brief poem where this is not so. Beardsley's further claim,
however, is that if linguistic norms, understood in a suitably broad
manner, fail to render the meaning of a literary work determinate,
then we must live with its indeterminacy. He raises a further difficulty for the actual intentionalist. How, we might ask, are authorial
intentions supposed to render meaning determinate, independently
of the well-informed reader's ability, under normal circumstances, to
tell what that meaning is? Beardsley writes:

> An ambiguous text does not become any less ambiguous because
> its author wills one of the possible meanings. Will as he will, he
> cannot will away ambiguity. There is something odd about the
> notion of 'willing' a meaning. It is as though we ordered someone,
> 'Say 'cat' and mean dog'. Can one do that? How does one do it?[23]

Another problem for someone adopting the Hirsch–Iseminger
strategy is that it is unclear what such a strategy dictates in cases
where the speaker's intended meaning falls *outside* the range of
'possible meanings' permitted by linguistic norms. To cite a classic
example, what are we to say about Mrs Malaprop's talk of 'a nice
derangement of epitaphs'?[24] In such a situation, it seems that there is
something determinate that the speaker says – either what her words
literally say or what she manages to convey to her audience, who
interpret her as talking of a nice arrangement of epithets. But neither

option seems open on the view under discussion. The former option is not what the speaker intends, and the latter option does not fall within the range of meanings allowed by the linguistic norms. Hirsch himself seems to hold that, since there is no 'determining will' in such a case, the utterance lacks a determinate meaning. Beardsley might respond that, if we can take the general idiosyncracies in Mrs Malaprop's use of language as part of the history of her use of words, then the 'conventional' meaning, broadly construed, is perfectly determinate. In any case, there is a need to clarify what the Hirsch–Iseminger view should say on this kind of case, and how plausible it is.

Robert Stecker's 'unified view'[25] can be seen as attempting to counter these objections while preserving a determinative role for actual intentions. Stecker formulates the unified view as follows:

> When the artist succeeds in expressing her intention in the work (which, of course, will commonly involve the exploiting of conventions and context) that is what we should identify with the meaning of the work, but when actual intentions fail to be expressed, conventions in place when the work is created determine meaning.[26]

Like Hirsch, Stecker holds that linguistic conventions are rarely sufficient to determine utterance meaning, but he has in mind the need to provide a context of utterance if we are to fix the reference of indexical expressions such as 'here' and 'now', demonstratives such as 'this' and 'that', and some other linguistic expressions. Thus he doesn't think that, when authors fail to express their intentions, the lack of a 'determining will' entails that meaning is indeterminate. However, once the unified view is amended to take account of the role of context, it becomes unclear what determinative role can be accorded to utterer's meaning. This difficulty manifests itself in two ways. First, 'success' in realizing one's semantic intentions seems to presuppose an intention-independent conception of utterance meaning – for success seems to be a matter of utterer's meaning actually being expressed by the utterance. Stecker argues, however, that we can think of expressive success in terms of an 'uptake condition' requiring that utterer's meaning be graspable by 'properly prepared' receivers.

However, this exposes a deeper difficulty with the unified view. Consider an example used by Stecker. If I say 'there is a fly in your suit' with the intention of communicating to you the presence of an insect in your broth, you are presumably quite capable of 'uptake'. But Stecker insists that, in such a case, the utterance meaning is that there is a fly in your *suit*, and thus that I *fail* to realize my semantic intentions. For this to be consistent with his proposed elucidation of expressive success, the resources available to a receiver engaged in 'uptake' must be limited to a knowledge of linguistic conventions plus a knowledge of features of the context of utterance implicated by those conventions. Let me term the meaning that would be ascribed by an interpreter with just these resources the 'contextualized conventional meaning' (CCM) of an utterance. If the measure of expressive success is conformity between utterer's meaning and CCM, however, and if, as is claimed by the unified view, it is CCM that determines utterance meaning when a speaker *fails* to realize her semantic intentions, then utterer's meaning seems redundant in the unified view of utterance meaning. For it appears that, on this view, utterance meaning is identified with CCM either directly, if the speaker fails, or indirectly, if the speaker succeeds, in her communicative intentions. Thus it seems preferable simply to identify utterance meaning with the CCM that receivers should ascribe.[27]

Suppose, on the other hand, that we allow that 'uptake' can involve the sort of interpretative intelligence that enables one to grasp what speakers intend to say even when their words fail them, as in the 'fly in your suit' example. Then I will *realize* my semantic intentions when I utter 'there is a fly in your suit' as long as, by employing such interpretative intelligence, you are able to grasp what I am trying to communicate. The meaning of my utterance, on the unified view so modified, will relate to insects in broth rather than tailoring requisites.

But, if these richer resources are permitted where speakers succeed, they should surely also be allowed when speakers *fail* in their semantic intentions. Imagine a Hungarian victim of a wholly inadequate English–Hungarian phrase-book, who possesses a rudimentary knowledge of English syntax but an impoverished English vocabulary.[28] Entering a London bank, he attempts to utter what he believes is the English equivalent of the Hungarian sentence whose conventional meaning is 'I want to withdraw some money'. The English sentence paired with this Hungarian sentence in the phrase-book, however, is 'I want to arrange a loan'. Suppose that, in attempting to utter this English sentence, the speaker produces a malapropic variation on the sentence in the phrase-book – say 'I want to derange a loon'. The bank teller, employing her customary interpretative intelligence, understands him to have said, in English, that he wishes to arrange a loan. If the unified view interprets success in terms of uptake richly construed, then utterance meaning in cases of speaker failure like the one described should also be the meaning ascribable by interlocutors capable of such uptake. Thus it appears that, whether we succeed or fail, utterance meaning will be identical to the meaning that would be ascribed to our utterance by appropriately skilled interpreters able to draw on knowledge of linguistic conventions, context, and interpretative intelligence – we might term this the 'hermeneutically enriched contextualized conventional meaning' (HECCM) of the utterance. Again, therefore, utterer's meaning seems to play no necessary part in determining utterance meaning.

The proponent of actual intentionalism might seek to evade this kind of objection by offering an alternative account of what is required for an utterer to succeed in her intentions. Such an account has been proposed by Paisley Livingston in elaborating a subtle intentionalist view that he terms 'partial intentionalism'.[29] Livingston seems to grant that the kind of argument just considered applies to a work's 'explicit content', which is determined by textual, conventional, and contextual variables. The artist, in intending that his work have a particular explicit content, relies upon such variables as the *means* whereby content is to be articulated, and fails if the meaning determined by such means is not the one intended. But, Livingston argues, this does not apply to some aspects of a work's 'implicit content'. Implicit content, it is claimed, sometimes derives from the speaker's intention. Furthermore, he maintains, implicit content includes those background assumptions, discussed in the previous chapter, that readers take to be true in a story. It is, Livingston maintains, the author's intention that certain things be implicitly true in the story that determines the unstated background.

Again, however, we need to ask when, given an artist's intentions, she *succeeds* in conferring implicit meanings on her story. Livingston proposes what he terms the 'minimal success condition'. The partial intentionalist thesis about fictional truth is that 'in determining what is true in a given fiction, the reader, viewer, spectator, etc., should adopt the thoughts and background premises that the author(s) of that fiction settled on in creating the work, yet only in so far as these assumptions mesh sufficiently with the features of the utterance'.[30] 'Meshing' requires being consistent with a work's explicit content, but also carries stronger implications concerning relevance and integration: 'if there is a sense in which an extraneous hypothesis is consistent with data, but bears no meaningful integrative relation with them, we would say that the two do not mesh'.[31]

Crucially, however, Livingston's test for whether an artist realizes her intention is *not*, as we took to be the case with the unified view, whether a reader ignorant of that intention would view the intended reading as correct, or as possible. It is, rather, whether a reader who *knew* of the artist's intention, as expressed, perhaps, in her diaries, would view the intended reading as making the best sense, or at least as making good sense, of the other data.[32] It is this understanding of the minimal success condition that allows us to entertain the possibility that certain things might be implicitly true in a fiction even though they are not part of either its CCM or its HECCM.

Livingston's 'minimal success condition' seems to evade our objections thus far to actual intentionalism. By locating the determination of implicit content in the hands of the informed reader, we establish a mechanism for determining story-meaning and avoid obscurantism. But, by making a knowledge of authorial intention a prerequisite for the informed reader's judgement, we preserve a determining role for actual authorial intention. However, we may wish to resist some of the judgements to which such a partial intentionalism would commit us. For example, imagine a latter-day Pierre Menard who produces a text word-for-word identical with *One Hundred Years of Solitude* with the intention, written in his diary, that it be true in *his* story that there is a naturalistic explanation of all of the supposedly 'magical' events in the narrative, and that the narrator is in fact deceived. It seems conceivable that such an intention might satisfy Livingston's 'meshing' requirement. For all sorts of elements in the story might appear in a completely new light, and make sense, to an interpreter who read the text with knowledge of the author's intentions. I think we need to introduce further constraints to exclude this kind of example. And, once we introduce these constraints, it becomes clear that, as with the unified view, the real determinant of work meaning is 'uptake', in some sense to be clarified, by the informed reader.

The informed reader, we may say, brings to her encounter with the text of a literary work just those kinds of resources that the author intends to be used in understanding the work. If the author intends knowledge of her intentions to be among those resources, then such knowledge should enter into the informed reader's judgements about story meaning. We have indirect evidence as to the kind of 'informed reader' that the author has in mind, for she will presumably take steps to make available to her readers whatever resources she intends that they use. So, if our latter-day Pierre Menard makes no effort to reveal his intentions save by inscribing sentences in his diary, we can assume that, unless he is perverse, he did not intend readers of his story to avail themselves of external evidence of his intentions in interpreting the story. Given that readers who possess the interpretive resources intended by the author – which exclude externally grounded knowledge of authorial intention – presumably fail to interpret the work in the manner intended, the author fails in his semantic intentions.

The problem in this case, we might say, is that the author's intentions failed to enter in an appropriate way into the acts of utterance generative of the texts. To see why this matters, we need to bear in mind that, if we are to ascribe to an agent a genuine intention to produce some effect, we must also ascribe some intended means whereby the effect is to be produced. An author's semantic intentions, we may say, involve not just an intended end – the audience making-believe certain things – but also an intended means – the audience doing so by making use of certain kinds of resources. In fact, this conclusion follows from the more general view of intentions defended by Livingston, which clearly acknowledges the integration of both an end and a means of achieving that end in the specification of an intention. An intention, we are told, 'represents some targeted situation or state of affairs as well as some means to that end'.[33] The author of an utterance requires 'at least a schematic idea . . . of the processes by means of which this utterance is to be realized'.[34]

'UPTAKE' THEORIES OF INTERPRETATION

Our enquiries thus far have uncovered reasons to doubt whether utterer's meaning can play the sorts of determining roles in a theory of utterance meaning proposed by actual intentionalists, and have suggested that what should play that role is how speakers would be understood by appropriate members of their target audience. But an adequate account of utterance meaning in terms of 'uptake' is no less elusive than one in terms of utterer's meaning. There is an obvious need to clarify the notion of 'uptake' by an 'appropriate' audience. How is the 'appropriate audience' for a given utterance to be determined in a principled way? This is where the intentions of the author might play an indirect determinative role. For, as just suggested, it is plausible to think that the relevant interpretative community is in some way determined by the utterer's intention that receivers bring certain skills or knowledge to their interpretative endeavours. But we can then ask whether possession of the precise skills assumed by the speaker is constitutive of the interpretative community whose uptake determines utterance meaning, or whether the speaker can misrepresent the interpretative skills of her intended audience (as, presumably, does Mrs Malaprop). A second question is whether there are more general constraints on 'uptake' if the latter is to determine the utterance meaning of the work. For example, should we allow receivers only a knowledge of relevant linguistic conventions and relevant features of the context of utterance (where 'relevance' may be partly determined by authorial intention) – in which case, utterance meaning will be something like CCM? Or should we allow receivers to employ richer interpretative resources, so that utterance meaning can take account of the employment of interpretative intelligence on the audience's part and be more like HECCM? A third question is whether it is *actual* 'uptake' by the intended interpretative community that determines utterance meaning, or some idealization of actual uptake. Presumably the stupidity or general lack of interpretative skills of the person I am addressing should not, as a rule, prevent me from saying what I intend to say. A final question is whether, as Beardsley maintains, the kinds of norms to which interpreters are allowed to appeal in their 'uptake' of literary works differ from those to which legitimate appeal can be made in ordinary conversational contexts.

Obviously, much more needs to be said on these issues before we can be happy with an 'uptake' account of utterance meaning. But the latter is worth pursuing only if we can answer certain more general criticisms of 'uptake' theories. These criticisms stem from a distinctive fact about prevailing 'uptake' theories. Proponents of such theories still identify utterance meaning with *intended* meaning of some sort. It is not, on such theories, the *actual* semantic intentions of the utterer that determine utterance meaning, but rather, the semantic intentions that would be *ascribed* by members of the relevant interpretative community. Such 'uptake' theories are usually classified as kinds of 'hypothetical intentionalism' (HI).

If it is ascribed semantic intentions rather than actual semantic intentions that determine utterance meaning, this can be understood in at least two different ways. First, utterance meaning might be identified with the meaning that a suitably informed receiver would ascribe, as intended, to 'an idealized, hypothetical [utterer], an [utterer] who can be held responsible for everything in the [utterance], being aware of all relevant features of context, conventions, and background assumptions, an [utterer] for whom we may imagine that everything is there by design, on purpose'.[35] Second, utterance meaning might be identified with the meaning that a suitably informed receiver would ascribe, as intended, to the actual utterer, given the evidence such a receiver would possess precisely in virtue of being 'suitably informed'.[36] In this case, meaning depends on the ascription of hypothetical intentions to the actual utterer, whereas in the former case, we are ascribing intentions to an idealized hypothetical utterer.

The second version of HI has received more attention than the first, but neither offers a convincing account of certain kinds of situations where our intuitive sense of what is said fails to correspond to the utterance meaning yielded by the HI analysis. Consider first the claim that utterance meaning is identical to the semantic intentions justifiably ascribed to the actual utterer. The obvious objection is that there are circumstances in which the hearer, in ascribing certain semantic intentions to the utterer, will also take the utterer to have *failed* to realize those intentions in virtue of *failing to say what she intended to say*. For example, it would be natural to describe the 'fly in your suit' scenario as follows: S *said* that there was a fly in his interlocutor's suit, though he obviously meant to say that there was a fly in his soup. If the HI theorist is tempted to adopt the 'hermeneutically enriched' conception of 'uptake' and maintain that, given the ease with which the utterer's meaning can be grasped in such cases, the utterance meaning *is* that there was a fly in the soup, other examples prove more difficult. Imagine a variation on the Hungarian phrase-book example, where the bank teller has, by chance, encountered another foreign customer labouring under the same misconceptions, and therefore ascribes to the traveller the desire to withdraw money from his account. It seems implausible to say that the utterance meaning is given by this ascribed semantic intention, since, had the traveller chanced upon any other bank teller in London, a quite different semantic intention would have been ascribed. Thus, it would seem, the HI theorist must place constraints on the kinds of knowledge that can inform those ascriptions of semantic intentions to utterers that are determinative of utterance meaning. Idiosyncratic knowledge that transcends the sorts of cognitive and interpretative resources we can assume in a representative receiver of the appropriate kind are, it might be argued, rightly excluded.

However, this undermines the central HI contention that what determines utterance meaning is ascribed intentions. For, if we place certain restrictions on the kinds of resources upon which the audience can draw in ascribing semantic intentions, this amounts to an acknowledgement that what is really at issue is conformity to certain principles for ascribing utterance meaning. These principles may closely track ascribed semantic intentions, and may thereby bring about a coincidence of utterance meaning and ascribed semantic intentions in many cases. But this coincidence is an artefact of the interpretative principles, and not an indication that utterance meaning is a function of the ascription of semantic intentions to actual utterers per se.

The 'hypothetical utterer' version of HI fares no better overall. It can grant, in 'fly in your suit' kinds of cases, that the semantic intentions I ascribe to the actual speaker differ from the utterance meaning of her utterance. This difference can be acknowledged because the semantic intentions I ascribe to the actual speaker may differ from the semantic intentions I ascribe to the hypothesized 'ideal utterer', and it is the latter that determine utterance meaning on the view under discussion. But, as Stecker points out, the 'hypothetical utterer' account seems to have no plausible story to tell about scenarios where the uttered vehicle is defective.[37] Take Mrs Malaprop's utterance. While it is possible to ascribe a CCM to that utterance, the vehicle is surely not one that an ideal utterer fully cognizant of the semantic and pragmatic norms of the language would use. Or, if we can conjure up some scenario in which such an ideal utterer would avail herself of such a vehicle, the broader semantic intentions we would have to ascribe to such an utterer will hardly furnish us with a plausible utterance meaning for Mrs Malaprop's utterance.

A further problem with the 'ideal utterer' version of HI is that, as in the case of Stecker's 'unified view', the utterer's semantic intentions seem to play a secondary role in the account of utterance meaning. For an 'ideal utterer' is, by definition, one who masters and flawlessly draws upon the relevant interpretative norms, appropriately contextualized, to produce an utterance that realizes her semantic intentions. But then the utterance meaning is given by those highly contextualized norms, construed in either a thin or 'hermeneutically enriched' manner.

We have seen that identifying utterance meaning with actual intentions fails, upon inspection, to ascribe a genuine determining role to such intentions, that role being more appropriately ascribed to the 'uptake' of the intended audience. But 'hypothetical intentionalist' accounts that construe uptake in terms of ascribed intentions are also flawed. This suggests that we should question the assumption that uptake must be construed in such terms. This assumption is grounded in a criticism of conventionalist accounts of utterance meaning: only if we take a vehicle to be employed to realize the semantic intentions of an utterer can we bring our knowledge of conventions and context, and our more general interpretative skills, to bear upon it in a coherent manner. Given this criticism, it is natural to conclude that receivers of utterances are in the business of ascribing semantic intentions. But all that actually follows is that receivers only ascribe utterance meaning to that which they regard as the product of an intentional act of utterance. This allows for an alternative formulation of the uptake view that does not identify utterance meaning with ascribed semantic intentions of any kind, but with the meaning that a properly informed receiver, correctly applying the appropriate interpretative norms, would ascribe to a vehicle taken to be intentionally used to make an utterance of a given kind. 'Interpretative norms' here, may, where appropriate, include linguistic and generic conventions, and the more general heuristic principles involved in interpretative intelligence.

Let me term this kind of uptake theory 'interpretationalism'. The interpretationalist acknowledges that interpretative norms exist first and foremost to enable utterers to realize their semantic intentions. In the absence of such norms, an utterer could not expect her meaning to be grasped. But it is usually built into the understanding of interpretative norms that the meaning yielded by their correct application to an utterance may not correspond to the utterer's meaning, and that this may be apparent to the interpreter.[38] The interpreter ascribes an utterance meaning by bringing the appropriate norms to bear on what she takes to be an intentional use of a vehicle. But the criterion for correctness in ascription of utterance meaning is conformity with the norms, not compliance with actual or hypothetical semantic intentions.

As already noted, utterers' intentions *may* have a determining role in *picking out the interpretative norms* which, in turn, determine utterance meaning. In the first place, it might be argued that utterers' intentions determine the *kind* of utterance produced. For example, if

Jane, just prior to her death, generates a text which she intends to be a poem, but after her death her literary executors mistake it for a laundry list, it is the relevant norms for interpreting poetic utterances that determine the meaning of her utterance. More significantly, as noted above, it might be argued that it is an utterer's intentions to be understood by the norms of a given interpretative community that indirectly identify the norms whose correct application determines the meaning of her utterance.

In a very interesting paper which examines how speakers – including Mrs Malaprop – are able to 'get away with it' in successfully comunicating to an audience a meaning falling outside the range of CCMs of the vehicle employed, Donald Davidson has drawn attention to certain interpretative norms that determine utterance meaning in ordinary conversational contexts.[39] These norms prescribe the use of what we earlier termed 'interpretative intelligence'. Speakers assume such norms in their communicative endeavours, expecting the audience to make reasonable judgements as to their semantic intentions and to ascribe utterance meaning accordingly. In such contexts, utterance meaning is not plausibly identified with CCM, and one who insists on identifying the former with the latter employs inappropriate interpretative norms. But – recall our London bank teller who has already encountered users of the inadequate phrase-book – this doesn't mean that the norms governing ascription of utterance meaning in ordinary conversational contexts *always* require that hearers ascribe utterance meanings that comply with what they identify as utterer's meaning. It is the relevant interpretative norms – even ones designed to be as sensitive as possible to utterer's meaning – that determine utterance meaning. Utterance meaning in such contexts, then, is to be identified with what we have termed hermeneutically enriched contextualized conventional meaning (HECCM).

This allows us to consider other interpretative contexts in which different interpretative norms determine utterance meaning. Identifying utterance meaning with HECCM in conversational contexts is appropriate because, in such contexts, speakers employ language in pursuit of various ends whose realization requires that the target audience grasp basic utterer's meaning. If this is done, the *vehicle* by means of which the utterer communicates this meaning to his audience is quite irrelevant. It functions only as a means of communicating basic meaning, and thereby allowing higher-order meanings to be grasped and other conversational ends to be advanced. Failure to use the conventionally sanctioned vehicle is philosophically un-interesting for a theory of communication. But there are other contexts in which the vehicle serves additional functions, and where it may be more appropriate to identify utterance meaning with unen-riched CCM. In academic contexts, for example, the vehicle used by a student to communicate utterer's meaning matters, because a certain precision and clarity in the linguistic medium is one goal of the exercise.

This extends, for more interesting reasons, to interpretation in the arts. For in contexts of artistic appreciation, we can never treat an artistic vehicle as a mere conduit for an artistic statement.[40] In terms of the conceptual framework introduced in Chapter 1, our apprecia-tive attention to a product of artistic activity takes, as its focus, an artistic content *as articulated in a vehicle in virtue of an artistic medium.* This is so for two reasons. First, as Richard Wollheim argued for pictorial representation,[41] a properly artistic interest is always concerned with the way an artistic content has been articulated in a medium, not merely with the articulated content as such. Second, there is a particularly intimate relation between the artistic content articulated through an artistic vehicle and the vehicle itself, in contrast to the meanings communicated through ordinary linguistic vehicles in conversational contexts. This is because the 'meanings' articulated through artistic vehicles depend upon a much richer array of discriminable features of those vehicles. This, as we saw in Chapter 1, is what Goodman termed the relative 'repleteness' of artistic symbols. The precise 'how' of the articulation of an artistic content may bear crucially on both basic and higher-order contents rightly ascribable to the vehicle as utterance. For both of these reasons, it would run counter to our interests in appreciating artworks to allow the artistic content articulated through an artistic vehicle to float free of the CCM of that vehicle and track our ascrip-tions of utterer's meaning to the artist. This would frustrate our attempts to understand the work through detailed exploration of the properties of the vehicle, and would also make it difficult to take a legitimate interest in the manner of articulation of that artistic content. Furthermore, it would render the utterance meanings of works internally incoherent where, as is often the case, some of their higher-order meanings depend upon the manner in which a medium has been used to articulate a basic artistic content – as, for example, in any artwork that comments, in this manner, on other artworks.[42]

In endorsing the idea that the utterance meanings of literary artworks should be identified with the CCM ascribable by appropriately informed receivers, it may seem that we are rehabilitating Wimsatt and Beardsley's anti-intentionalism, and to a large extent, we are. But our understanding of the anti-intentionalist view of interpretation has been enriched by our consideration of intentionalist alternatives. This has led to a better appreciation of the significance of 'uptake' and of the reasons why uptake should not be seen as a matter of ascribed semantic intentions. Furthermore, in considering the different kinds of interpretative interests that uptake serves in different contexts, we have put on a firmer foundation Beardsley's claim that interpretative standards in literature differ from those that obtain in ordinary conversation.[43] In so doing, we have to some extent finessed the problem which I raised for uptake theories in general, of clarifying both the audience whose uptake determines utterance meaning and the resources upon which this audience can draw. For, if interpretationalism is correct, there is no single answer to that question. Rather, we should expect that a principled answer to that question for a given context of utterance will identify the interpretative norms in place in that context and the interpretative interests served, in that context, by those norms.

But there are at least two significant ways in which the interpretationalist may disagree with Wimsatt and Beardsley. First, she may allow that, even in the context of literary interpretation, there are some interpretative norms that do assign a crucial role to either actual or hypothetical intentions. One kind of example arose earlier when we looked at Wimsatt and Beardsley's treatment of allusion. Here, I suggested, it is part of our interpretative practice that we only take a poem to allude to another poem when we ascribe to the actual author an intention to make such an allusion, and, plausibly, we only rightly take a poem to be allusive when the author did indeed have such an intention. Similar considerations, I further suggested, apply to the judgement that a text is ironic or a remark is sarcastic. For the interpretationalist, this can be granted without difficulty, since it is merely a recognition that the interpretative norms, whose application by qualified receivers is determinative of meaning, include norms that accord a determinative or a regulative role to the semantic intentions of the author.

Second, while the interpretationalist broadly endorses an anti-intentionalist line on *interpretation*, she may insist that actual or hypothetical intentions do play a role in the *evaluation* of works. Given that the relevant interpretative norms sustain the view that a work's artistic vehicle articulates a particular artistic content, our sense of the work as an artistic achievement may be affected by what we know about what the artist intended to articulate in the work. This is simply one respect in which knowledge of a work's history of making may affect our judgements of artistic value. Just as it may matter whether an artist like Vermeer produced his canvasses by drawing freehand or by tracing over the image made in a camera obscura,[44] so it may matter whether a stunning metaphor in a poem results from the intelligence of the poet or from a linguistic error. More significantly, our belief that an artist failed in her intentions may, indirectly, bear upon how we interpret the work. For, in trying to ascribe higher-order content to an artwork, we seek to bring together in a complex but coherent pattern the different elements of which the work is composed. But, if we believe that some element is there as a result of error, we may settle for an interpretation of the rest of the work that does not incorporate this element. Again, this is a particular 'intentionalist' application of more general interpretative principles also to be seen in our willingness to discount what seem to be 'loose ends' in interpreting a work we take to be unfinished.

INTERPRETATIVE PLURALISM AND INTERPRETATIVE MONISM

In examining different accounts of the constraints that govern right reading of a literary work, we have seen how some intentionalist arguments assume that there is a need to render meaning determinate. It is for this purpose that Hirsch thinks we need to posit a 'determining will'. And anti-intentionalists like Beardsley have seen a need to respond to such arguments, not by denying the demand for determinacy in the meaning of literary works, but by arguing that conventional meaning, suitably understood, *is* determinate. Where conventions fail to disambiguate a text, the text is determinately *ambiguous*. But what grounds this demand for determinacy in literary meaning, and how determinate should we take the meaning of a literary work to be? If we look to critical practice, what is striking is the diversity of readings offered of a given work – as, for example, in the conflicting readings of Wordsworth's 'A Slumber Did My Spirit Seal' cited earlier. Should we nonetheless maintain that there is a single right unified reading of a work – for example, the

reading that best complies with the utterance meaning of the work –
so that any particular critical interpretation must either be included
in this unified reading, or be mistaken? Hirsch, we may recall,
maintains that the very practice of criticism requires determinacy of
meaning, since the critic's task is to discern the meaning of the work
and inform the reader of this. Without the determinacy that comes
from the exercise of a 'determining will', Hirsch maintains, there will
be no 'objectivity' in interpretation, but just the different voices of
different critics with their different critical perspectives.

Others, however, have maintained that the very diversity of critical
readings of a literary work is to be celebrated rather than legislated
away.[45] Such diversity is viewed as an indication of the richness of
meanings that literary works have to offer. Some writers, such as
Roland Barthes and Michel Foucault, have endorsed what Foucault
terms the 'proliferation of meaning',[46] rejecting, as repressive and
ideologically based, the practice of constraining the interpretation of
literary texts by referring them to an author. For Foucault, such talk
of an author simply reifies what are in fact particular interpretative
practices widely accepted within the critical community. He refers
here to the 'author function', writing of it that

> aspects of an individual which we designate as making him an
> author are only a projection, in more or less psychologizing terms,
> of the operations that we force texts to undergo, the connections
> that we make, the traits that we establish as pertinent, the continu-
> ities that we recognize, or the exclusions that we practice.[47]

Barthes expresses a related view in terms of the 'écriture' thesis that
the texts generated by literary authors are to be viewed as pieces of
writing that are, by the very process of their creation, divorced from
their origins. 'Texts', as Barthes terms them, are to be distinguished
from 'works', the kinds of semantically constrained entities with
which literary critics have traditionally taken themselves to deal. A
text, for Barthes, 'answers not to an interpretation, even a liberal
one, but to an explosion, a dissemination'.[48]

It is clearly possible to treat the products of literary activity as
'texts', in Barthes' sense, and to seek various values in the 'proliferation of meaning', and the fruits of such a practice may on occasion
prove significant. Rather than enquire further into these matters,
however, I want to look at attempts, by writers belonging to a more
analytic tradition, to argue for the proliferation of meanings in

literary interpretation without always drawing, as does Barthes, upon a distinction between works and texts. Susan Feagin, for example, suggests that we see the tolerance, in critical practice, of a plurality of apparently incompatible readings of a literary work as a reason to re-evaluate our understanding of the legitimate goals of interpretation and the sorts of standards to which it is accountable.[49] She argues that we should not think of radically differing interpretations of a literary work as 'incompatible'. Such a characterization rests on the mistaken assumption that literary interpretation aims at discovering some independently existing meaning of a work. Rather, we should view interpretation as a creative activity whose goal is to provide the reader with 'a theoretical framework of understanding' for a work, a framework which renders it coherent and permits the reader to ascribe a sense to it. We then evaluate different such frameworks not in terms of whether they correspond to the 'true meaning' of the work, but in terms of how the readings they engender enrich our experience both of the work and of the world. Even historically anachronistic interpretations, she claims, 'contribute to the enrichment of experience . . . of the work'.[50] Alan H. Goldman argues for a similar conclusion, arguing that the aim of interpretation is 'to maximize the artistic value of the interpreted work',[51] where to accomplish this goal may require that we depart from what would be regarded as historically accurate interpretation.

One kind of ground for the idea that interpreters should seek to proliferate meanings is the view, cited by Feagin, that it is a mistake to think that there is an independently existing meaning of a work which could make certain interpretations 'true' and others 'false'. Writers such as Robert Matthews and Denis Dutton have defended such a view, holding that, while some interpretations are more acceptable than others, this is to be explained in terms of relative plausibility as measured against some disciplinary norm of acceptability rather than in terms of truth.[52] Interpretations, it is claimed, are always *underdetermined* by all possible evidence available to an interpreter. But opponents of such a view have challenged these claims, arguing that a plausible interpretation is one that is plausibly *true*,[53] and that the underdetermination thesis rests upon too thin a conception of available evidence.

Robert Stecker has tried to mediate this debate, claiming that the participants are to some extent arguing at cross-purposes.[54] What Stecker terms 'critical monism' is, he maintains, compatible with what he terms 'critical pluralism'. The two views are characterized as follows:[55] Critical pluralism (CP) is the view that 'there are many acceptable interpretations of many artworks that cannot be conjoined into a single correct interpretation'. This view allows not only that there are many acceptable interpretations of a given work but also that some interpretations are unacceptable. But what the critical pluralist will deny is that the aim of interpretation must be the search for a single correct interpretation. Critical monism (CM), on the other hand, is the view that 'there is a single, comprehensive, true (correct) interpretation for each work of art', one that comprehends the entire work and that conjoins all true interpretations of the work.

Stecker's claim that CP and CM are compatible turns on the distinction between (1) truth or correctness, and (2) acceptability. We can locate the quest for 'true' or 'correct' interpretations of a literary work in the context of the project of understanding a work as the product, for the most part, of design by its historical creator. Given Stecker's commitment to a form of actual intentionalism, this project requires that we attempt to understand the writer's intentions, and also the relevant background conditions, linguistic norms, literary traditions, etc. CM, then, is the claim that all interpretations that are correct as defined relative to the aims of this project can in principle be conjoined into a single true interpretation which gives us the basic and higher-order utterance meaning of the work. But CM can be reconciled with CP once we recognize that there are various legitimate aims of art interpretation, in addition to determining the 'true' meaning of a work, and that the acceptability of an interpretation is relative to one's interpretative aim. Such aims might include 'making a work relevant or significant to a certain sort of audience, . . . identifying what is cognitively valuable in a work, or . . . enhancing the reader's aesthetic experience of a work'.[56] Interpretations of works that satisfy such aims can be acceptable, even if they are incompatible with the utterance meaning of the work, because they do not *aim* at grasping utterance meaning. Thus, while an interpretation may aim at 'understanding a work as the product of the intentional activity of the historically situated artist', an interpreter may also merely try 'to achieve *an* understanding of a work', where the acceptability of the latter is a matter not of getting things right with respect to the intentional activity and historical situation of the artist, but of 'render[ing] the work coherent in a way that promotes appreciation'.[57] Acceptable interpretations that aim in this way at maximizing the value of the work to the receiver are constrained to a certain extent in that they must be 'consistent with *some* facts about the work',[58] but this also allows them to conflict with other such facts.

A difficulty with Stecker's proposal for reconciling CM and CP, however, is that, while the defence of CM seems to require a broadly contextualist conception of the literary work, the defence of CP seems to require a textualist conception.[59] On the one hand, if we are to restrict *true* interpretations of literary works to those that respect the context in which their texts originate, then the relevant features of that context must be constitutive features of *the work*. On the other hand, if the different 'acceptable' interpretations posited by the critical pluralist are to be interpretations of the work, then the work cannot have, among its constitutive properties, properties that are incompatible with those ascribed in those interpretations. In what sense can an anachronistic interpretation of *Hamlet*, for example, be an acceptable interpretation of the *work*, if, as the defence of CM requires, we take the work to incorporate aspects of the context of creation of the text which rule out the possession of anachronistic properties? Should we not say that the different 'acceptable' interpretations are of the *text* of the work, rather than of the work itself? In fact, elsewhere Stecker seems to make this very point, noting that 'a work can be successfully intended to mean, in part, *p*, and, at the same time, the text of the work can be construable as meaning not-*p*'.[60]

In his more recent work, Stecker has reiterated both his contextualism and his claim to have reconciled CM and CP, and has tried to meet the above objection by insisting on the legitimacy of interpretations that identify what a work *could* mean in what he terms the 'pragmatic' sense: 'We assert that a work could mean something relative to a point of view or set of constraints. We ignore or bracket off something we do know about the work for the purpose of pursuing a particular interpretive aim'.[61] But do works, construed contextually, have 'pragmatically possible' interpretations in this sense? Once we 'bracket off' what are, for the contextualist, constitutive features of the work, it is no longer *the work* that can be taken to have the ascribed meanings, but an entity, or a class of entities, that would resemble the work in certain respects. Here is one reason to think this. For the contextualist, both a vehicle and a context of utterance enter into the identity of the work. But, in that case, if we allow for genuine interpretations of a work that bracket features of context, we should be equally open to genuine interpretations that bracket features of the vehicle itself.[62]

In Chapter 2, we saw why a contextualist conception of literary artworks seems preferable to a textualist conception. We have now seen why contextualism supports CM but is not compatible with the sort of critical pluralism for which Feagin argues. Of course, the contextualist may grant that there is a plurality of acceptable interpretations none of which require that we 'bracket off' constitutive features of the work. Arguably, if we reject actual intentionalism and hold to an interpretationalist view of a work's semantic properties, this will permit such a plurality of acceptable interpretations. But, if we wish to venture interpretations that 'bracket off' constitutive elements of the work, these must be taken as readings of the *text* of the work, not as readings of the work itself. We can thereby protect the *work* from the 'proliferation of meanings' celebrated by Foucault, while allowing for such a proliferation in respect of the *text*. On this, at least, Barthes and Foucault seem to be right.

CHAPTER 6

THE NATURE OF FICTIONAL CHARACTERS

PHILOSOPHICAL PROBLEMS WITH FICTIONAL CHARACTERS

In Chapter 3, we saw that the fictionality of a narrative depends upon what the author of the narrative does with language. In arguing to this conclusion, we rejected the alternative suggestion that the difference resides in the very language employed in fictions. The latter, according to this suggestion, differs from the language employed in non-fictions in its meaning or reference, or in its being assessable as true or false. To put this point slightly more formally, the difference between fiction and non-fiction is a matter not of *semantics* – of the meaning, reference, and truth-conditions ascribable to the elements of which the language is composed – but of *pragmatics* – of the things that language-users are able to do with language in virtue of its semantic properties. The conclusion we drew from this was that, given what a sentence *S* independently means, and what would make it true, the author of a fictional narrative either (1) *pretends* to assert the sentence, or (2) intends that the audience *make-believe* that the sentence is true. We also saw reasons to prefer the second of these views.

In the previous two chapters, we looked at how the reader of a fictional narrative is able to work out what he or she is supposed to make-believe, given the text of the fiction. In order to do this, the reader must first understand the meaning of the sentences making up the narrative, and then determine what is true in the story in virtue of its being made up of those sentences. If, as we have assumed, the words employed in a fictional narrative have their standard meanings, this might seem unproblematic. Consider, for example, the opening paragraphs of *Bleak House*:

London. Michaelmas Term lately over . . . Implacable November weather . . . Smoke lowering down from chimney-pots, making a soft black drizzle, with flakes of soot in it as big as full-grown snow-flakes . . . Dogs, undistinguishable in mire. Horses, scarcely better; splashed to their very blinkers. Foot passengers, jostling one another's umbrellas, in a general infection of ill-temper, and losing their foot-hold at street-corners . . .

Fog everywhere. Fog up the river, where it flows among green aits and meadows; fog down the river, where it rolls defiled among the tiers of shipping . . . Fog on the Essex marches, fog on the Kentish heights.[1]

There is no obvious difficulty here working out what the sentences mean and what we are being invited to make-believe. We are to imagine London on a foggy November day in Victorian England, with people and animals going about their business in the way described. We are, in other words, being invited to make-believe that, at a particular time of the year, a given place (London) and its inhabitants are suffering under certain meteorological conditions.

But consider now the opening lines of two other famous literary works. Virginia Woolf's *Mrs Dalloway* opens with the line: 'Mrs Dalloway said she would buy the flowers herself', while the memorable opening line of Franz Kafka's *Metamorphosis* is: 'As Gregor Samsa awoke one morning from uneasy dreams he found himself transformed in his bed into a gigantic insect'. In this case, it would seem, we are being invited to make-believe something concerning Mrs Dalloway, in the first instance, and Gregor Samsa, in the second. But Mrs Dalloway and Gregor Samsa, it seems, are *fictional characters*, creatures of the author's imagination. So how are we to understand sentences that seem to be inviting us to imagine that certain events befall *them*?

Why does this present a problem? Consider what seems to be involved in understanding sentences in *non*-fictional contexts that appear to be similar in structure to our pair of opening lines. Suppose I write: 'George Orwell wrote *Animal Farm*. The author of *Animal Farm* was a lifelong socialist who became disillusioned with Soviet communism.' Here is a natural way of thinking about what I am doing in each of these sentences. The subject expression *picks out* the thing I want to talk about, and the predicate expression *says something about* that entity. In the case in hand, I have used two different expressions to pick out the same individual, and I have predicated two different things of that individual. As it happens, both of these things are true of that individual, but I might have said something false – if, for example, I had said 'George Orwell wrote

Brave New World'. Whether such a sentence is true or false depends upon whether the thing picked out by the subject expression satisfies the predicate expression. When I utter any of these sentences assertively, you know what I mean and also know what I want you to believe. And if I author a fiction containing these sentences, presumably I am pretending to assert these same things, or intend you to make-believe them as part of the story.

But, in our fictional sentences whose grammatical subjects are given by the expressions 'Mrs Dalloway' and 'Gregor Samsa', the very fact that we view these expressions as names of fictional characters suggests that they fail to pick out an entity. There is, we assume, no such person as Mrs Dalloway or Gregor Samsa. But, if the grammatical subject of a sentence fails to pick out an entity, then there is nothing of which we predicate some property in the rest of the sentence. So it isn't clear what such a sentence *says*, in which case it is just as unclear what Woolf or Kafka can have pretended to assert, or have intended the reader to make-believe, in inscribing that sentence.

This problem is not merely of concern to those of us who are interested in understanding the workings of fictional narratives. For the same problem arises outside of the context of fictional narratives, where we seem to be able to talk meaningfully, and often truly, using subject-expressions that do not, at least at face value, refer to anything. For example, most of us will claim both to understand and believe to be true what is expressed by the sentence 'The unicorn has a single horn in the middle of its forehead'. Even more puzzling is our ability to speak both meaningfully and truly when we utter a sentence like 'Unicorns don't really exist', since, on the view of sentence meaning that we have been assuming, the meaningfulness of this sentence seems to require that there *exist* unicorns in order for us to pick out the things to which we are *denying* existence.

The patent meaningfulness of such sentences has spurred philosophers of language more generally to seek an account of how we can meaningfully and often truly talk 'about' that which doesn't exist. Given an answer to this more general question, we might hope that this will also solve our more immediate puzzlement concerning sentences in fictional narratives 'about' fictional characters. We can distinguish three kinds of strategies that have been adopted in attempts to explain how we can talk 'about' such apparent non-entities as Mrs Dalloway, Gregor Samsa, unicorns, and the present king of France. The first strategy, generally associated with the philosopher Alexius Meinong, who first proposed such a view,[2] seeks to establish that there *are* entities corresponding to names such as 'Mrs Dalloway', but that these entities (or objects) do not exist, enjoying rather some other kind of 'being'. The second strategy, this time associated with the philosopher Bertrand Russell,[3] is to argue that we are puzzled only because we have mistaken the *surface structure* of sentences such as 'George Orwell wrote *Animal Farm*' or 'The author of *Animal Farm* was a lifelong socialist' for the *logical structure* of these sentences. The logical structure of a sentence displays how what it says depends upon its composition, and makes clear the logical relations in which it stands to other sentences. Once we correctly identify the logical structure, or logical form, of our problematic sentences, it is claimed, their meaningfulness is obvious. A third option, at least for fictional narratives, is to argue (1) against the Russellian, that the logical structure of our problem sentences *is* reflected in the surface structure, but also (2) against the Meinongian, that there are no entities that can serve as the referents of the subject-expressions of such sentences. It can then be argued that such sentences are indeed meaningless, but that this is not a problem because, in our imaginative engagement with fictions, part of what we make-believe is that the conditions for their being meaningful are met – that, for example, there *is* a person denoted by the name 'Mrs Dalloway'. As we shall see, however, all of these approaches face difficulties in explaining at least some of the relevant phenomena.

'MEINONGIAN' SOLUTIONS

As we have seen, the most natural way of understanding how we are able to make claims about the world in uttering sentences whose surface structure is '*S* is *p*' is to take the surface structure as the logical structure. The *S* term, then, picks out what we want to talk about, and 'is *p*' predicates something of that entity. The Meinongian seeks to preserve this natural understanding by providing entities that can be picked out by the *S* term when no existing entity is so picked out. In the case of fictions, these entities are fictional characters. Fictional characters do not (really) exist, we might say, but they can be accommodated within a more general theory of 'non-existent objects'. Some sentences in which the names of fictional characters occur appear to support the idea that the latter enjoy some kind of being, even if they don't exist in the same way that ordinary people and places exist. We have no trouble understanding sentences like 'Mrs Dalloway is one of Virginia Woolf's most engaging creations', or 'Sherlock Holmes is much smarter than Inspector Linley'. But what sense can such sentences have unless fictional characters have some kind of being?

The basic assumption for the Meinongian is that, for every set of properties meeting certain conditions, there is an object correlated with those properties. Since only some sets of properties are realized in entities that exist in the world, only some objects are existent. Other objects have a different kind of being: they 'subsist', in Meinong's own terminology. If an object exists, then it is also 'complete' in the sense that, for every property of the relevant kind, it is determinate whether the object possesses that property. Non-existent objects, on the other hand, are usually incomplete. In this respect, we may note, they are like fictional objects, which, as we saw in Chapter 4, are characterized by 'narrative incompleteness'. It is claimed that we should admit such non-existent objects into our ontology in order to explain how we are able to think about and talk about entities that don't exist. It seems that there must be something about which we are thinking and talking, and this clearly applies in the case of our engagement with fictional discourse. A fictional character, then, is to be identified with a non-existent object correlated with just those properties predicated of that character in the fictional narrative.[4]

Meinongians differ as to which *kinds* of properties enter into the individuation of Meinongian objects.[5] Terence Parsons, for example, distinguishes between 'nuclear' and 'non-nuclear' properties, where only the former count for the purposes of individuation. 'Nuclear' properties of Sherlock Holmes would include being a man, being a detective, smoking a pipe, etc., while 'non-nuclear' properties would include 'being written about by me'. It is easy to see why the Meinongian might want such a distinction. For, if the latter kind of property entered into the individuation of objects, this would entail that an object written about by me is not the same entity as an otherwise identical object not written about by me. But a non-existent object can possess contradictory *nuclear* properties. One such non-existent object would possess the properties of being square, being round, and being the cupola on Berkeley College.[6] For our purposes, however, we need not go into further details of such matters.

The Meinongian commitment to non-existent objects is, for many, a good reason to seek an alternative account of those linguistic contexts in which we seem to be talking about entities that do not exist. On the one hand, the notion of 'subsistence', as a mode of 'being' distinct from existence, is hardly transparent, and without further clarification it is not clear how the Meniongian claim that there are objects correlated with every non-actualized set of (nuclear or otherwise) properties differs from the uncontroversial claim that we can individuate and presumably talk about such sets of properties themselves. A further challenge to any Meinongian account is to explain how, if we admit such non-existent objects to our ontology, we are able to refer to them, especially if, as we shall see, there are reasons to think that, for at least some referring expressions, reference requires some kind of causal link between the speaker and the referent.

At least as serious in the present context, however, are objections to a Meinongian solution to our concerns about *fictional characters* and about the sense to be made of sentences in fictions which feature expressions seemingly referring to such characters.[7] First, if fictional characters are non-existent entities, then they cannot be brought into existence by their authors, nor, it seems, do they depend for their being on their authors. But arguably this conflicts with our intuition that fictional characters are *created* entities that come into being through the activity of authors, and *dependent* entities in that they depend upon the activities of authors to bring them into being, and on literary works in order to persist in being. The only option open to the Meinongian seems to be the one adopted by Parsons, who maintains that fictional characters are non-existent entities that writers do not create, but *discover* and make *fictional*.

A second problem for the Meinongian arises when we consider cases in which we want to identify the same fictional character in different fictional narratives. This occurs not only when we have different fictions by a given author – the Sherlock Holmes character in different stories by Conan Doyle, for example – but also when an author wishes to incorporate in one of her fictional narratives a fictional character created by another author. In the case of the Sherlock Holmes character, this occurs in Nicholas Meyer's pastiche *The Seven Percent Solution*. A more established literary example is the character of Pamela, created by Samuel Richardson in his novel of the same name, but incorporated for satirical purposes into Henry Fielding's *Joseph Andrews*. If fictional characters are individuated by reference to what is true of a given character in a particular fictional narrative, then, even in the case of different stories by a single author, we have a different character in each narrative. A related problem is that, in the case of minor characters in fictions, it is quite conceivable that, in two narratives written by different authors quite independently of one another, what are intuitively different fictional characters will be correlated with the same set of properties, and thus, on the Meinongian account, will be occurrences of the *same* character.

Unfortunately for the Meinongian, responses that might address one of these problems only make the other more acute. We might allow for fictional characters to feature in different fictions by incorporating, into the set of properties with which a character is correlated, properties true of the character in more than one narrative. But the more inclusive we make this set, the more it will constrain future fictions, and the less inclusive we make it (for example, by only including things true of the character in every such narrative) the more likely we are to let in different characters in other fictional narratives who share that small set of properties. Furthermore, as Amie Thomasson points out in elaborating upon the sorts of difficulties that beset the Meinongian,[8] to draw in this way on different fictional narratives to generate a composite set of properties to constitute the set correlated with the fictional character presupposes that we already know *which* characters in different narratives are occurrences of this character – the very thing that the identity of the fictional character is supposed to determine. These problems are difficult for the Meinongian to surmount because they stem from the idea that fictional characters are non-existent objects that can at best be *discovered* rather than created by authors. For this prevents the Meinongian from taking account, in the individuation of fictional characters, of the circumstances in which a character might be created by an author, and the ways in which an author may borrow from another author. Perhaps this difficulty might be surmounted within the idiom of 'discovery' – two authors might be said to have discovered the same non-existent object – but this still leaves most of the above difficulties unresolved.

A third problem arises when we turn to what might be thought to be a strength of the Meinongian account – its ability to deal with those contexts, noted above, when we do seem committed to entities that are fictional characters – in comparing the sleuthing abilities of Holmes and Linley, for example, or in talking of a character as an artist's most engaging creation.[9] Writers have distinguished here between two kinds of contexts in which fictional names or descriptions occur.[10] When we are concerned with occurrences of names within the story, we can speak of occurrences in *fictional discourse*, whereas when we talk about fictional characters in relation to their authors or their relative qualities, we can speak of occurrences of fictional names in *discourse about fiction*. Suppose, like Parsons, that we take the relationship between non-existent entities and their nuclear properties to be the same as that between existent entities and the properties they possess. In both cases, according to Parsons, the entity *exemplifies* these properties. If, to make sense of the occurrence of fictional names in fictional discourse, a fictional character like Sherlock Holmes is to be correlated with the set of properties that are true of that character in the story, then two of the properties exemplified by Holmes are being a human being and residing at 221B Baker Street, since both of these things are true of Sherlock Holmes in the story. But, in discourse about fiction, it is definitive of an entity's being a *fictional* character, rather than a real person, that it does not exemplify these kinds of properties. Furthermore, the Sherlock Holmes character we talk about in discourse about fiction exemplifies such properties as being in a novel by Conan Doyle, whereas this is not true in the story, and thus is not exemplified by the fictional character that is supposed to make sense of our fictional discourse. Thus it appears that fictional characters will always exemplify contradictory properties, *not* because contradictory things are true *in the story* but because nothing can consistently serve to explain the use of fictional names in both fictional discourse and discourse about fiction.

Edward Zalta, another contemporary Meinongian, avoids this problem by distinguishing two kinds of relations in which an entity can stand to its properties. While existent entities exemplify their properties, non-existent entities *encode* those properties that are in the set by reference to which the entities are individuated. When talk of fictional characters occurs in discourse about fiction, however, a non-existent entity can indeed exemplify the properties predicated of it. Thus Sherlock Holmes encodes, but does not exemplify, the property of residing at 221B Baker Street, and exemplifies, but does not encode, the property of being a character in the stories written by Conan Doyle. But one could be forgiven for finding this distinction rather obscure, and the solution to the problem rather ad hoc. Furthermore, as Thomasson demonstrates, even if the Meinongian is allowed to avail herself of such resources, she has difficulty telling a consistent story about fictional narratives in which some of the characters are real people.[11]

Another way in which we might try to provide referents for fictional names is by taking the referents of such names to be individuals who exist in *other possible worlds*. If this strategy is to provide us with genuine referents for fictional names, we must also be 'realists' about possible worlds, something that many philosophers are reluctant to admit. But, even if we are willing to embrace such ontological extravagance, we fare little better than the Meinongian. In the first place, the incompleteness of fictional characters means that, for any given fictional character, there will be a multiplicity of candidates, existing in different possible worlds, who might be taken to be the referent of that character's name. To pick any one of these individuals as, say, Sherlock Holmes seems arbitrary, whereas to identify Holmes with all of the individuals in possible worlds who are sufficiently Holmes-like runs counter to our sense that, if the fictional name 'Sherlock Holmes', as that name occurs in fictional discourse, has a referent, it is an individual rather than a class of individuals. Nor does a 'possible worlds' approach help to reconcile the apparently inconsistent roles ascribed to fictional characters in fictional discourse and discourse about fiction. And, if fictional characters are identified with individuals in other possible worlds, they can be discovered but not created by the authors of the narratives in which they appear.

'RUSSELLIAN' SOLUTIONS

Rather than try to develop an account of fictional discourse that upholds our intuitive picture of how language manages to say things about the world – a picture that identifies the logical structure of sentences with their surface structure – we may now be tempted by an alternative strategy. Bertrand Russell attempts to resolve a number of philosophical puzzles that arise if we adopt this intuitive picture.[12] The 'logical form' or logical structure of a sentence represents the way in which the overall meaning and truth-conditions for that sentence are determined by its constituent elements. Russell focuses on sentences containing 'denoting phrases' as their grammatical subjects. A 'denoting phrase', for Russell, is a linguistic expression having one of the following grammatical forms: 'an x', 'some $x$es', 'every x', 'all $x$es', 'the x'. Not all denoting phrases actually denote anything. 'The author of *Animal Farm*' and 'the present queen of England' denote one thing, 'the woman who wrote *Animal Farm*' and 'the present king of France' fail to denote, and 'an English author' and 'an English monarch' denote ambiguously. We need denoting phrases, according to Russell, because we want to think and talk about many things with which we are not directly acquainted, and we can do this via our use of descriptions that employ denoting phrases.

Russell claims that, if we take the logical form of sentences containing denoting phrases as given by their *grammatical* form, then we cannot solve a number of linguistic puzzles. Some of these puzzles are already familiar from our discussion of fictional names, and arise when we have a denoting phrase that lacks a denotation. Consider the sentence 'The woman who wrote *Animal Farm* was a lifelong socialist.' If we take grammatical form as a guide to logical form, it seems that such a sentence fails to express a determinate proposition, so it is unclear what is involved in understanding such a sentence, or how such a sentence can have a determinate truth-value. We face a similar problem with 'negative existentials' having non-denoting denoting phrases as their grammatical subjects, as in 'The present king of France does not exist'.

Russell maintains that such puzzles can be solved only if we reject our intuitive picture of the logical form of such sentences. On the intuitive picture, as we have seen, the denoting phrases pick out a particular entity about which we wish to say something, and are thereby treated as individually meaningful elements making their distinct contribution to the meaning of the sentences in which they occur. Russell proposes that we reject this picture, and take the logical form of such sentences to be very different from their grammatical form. Properly understood, sentences with denoting phrases in the grammatical subject position are complex *existential propositions* which make a general claim about the kinds of thing that the world contains, rather than singular propositions predicating a property of a particular entity. So, for example, a sentence having the grammatical form 'an *M* *L*ed' – e.g. 'An English author wrote *Animal Farm*' – has the logical form: 'there is something or someone of which it is true both that they are *M* and that they *L*'ed'. More formally, using the standard notation of the predicate calculus, what such a sentence affirms is that:

$(\exists x)(Mx \ \& \ Lx)$.

In the case of sentences whose grammatical subjects are *definite descriptions* having the grammatical form 'the *M*' – e.g. the sentence 'The woman who wrote *Animal Farm* was a lifelong socialist' – the claim is that one and only one thing satisfies the predicate 'is *M*' and that that thing is *L*. Again, more formally, the logical form is claimed to be:

$(\exists x)\{[Mx \ \& \ ((y) \ (My \rightarrow y = x)] \ \& \ Lx\}$

Since this logically entails that there is one and only one person who satisfies the predicate 'is *M*' – formally,

$(\exists x)[Mx \ \& \ (y) \ (My \rightarrow y = x)]$ –

it is *false* if there is no such unique individual.

Russell's strategy, then, is to reformulate all sentences containing denoting phrases as grammatical components as sentences *not* containing such components, then take the latter sentences to give the *logical form* of the former sentences. This solves the original puzzles because the resulting sentences – which make general claims about the sorts of things that the world contains – are perfectly meaningful, and can be assigned a determinate truth-value – true or false – according to whether the world really does contain such things.

Russell's account would allow us to make sense of sentences containing non-denoting denoting phrases – such as 'the woman who wrote *Animal Farm*' – and that account can also be applied to such phrases when they occur in fictional contexts. Consider, for example, the opening sentences of Aldous Huxley's *Brave New World*:

A squat building of only thirty-four storeys. Over the main entrance the words, CENTRAL LONDON HATCHING AND CONDITIONING CENTRE, and, in a shield, the World State's motto, COMMUNITY, IDENTITY, STABILITY.
The enormous room on the ground floor faced towards the north.[13]

Although the subject-expression in the third sentence is a non-denoting definite description, Russell's analysis would explain both how we can understand that sentence and how we can know what it is that we are to make-believe – roughly, that there is one and only one thing that is an enormous room on the ground floor of the building characterized in the opening paragraph, and that that thing faced towards the north.

Furthermore, we can easily extend this analysis to sentences in fictional discourse that contain, in subject position, *names for fictional characters*, if we follow Russell in his treatment of proper names as ordinarily understood.[14] Russell and a number of other philosophers, such as Frege, Wittgenstein, and Searle, see ordinary proper names like 'George Orwell', 'Aristotle', and 'Bertrand Russell' as a kind of shorthand for some set of definite or indefinite descriptions that a speaker or community of speakers associates with that name. The meaning of the name, on the canonical version of such a 'descriptions theory' of proper names, is given by this set of descriptions, and the referent is the individual, if any, who satisfies all, or a sufficient number, of those descriptions. Thus the name 'George Orwell' might be taken as shorthand for a set of descriptions that includes 'the man born Eric Blair', 'the author of *Animal Farm*', 'the author of *1984*', 'the author of *Down and Out in Paris and London*', 'the author of *The Road to Wigan Pier*', etc. But if proper names are disguised descriptions, then Russell's theory of the logical form of sentences containing denoting phrases in subject position can be applied to sentences containing ordinary proper names in subject position. To get the logical form of such a sentence – say 'George Orwell was a lifelong socialist' – we simply replace the name by the set of associated descriptions and treat the sentence as a complex existential proposition, stating that there is one and only one individual who satisfies the set of descriptions and that the individual in question was a lifelong socialist. In the case of fictional characters, the set of descriptions to be associated with the name of a character consists of those things that are true of the character in the story. We understand a sentence containing such a name – say 'Mrs Dalloway said she would buy the flowers herself' – as saying that there is one and only one individual who satisfies the set of descriptions associated with the name 'Mrs Dalloway' and that the individual in question said that she would buy the flowers herself. It is this that we are then invited to make-believe.

There are, however, at least three serious difficulties confronting a Russellian account of talk about fictional characters. First, while it explains how sentences containing non-denoting names and descriptions can be both meaningful and determinately true or false, it has the unfortunate consequence that all such sentences are false, unless, purely by chance, there is some actual individual who satisfies the descriptions associated with the name and has the property predicated of the character. This is unfortunate because it fails to respect what may strike us as an obvious difference in truth-value between the following two sentences: (1) 'Pegasus has wings', and (2) 'Pegasus has a single horn in the middle of his forehead'. Since the description associated with the name 'Pegasus' – something like 'the winged horse mounted by Bellerophon' – is not satisfied by any actual entity, both (1) and (2), interpreted as existential propositions with the description substituted for the name, come out false. But we are strongly inclined to say that the first sentence is true while the second is false. Similarly, in fictional discourse, we want it to be true, in our understanding of the story, that Mrs Dalloway said she would buy the flowers herself. But, since no actual individual satisfies the set of descriptions associated with the name 'Mrs Dalloway' in virtue of the narrative, the existential proposition that is expressed by the opening sentence of Woolf's novel, on the Russellian account, is false. Similarly, we want to say that 'Sherlock Holmes lived at 221B Baker Street' is true, whereas 'Sherlock Holmes lived in the White House' is false, but they come out equally false on a Russellian account.

A second problem with the Russellian account is that it does not obviously extend to occurrences of the names of fictional characters in discourse about fiction. If, for example, we substitute, for the name 'Sherlock Holmes' in the sentence 'Sherlock Holmes was created by Arthur Conan Doyle', the set of descriptions gleaned from one or more of the narratives, we turn an uncontroversially true claim (save for a Meinongian) into one that is not merely false but bizarre, ascribing to Conan Doyle the God-like ability to bring human beings into existence. The Russellian must therefore hold that, in discourse about fiction, the names of fictional characters are shorthand for a *different* set of descriptions – of the form 'the fictional detective who does the following things in the stories . . .' Such a strategy is not obviously wrong, however, for as we have already seen in examining the Meinongian account, it may not be possible to provide an account of fictional names that applies univocally to occurrences of such names in both fictional discourse and discourse about fiction.

But a third objection represents a more serious challenge to a Russellian account of sentences containing names of fictional characters. As we have seen, to extend Russell's account of the logical form of sentences containing denoting phrases to sentences that contain occurrences of fictional names, we require what is usually called the 'descriptions theory' of proper names. According to the latter, the linguistic roles played by ordinary proper names depend upon sets of descriptions associated with those names. The associated descriptions may be seen as synonymous with the name, in which case what we mean by using the name is something like 'the entity that satisfies all (or a sufficient number) of these descriptions'. The name 'George Orwell', then, will be synonymous with the set of descriptions canvassed above. Alternatively, it may be said that, though not synonymous with a proper name, the associated set of descriptions picks out the *referent* of the name. The referent of 'George Orwell', then, will be the individual, if any, who did all (or a sufficient number) of the things listed in the associated descriptions. A further difference between varieties of the descriptions theory, alluded to in the preceding sentences, relates to whether the meaning of a name is given, or the reference of a name is fixed, by *all* of a set of associated descriptions, or by a *sufficient (weighted) number* of them. Descriptions theories taking the latter option are known as 'cluster' theories. When challenged by apparent counterexamples, descriptions theorists have usually retreated to the weaker formulations, of which the weakest is a cluster theory of how the reference of a name is fixed. But, if we accept Saul Kripke's highly influential arguments in *Naming and Necessity*, all versions of the descriptions theory are incorrect.[15] And, if this is so, then there is no path from Russell's theory of denoting phrases to an account of the names of fictional characters.

In arguing against different versions of the descriptions theory, Kripke presents us with various hypothetical circumstances in which the theory seems to misrepresent either the meaning or the reference of a proper name. Descriptions theories of meaning can be challenged by describing possible worlds in which, so it is claimed, a particular individual – say Aristotle – might correctly be said to exist, even though the individual in that possible world whom we take to be Aristotle did none of things done by Aristotle in the actual world, and thus satisfied none of the descriptions associated with the name 'Aristotle' by the descriptions theorist. Descriptions theories of reference-fixing can be challenged by describing ways in which the referent of a name in the actual world might not satisfy *any* of the descriptions associated with the name. For example, it could turn out that Aristotle did none of the things we believe him to have done.

Given the intuitive force of these kinds of hypothetical examples, Kripke proposes an alternative model of the linguistic functioning of proper names that purportedly makes better sense of our intuitions. In setting out this model, he introduces the term 'designator' as a general term covering proper names, definite descriptions, and also demonstrative expressions such as 'that table'. He distinguishes two ways in which a designator might relate to the thing(s) that it designates when we take into account not just the actual world but various counterfactual situations expressible in terms of other possible worlds. A 'rigid designator' is a linguistic expression that designates the same object in every possible world in which it designates anything at all. In the case of designators that originate in our linguistic community, the object it designates in every such possible world is the object, if any, that it designates in the *actual* world. A 'non-rigid designator', on the other hand, can designate different objects in different possible worlds.

Proper names, Kripke argues, always function as rigid designators – we use them to talk about the same individual in different counterfactual situations. Definite descriptions, on the other hand, standardly function as non-rigid designators. So 'the tutor of Alexander', supposing that it designates Aristotle in the actual world, may designate other individuals in other possible worlds, depending upon who taught Alexander in each of those worlds. But 'Aristotle', in its standard use in our language, can only designate, in any possible world, the individual, if any, that it designates in the actual world. Since 'Aristotle' is a rigid designator, we are able to talk legitimately about Aristotle in possible worlds in which he fails to achieve any of the things that we associate with his name – hence the failure of the descriptions theory, in any of its forms, as a theory of meaning. The failure of the descriptions theory as a theory of reference-fixing follows once we are persuaded, by the kinds of hypothetical examples set out by Kripke, that the actual referent of a proper name can, in standard cases, be an individual who fails to satisfy any of the associated descriptions. A name is not standardly connected to a designated individual through the satisfaction of a set of associated descriptions, Kripke claims,[16] but through a causal-historical 'chain of communication' which links a speaker's use of a name to a particular individual. A speaker is thus able to pick out such an individual, even if she knows little or nothing about their achievements, because she belongs to a historically enduring linguistic community that has transmitted the reference. At the beginning of the chain there is standardly a 'baptism' of some kind, involving a direct encounter between the person who introduces a naming expression and the entity that is named. The name itself may undergo change or corruption over time, but, as long as the chain of transmission is not 'broken' by certain kinds of occurrences, a contemporary speaker can designate the individual originally 'baptized' by using a proper name she inherits from the linguistic community to which she belongs. Thus, in using the name 'Aristotle', I am able to designate a particular individual with whom I have no direct contact, who may have done none of the things I associate with the name, and who may not have been called 'Aristotle' by his contemporaries.

This is, of course, a much abbreviated and simplified version of Kripke's arguments against the descriptions theory, but it may suffice for present purposes. It should be clear that, barring an answer to Kripke, the Russellian account of sentences containing names of fictional characters cannot work. If 'Mrs Dalloway', 'Gregor Samsa', and 'Sherlock Holmes' are genuine proper names, then Kripke's arguments establish that none of these names is synonymous or necessarily co-referential with any set of associated descriptions. And, without some equivalence between fictional names and sets of descriptions, we cannot apply Russell's theory of denoting phrases to explain the meaning of sentences such as 'Sherlock Holmes lived at 221B Baker Street'. On Kripke's account, names do serve to pick out particular entities about which we are able to say something in virtue of an appropriate causal-historical connection between our use of the name and that entity. It might be thought that this provides solace to the Meinongian, who holds that the names of fictional characters do indeed refer to entities, albeit non-existent ones. But, if we are tempted to say that 'Sherlock Holmes' refers to a Meinongian fictional character, this temptation rapidly fades when it is asked how, on the Kripkean picture, we would be able to secure reference to such an entity? This reinforces our earlier concern as to how we might refer to non-existent entities, since it is difficult to imagine a causal-historical connection of the sort Kripke proposes.

ALTERNATIVE STRATEGIES

In light of our discussion thus far, what options remain? Three possibilities have been proposed, two of which attempt to rehabilitate Meinongian or Russellian intuitions while the third is Kripke's own response to the puzzles posed by non-denoting expressions. In each case, it is acknowledged that we require different treatments of fictional names in the contexts of fictional discourse and of discourse about fiction. I shall set out the three alternatives, beginning with Kripke's own account in his unpublished paper 'Vacuous Names and Mythical Kinds'.

Russell, as we saw, took the existence of non-denoting denoting phrases and non-denoting names as a reason to reject our intuitive picture of how language makes determinate claims about the world. Kripke, however, thinks that this way of proceeding is perverse. Given that we naturally take the principal function of proper names to be to pick out particular individuals about which we wish to talk, we should seek an account of how successful reference to individuals might occur, and then explain how, under other circumstances, we can make sense of uses of names where reference is not secured. When we read fables 'about' unicorns or fictional stories 'about' characters like Sherlock Holmes, we *pretend* that the conditions for successful reference have been satisfied, as part of our more general imaginative engagement with the fable or fiction. He offers what he terms the 'pretence principle': 'When someone spins a story or something like that and uses various names which don't refer to anything real, then the story is just that, it's a story, it's a pretense. Part of the pretense is that these names are names just like ordinary names, that the ordinary conditions for reference are satisfied, even though in fact they are not.'[17] So, in reading the fictions of Conan Doyle, we make-believe that there is an actual individual who stands in an appropriate causal-historical relationship to the name 'Sherlock Holmes' as employed in the narrative, and then make-believe that we are being told various things about that individual.

Kripke then focuses on the different contexts in which we say that fictional characters exist or don't exist. In fictional discourse, where our concern, as authors or as readers, is with what is true in the story, we say such things as 'Hamlet exists', or 'Macbeth's "dagger" doesn't exist', understanding such claims as having an implicit 'in the story' qualifier. Such talk is part of our pretence that there are individuals who stand in appropriate causal-historical relationships to the names used in the narrative. In discourse about fiction, we can talk explicitly about *fictional characters*, such as Hamlet and Macbeth. A fictional character, Kripke maintains, exists as long as the relevant works exist.[18] Of greater concern to Kripke, however, are contexts in which, talking outside of the story, we truly say such things as 'Hamlet never existed' or 'unicorns never existed'. Does it make sense, in such contexts, to add that there are circumstances under which we might find out that Hamlet or unicorns *did* exist, or that, if they didn't, they nonetheless *would have* existed under certain counterfactual conditions?

According to Kripke, names for species are like proper names in that they *rigidly* designate their objects, where what they designate is determined by some kind of causal-historical connection rather than by associated descriptions. He therefore denies that, were archaeologists to discover remains consistent with the descriptions of unicorns in the fables, this would establish that unicorns really existed. What matters, rather, is the intentions of the tellers of the fables and the causal-historical relationship, if any, between their use of the term 'unicorn' and the beasts whose remains we discover. Suppose now that the term 'unicorn' as employed in the fables does not stand in an appropriate causal-historical relationship to any actual kind of beast. Then, Kripke argues, we cannot sensibly say that there are conditions under which there might have been unicorns, because we have no way of determining which of many possible species in other possible worlds is the species unicorn. The problem is that all we know about unicorns is that they are a species and they have a certain surface appearance. But there are many possible species that fit these requirements, and only one of them could be unicorns. More significantly, having the appearance properties ascribed to unicorns in the fables would not identify something as a unicorn, given Kripke's critique of the descriptions theory.

Kripke applies the same analysis to proper names that occur in fictional narratives. Were we to discover that there was an actual individual in Victorian England who did the things narrated in the Sherlock Holmes stories, this would not show that Sherlock Holmes actually existed. What would be necessary is that Conan Doyle intended to refer to an actual existent and that his employment of the name 'Sherlock Holmes' in the narrative stood in the right kind of causal-historical relationship to the individual in question. If this was not the case, then, again, we can make no sense of the claim that Sherlock Holmes *might have* existed, because we would have no way of picking out a particular individual in another possible world as Sherlock Holmes. What we *can* do is identify individuals in other possible worlds who do the things narrated of Sherlock Holmes in the stories. Such individuals can be said to play the 'Holmes role' in their respective worlds, but none of them is Holmes, because none of them stands in the right causal relationship to our use of 'Holmes', which goes back to Conan Doyle.

Amie Thomasson picks up on Kripke's claim that, at least in some contexts, fictional names are rightly seen as referring to fictional characters, and seeks to clarify the ontological status of the latter. We noted above that Kripke was prepared to grant the existence of fictional characters as the referents of expressions in discourse about fiction. He writes that, in the latter context, 'a fictional character . . . is not some kind of shadowy person; it is an entity of a different sort which exists provided the appropriate works of fiction have been written. In some sense it's not anything over and above these works'.[19] Fictional characters are described, here, as real-world existents that (1) depend for their existence on the existence of works of fiction in which they 'appear'; and (2) are 'in some sense' nothing over and above the works themselves.

Thomasson tries to clarify what such existents *are* and how they relate to fictional characters as construed by the Meinongian. Her claim is that fictional characters belong to an ontological category that has been largely ignored, the category of 'abstract artefacts'. They must be viewed as artefacts because they are brought into existence by authors. But they are *abstract* artefacts because, unlike concrete artefacts such as paintings or works of sculpture, they cannot be ascribed any spatio-temporal location. Abstract artefacts differ from abstract entities as normally construed – entities such as numbers and properties – because it is usually assumed that the latter cannot be brought into existence or destroyed.

But if the names of fictional characters refer to abstract artefacts, this raises Kripkean worries about how we are able to refer to such entities. Thomasson proposes that authors are able to bring fictional characters into existence by a form of 'baptism' that occurs when they are writing the fictional narratives in which the characters have a place. She acknowledges that neither of the means of 'baptism' recognized by Kripke can apply to the naming of fictional characters. On the one hand, the referent cannot be picked out indexically, as in the case of the literal baptism of an infant. On the other hand, it isn't clear how baptism of a fictional character could be accomplished by means of a reference-fixing description, as in the case of the name 'Jack the Ripper', although perhaps a description like 'the character I am writing about at this moment' is a possibility. Thomasson suggests that the baptism of fictional characters be understood in the following way:

Although there can be no direct pointing at a fictional character on the other side of the room, the textual foundation of the character serves as the means whereby a quasi-indexical reference to the character can be made by means of which that very fictional object can be baptized by author or readers. Something counting as a baptismal ceremony can be performed by means of writing the words of the text or it can be merely recorded in the text, or (if the character is named later, for example by readers), it can remain unrecorded in the text.[20]

If this account of the 'baptism' of fictional characters is plausible, Thomasson's account of fictional characters as abstract artefacts neatly evades some of the most powerful objections against the Meinongian identification of fictional characters with non-existent objects. First, most obviously, we get round the objection that, on a Kripkean account of how names refer, we cannot refer to non-existent objects. Second, if fictional characters are artefacts, then they are the creations of authors, and depend upon the novels in which they appear for their continued existence. And third, since, as artefacts, fictional characters are individuated not merely by reference to the properties ascribed to them in the story but also by reference to an act of creation by the author, we get round the difficulties with the individuation of characters that confront the Meinongian. In answer to the question, 'When do we have the same character in different fictional narratives by one or more authors?', we can ask whether the authors' employment of a character in a given narrative stands in the right kind of causal and intentional relations to an original baptism of the character in question. In the case of *The Seven Percent Solution*, for example, we can ask whether Meyer's employment of the name 'Sherlock Holmes' with reference to one of the fictional characters in his novel is both *intended* to refer to the fictional character created by Conan Doyle, and stands in the right kind of causal-historical relation to Conan Doyle's act of 'baptism'.

However, as will not surprise us given what we have seen thus far, there are problems when we try to apply the abstract artefact theory of fictional names to contexts of both fictional discourse and discourse about fiction. Kripke, we will recall, introduces the idea of fictional characters as real-world existents in order to account for discourse about fiction. Thomasson follows Kripke in holding that such an account of what we are talking about in discourse about fiction can accommodate our saying truly, in such discourse, such things as that 'Hamlet does not exist'. This is to be paraphrased as saying that Hamlet is not a (real) person – i.e. that Hamlet is a fictional character. More troubling, however, is our talk about fictional characters in fictional discourse, either as authors inviting the reader to make-believe or as readers entertaining what they take to be true in the story. When the opening sentence of *Metamorphosis* tells us that Gregor Samsa awoke from an uneasy sleep to find himself transformed into a gigantic insect, this cannot be understood as predicating such properties of an abstract artefact, for abstract entities do not sleep and cannot be transformed into concrete entities like insects. In response to this objection, Thomasson suggests that, when names for fictional characters occur in statements in fictional discourse, we must paraphrase such statements as claims about what is the case 'according to the story'. But this doesn't immediately solve the problem, in that it is not true that according to the story an *abstract artefact* has the property in question: the paraphrase will have to be more comprehensive, perhaps substituting a set of descriptions for any occurrence of the fictional name.

The latter idea is central to Gregory Currie's account of fictional discourse. Currie proposes that we treat fictional names in a fully Russellian manner, viewing them as semantically equivalent to a set of descriptions expressing what is true of the character in the story.[21] This is not to reject Kripke's critique of the descriptions theory of names, but to hold that what appear to be names in works of fiction are not genuine names but are disguised descriptions, as Russell wrongly thought ordinary proper names to be. We evade the other serious objection to a Russellian account of names of fictional characters – that all sentences containing such names are false – by taking all sentences that occur in fictional discourse as implicitly prefixed by 'in the story'. Thus a sentence like 'Sherlock Holmes took out his pipe and began to smoke' is rendered as an existential proposition concerning the story, of the form: In the story, there is one and only one individual who fits the description D and this individual took out his pipe and began to smoke. Currie does not, however, think that such an account can make sense of the different kinds of things that we say in discourse about fiction, and offers a different analysis of the latter.

It seems unlikely that a single account of the names of fictional characters can deal with their occurrence in both fictional discourse and discourse about fiction – something acknowledged by all parties in the contemporary debate just surveyed. Each of the three views has relative strengths and weaknesses. For example, Currie's view is ontologically deflationary but requires that we deny that the 'names' of fictional characters really function as names. Thomasson clarifies what kind of thing a fictional character is in our discourse about fiction, but we may prefer either Currie's modified Russellian account or Kripke's account as a way of making sense of fictional discourse. In the end, it is likely that our preference for one or another kind of account of fictional characters will depend in part on our broader sympathies in metaphysics and the philosophy of language, sympathies we cannot further explore in the present context.

CHAPTER 7

LITERATURE AND THE EMOTIONS

Charles is watching a horror movie about a terrible green slime. He cringes in his seat as the slime oozes slowly but relentlessly over the earth destroying everything in its path. Soon a greasy head emerges from the undulating mass, and two beady eyes roll around, finally fixing on the camera. The slime, picking up speed, oozes on a new course straight toward the viewers. Charles emits a shriek and clutches desperately at his chair. Afterwards, still shaken, Charles confesses that he was 'terrified' of the slime.[1]

Kendall Walton's tale of Charles and the green slime introduces his discussion of what is usually termed the 'paradox of fiction', one of the supposed 'paradoxes' relating to our affective responses to fictional works. Walton describes a familiar reaction to a cinematic, rather than a literary, fiction. But, while it might be argued that the cinematic medium serves to accentuate our affective responses, it is unlikely that there are many readers of literary fictions who have not, on at least some occasions, found themselves moved by a narrative to affective states most naturally described as pity, anger, sorrow, fear, etc. Contemporary readers of Dickens' *Old Curiosity Shop* were reduced to tears by the slow and painful death of Little Nell as this unfolded in weekly instalments in the magazine *Master Humphrey's Clock*,[2] and it was surely Dickens' intent that the same readers be moved to outrage at the treatment meted out in Victorian social institutions to the youthful protagonists of such novels as *Nicholas Nickleby* and *Hard Times*. And a reader of *Anna Karenina* who failed to be moved by Anna's fate might be thought to have missed something as crucial to the appreciation of the work as the irony in Swift's *A Modest Proposal*. Indeed, whole genres of literary works – from ghost stories to Harlequin romances – seem to have as one of their principal goals the eliciting of strong feelings in the reader.

It seems so obvious that we are moved in different ways by literary works, and that this may itself be a principal reason why readers choose to engage with these works, that we might wonder how this could be thought to engender any kind of problem. But, as we shall see, our affective responses to literary and other fictions, when viewed in the context of other plausible assumptions, generate at least two distinct paradoxes. The 'paradox of fiction', illustrated by Charles' reaction to the slime, arises if we ask whether we should accept Charles' own description of his experience. Can we reconcile his claim to have been 'terrified' with his presumed awareness that he is watching something fictional? Similarly, since readers of *Anna Karenina* are surely aware that Anna is a character in a fictional narrative that they are reading, how can they genuinely pity her? Another kind of paradox purportedly arises in respect of both tragedy and works belonging to the 'horror' genre. How, it might be asked, can we explain the fact that receivers seek out by choice works that, so it seems, arouse unpleasant emotions such as pity and fear? We shall look at each of these paradoxes in turn and consider how best to make sense of our affective responses to fictions.

THE 'PARADOX OF FICTION'

The paradox of fiction arises when we try to reconcile what strikes us as the natural way to describe our affective responses to fictions with a more general philosophical theory of the emotions. If we reflect on the phenomenology of our engagement with fictions, it is natural to talk, in the manner of Charles, of being frightened or even terrified by ghost stories or horror movies, and of feeling pity for Anna Karenina. Charles assumes that, because it feels to him as if he is terrified of the slime, it follows that he is indeed terrified of the slime. But the idea that emotions can be identified with, and individuated in terms of, distinctive kinds of qualitative feelings has been called into question by philosophers who have enquired into the nature of emotions. Here are two reasons why we might question a purely phenomenological conception of the emotions. First, it is not clear that we are able to distinguish between different kinds of emotional states purely in terms of how they 'feel'. Can I really tell if I am afraid or just anxious by merely reflecting upon the qualitative nature of my experience? Second, we surely want to ascribe the same kinds of emotional states to different individuals, but it is implausible to think that the basis for doing so could be phenomenological identity or similarity.

A more satisfactory account of the emotions, it is claimed, must take account of two things. First, emotions such as fear, pity, love, and hate involve not just a particular kind of affective attitude, but also an 'intentional object' of that attitude. A person may pity the homeless person panhandling in the rain, be afraid of heights, and love his cat, but it is difficult to make sense of objectless instances of these emotions. An 'intentional object' of an emotion need not actually exist, of course, which is why we do not commit ourselves to the existence of ghosts, God, or Satan if we cite these as the intentional objects of people's fear, love, and hate. But, it is further claimed, if one's affective relation to such an intentional object is to be, say, fear rather than pity, one must have certain cognitive states relative to that intentional object. It is because I *believe* that the homeless panhandler is suffering, and perhaps suffering unjustly, that I pity him. Had I believed, rather, that he posed a danger to my well-being or to the well-being of one close to me, then my feeling towards him would be properly described as fear rather than pity. Similarly, if you really love your cat, then you must *desire* to do things that further your cat's well-being, whereas if I am afraid of heights, then I must *want* to avoid placing myself in elevated locations.

According to what is termed a 'cognitivist' view of the emotions, there is an essential cognitive component to emotional states like pity and fear. Only if one has certain kinds of beliefs, and perhaps also certain kinds of desires, can one be said to genuinely pity someone, or to be genuinely afraid of something. This doesn't mean that we have to deny that emotions also have an affective component. When someone is afraid of climbing out onto the 25th-storey balcony, they experience various kinds of affective and physiological symptoms, such as sweating, accelerated heart-rate, queasiness, etc. But to experience such symptoms in the absence of the relevant cognitive states is not to have the emotion of fear, it is claimed. Furthermore, so cognitivists argue,[3] to have an emotion is not just to have certain beliefs and desires while at the same time experiencing certain physiological or affective symptoms. It is to experience the latter as a result of having the former. It is because someone's palpitations, sweating, and queasiness are caused by their belief that the balcony, on the other side of the door they are facing, is on the 25th floor that they are rightly described as being afraid of going out onto the balcony. Note that cognitivism requires that an agent's *beliefs* about the entity which is the intentional object of her emotional state plays a particular causal role in the generation of an affective response: it does not require that the entity *itself* play such a causal role. Thus the cognitivist does not face a problem explaining how we can have emotions whose intentional objects fail to exist. I can be afraid of a tiger lurking in the bushes as long as I believe that such a beast is there and threatens or endangers me or one close to me: yet there may not be any such tiger.

A cognitivist theory of the emotions calls into question our usual way of describing our affective responses to fictions because it is not clear that we satisfy the cognitive requirements for being in the emotional states that we naturally ascribe to ourselves. Most obviously, if I am to pity someone or fear something, then it seems that I cannot have the required *belief* – that the person I pity is suffering unjustly, or that the thing I fear endangers me or someone near to me – unless I believe that the intentional object of my posited emotional state *exists*. But, if I know that I am reading or watching a fiction, surely I *don't* believe this. What I believe, it seems, is that Anna Karenina is a fictional character in a story by Tolstoy, and that the slime is a fictional entity in a horror story. If I believed that the slime existed, then surely I would flee from the cinema immediately and inform the authorities of the danger. So, if the cognitivist theory of the emotions is correct, then it seems that my affective responses to fictions are not emotional states. Or, if they are, then I must be holding inconsistent beliefs – believing, for example, both that the slime doesn't exist (to explain why I remain in my seat) and that the slime does exist (to explain how I can satisfy the cognitive requirements for being genuinely terrified of the slime).

The paradox of fiction, then, arises for anyone who wishes, on independent grounds, to believe all three of the following claims:

1. We rightly ascribe to receivers of fictions, including ourselves, emotions such as pity and fear that have fictional characters as their intentional objects.
2. One can be in an emotional state such as pity or fear only if certain cognitive conditions are satisfied. One cannot pity, or feel fear for, an entity unless one has certain kinds of beliefs, and certain kinds of desires, concerning that entity and its situation.
3. As a matter of act, receivers of fictional narratives who are moved by those narratives do not satisfy the aforesaid cognitive conditions. They lack the required beliefs and desires concerning

the fictional characters that are the putative intentional objects of their emotions.

The existence of the paradox, or at least of the need to reconcile what appear to be inconsistent claims relating to our affective involvement with fictions, has long been recognized. Dr Johnson, for example, famously asked 'how the drama moves, if it is not credited'.[4]

Walton, whose own solution to the puzzle posed by Charles is to deny (1) and reject Charles' claim that he is genuinely terrified of the slime, considers and rejects a number of possible challenges to (3). One might, for example, maintain that readers who are moved by fictions do indeed inconsistently believe that the fictional protagonists *don't* really exist and that they *do* really exist. This would permit us to ascribe genuine emotions to Charles and his kind, albeit at the cost of viewing them as cognitively irrational. The charge of irrationality was famously levelled at those readers who are moved by the fate of Anna Karenina by Colin Radford, in a much-discussed paper.[5] But, given the ubiquity of affective responses to acknowledged fictions, it seems preferable to avoid any solution to the paradox that requires such extensive irrationality.

We take an agent's behavioural dispositions to be one of the clearest indications of what she really believes. Indeed, for some philosophers there is nothing more to ascriptions of beliefs than would be contained in claims about dispositions to act. Thus it is difficult to deny that Charles in particular, and receivers of fictions in general, believe that they are engaging with a fictional narrative rather than with real events that might harm them in some way. As noted, there is no evidence in Charles' case of the sorts of behavioural dispositions that we associate with the belief that an evil slime is about to devour one. As a number of writers have also noted, to believe that one is actually endangered by what one takes to be fictional would manifest a severely impaired grasp of basic metaphysical facts. For, as Alex Neill puts it, the 'ontological gap' between fictional characters and ourselves prevents us from causally interacting with them, and thus prevents them from physically harming us.[6] Equally, it prevents us from harming or helping them – by interceding, for example, to prevent Othello from killing Desdemona. Walton too writes of 'a definite barrier against *physical* interactions between fictional worlds and the real world'.[7] He is equally dismissive of other challenges to the third claim in our paradoxical triad. Even though Charles is clearly strongly affected by what he is viewing, the absence of any dispositions to appropriate action undermines the claim that he 'half-believes' the slime to be real, or that he has a 'gut belief' to that effect. For even 'gut beliefs' that one does not intellectually accept – such as the gut belief that flying is very dangerous, when one knows from reading the statistics that it is not – are manifest in one's dispositions to action.

Suppose, therefore, that we accept claim (3), and grant that we cannot reasonably ascribe to consumers of fictions the belief that the narrated events, when entertained as fictional, are really occurring or have really occurred. If there are independent reasons to accept a cognitivist theory of emotion, and if such a theory requires, for a genuine emotion of pity or fear, a belief in the reality of its intentional object (claim (2)), then it seems that, if we want to resolve the paradox, we must call into question the first claim in our triad. But there are different ways of doing this. One possibility is to maintain that our affective responses to fictions are indeed genuine emotions, but that their intentional objects are *not* fictional characters, but other entities that we believe to be real existents and that stand in some relevant relation to the fictional characters and events. One popular suggestion is that the objects of our emotional responses to fictions are not the fictional characters and events themselves, but *real people and situations* that are brought to mind by what is narrated in the fiction.[8] In reading *Anna Karenina*, for example, we are moved to genuine pity, but the intentional object of our emotion is not a fictional character but real people whom we believe to have suffered in the same kind of way that Anna suffers. In watching *Othello*, it is not Iago that we detest or the murder of Desdemona that inspires our horror and grief. Rather, we are moved to such genuine emotions because the fictional narrative brings to mind real incidents of treachery and deceit leading to tragic consequences as a result of human jealousy for those who are relatively innocent.

This strategy does indeed provide a way of reconciling the three claims in the triad, once we reformulate the first claim, but it is problematic in at least three respects. First, it seems phenomenologically false, in that we are rarely aware of extrapolating in this way from the content of the fictional narrative to some real-life counterpart. If such extrapolation occurs, it seems more likely to do so when we disengage from our reading of the fiction and reflect upon its more thematic meanings. Second, it is doubtful that the reader is usually aware of any specific real-life counterparts for the individuals and events that figure in the fictions that engender affective responses. If so, then it is difficult to see how reflection of a more amorphous kind upon 'suffering lovers in the world', for example, with no particular individuals or situations in mind, can account for the sharpness and particularity of our emotional responses. Again, phenomenologically speaking, it is Anna, not the general mass of star-crossed lovers, for whom we feel pity. And, in the case of many fictions that move us, we may not believe that there are or even could be any real-life counterparts. Must Charles believe that there really are people being devoured by green slime, or something very much like it, in order to be genuinely terrified of the slime? Finally, the posited relationship between the fictional narrative and the response of the receiver seems inadequate to account for the values that we ascribe to *the work* in virtue of our being affected in certain ways. If the narrative causes us to think of something else – real people or events – and it is to the latter that we respond, this seems irrelevant to the proper appreciation and evaluation of the work. Consider, as a comparison, the emotional response to a seascape by a visitor to an exhibition of paintings who is reminded, by the painting, of his or her summer vacation, and is thereby led to feelings of euphoria or despair (depending upon how the vacation went!).

There is, however, an alternative account that might be thought to preserve the insights in the preceding proposal without entailing the dubious consequences. According to what is usually termed the 'thought theory',[9] the genuine emotions evoked in receivers of fictional works are responses not to events in what is taken to be a fiction, nor to real people of whom we are reminded by the fiction, but to the very *thought* of the narrated events occurring. It is the very thought of being consumed by green slime that terrifies Charles, even though he is under no illusion about his location in the cinema and under no misapprehension that there are real green slimes loose in the world. Just as, in real life, we can be emotionally moved by merely thinking about a particular kind of occurrence – we can, for example, become embarrassed by merely thinking about committing a particularly egregious social faux pas – so, in reading fiction, we can be genuinely emotionally moved by merely thinking about what is narrated. Here, it seems, we preserve the particularity of the narrative, and do not refer the reader outside of her engagement with the text in order to find the intentional object of her emotion. This also seems to respect the phenomenology of our experience, and the intrinsic relationship between the work and our responses to it. And, furthermore, there is no problem with fictions that narrate events whose actual occurrence we deem either unlikely or even impossible.

The suggestion is that it is the thought of the green slime that causes Charles to be terrified. And the thought of the green slime, as a mental representation in Charles, both exists and is believed by Charles to exist. But, if he is genuinely terrified, what is he terrified *of*? Not, surely, of his thought, but, as Peter Lamarque puts it in expounding and defending the thought theory, of the *content* of his thought:

> We need to distinguish what Charles finds frightening, which specifies either a general type (slimy things) or some feature of the particular instance; what he is frightened *by*, which specifies the cause of the fear; and what he is frightened *of*, which specifies the intentional content of the fear. The thought of being devoured by the slime is a frightening thought for Charles. He is frightened by that thought, made vivid by the images in the movie. What he is frightened of is *the imagined slime*, which is not a mysterious 'ficti-tious entity', certainly not a kind of slime, but a kind of imagining. 'Slime' characterizes the intentional content of his fear (and his imaginings); it is a slime-fear, not, say, a vampire-fear.[10]

The thought theory requires that we reject, or at least amend, the standard formulation of the cognitivist theory of emotions outlined above. For, as we saw, proponents of the latter, such as Currie, assume that, in order to experience genuine fear, I must believe that the intentional object of my fear both exists and endangers either me or someone close to me, and this belief must play an essential part in causing my affective reaction. But, while Charles believes that the content of his thought exists, as a mental representation, he does not believe that this representation endangers him, nor does any such belief cause his response. The thought theorist maintains that it is not only *beliefs* about the intentional object of an affective state that can cause genuine emotions, but also the very act of entertaining the thought of that object. As Noel Carroll, another proponent of the thought theory, puts it, it is only if we take it to be an 'article of faith' that genuine fear requires genuine belief that we will see ourselves forced to choose between either ascribing irrational beliefs to Charles or denying that he is genuinely afraid: the solution to the paradox of fiction is to recognize that 'it is reasonable to think that thought contents, as well as beliefs, can produce emotional states'.[11]

The thought theory does indeed seem to avoid the pitfalls seen to confront the proposal that the intentional objects of our affective reactions to fictions are real people or events that we associate with what is described in the fiction. The content of the thought that is the intentional object of our emotion can be as specific as the fictional narrative demands. Thus, as Lamarque argues, in reading *Anna Karenina* the content of the thought that arouses my pity is not just someone or other who resembles the depicted character, but the very particular individual that is central to my imaginings when I read the story. Genuine pity, he maintains, can be aroused by the thought of Anna and her predicament, and our sympathetic imagining of what that predicament must be like.[12] Nor does the thought theory have a problem with fictions that narrate events whose actual occurrence we deem either unlikely or even impossible, since the capacity of a thought to affect us does not depend upon any belief about the real existence of its content. Perhaps most significantly, the thought theorist locates our affective responses to fictions in the context of our imaginative engagement with the details of the story, rather than in reflections upon matters external to the fiction that are merely caused by that imaginative engagement. This both respects the phenomenology of our experience, and preserves the intrinsic relationship between the work and our responses to it.

Nonetheless, there is some resistance to the suggestion that genuine emotions can be grounded in thoughts that are merely entertained but not endorsed. If one holds that genuine emotions do indeed require genuine beliefs, and if one accepts the arguments against alternative solutions considered thus far, this seems to force the conclusion that our affective responses to fictions are not genuine emotions at all, but 'quasi-emotions'. Quasi-emotions are said to involve the same kinds of physiological effects and psychological affects as their real counterparts, but to lack the necessary cognitive component. Charles is quite correct if he says that he 'feels' terrified of the green slime, but having all of the feelings that attend being terrified is not sufficient actually to *be* terrified. What Charles experiences, then, is not fear but 'quasi-fear'. Both Walton and Currie propose resolutions of the paradox along such lines,[13] and both concur with the thought theorists in thinking that an adequate account of our affective responses to fictions must situate those responses in the context of our imaginative engagement with the fictional narrative. According to Walton, the receiver of a fiction comes to believe that certain things are true in the story and thus that, to engage properly with the fiction, one should make-believe those things. But this belief about what is fictionally true may produce physiological and affective responses in the reader. It is Charles' belief that it is fictionally true that the slime is heading towards him that causes him to experience those feelings constitutive of 'quasi-fear', according to Walton. But, since this occurs in the context of Charles' imaginative engagement with the fiction – his making-believe that certain things are occurring – his quasi-fear provides further input to the game of make-believe that Charles is playing, and makes it true *in that game* that Charles is actually afraid. Thus, in the game of make-believe that Charles is playing as a result of viewing the film, it is indeed true that he is afraid of the slime, but he is not *really* afraid: what he really experiences is quasi-fear. Nor is his being afraid true in the film itself: rather, it is true in the expanded fiction generated by Charles' imaginative engagement with the fiction. A similar analysis is offered of other kinds of affective responses to fictions. For example, it is my belief that it is fictionally true that Anna is driven by her grief to throw herself in front of the train that causes me to experience the feelings constitutive of quasi-pity, and this makes it true in the game of make-believe I am playing with the novel that I really pity Anna.

Currie's account, while similar to Walton's, differs in two crucial respects. First, the feelings constitutive of quasi-fear are generated, not by the *belief* that certain things are make-believe in the fiction, but by the reader's *making-believe* that those things are true. Currie argues that it is difficult to understand how the mere belief that certain things are fictionally true could generate the kinds of strong feelings that Charles and others experience in their engagements with fictions. It is the activity of making-believe that certain things occur that moves us, so Currie maintains, not our beliefs as to what we are required to make-believe. Currie's account thus more closely resembles that of thought theorists like Lamarque. It is the content of Charles' imagining, as Lamarque would put it, that causes the affective response, but this response, for Currie, is quasi-fear rather than genuine fear. The second difference between Currie and Walton is that the former does not additionally claim that, in virtue of the quasi-fear aroused in Charles, it is part of his larger make-believe that he is really afraid.

We may wonder at this point whether the difference between

Currie and Lamarque is more than terminological, and Currie himself is willing to entertain this possibility.[14] Should we impose a strong cognitive requirement on the ascription of emotions like fear and pity, so that such emotions require a genuine belief about the existence and nature of the intentional object of the emotion? Or should we adopt a broader conception of such emotions that encompasses affective states caused by either genuine beliefs or the unendorsed entertainment of thoughts? A further ingenious proposal, however, is made by Alex Neill, who suggests that the appropriate constraints may not be uniform across the spectrum of the emotions.[15] While we may genuinely pity Anna Karenina, he claims, Charles cannot genuinely fear the green slime.

Neill, like Walton and Currie, begins with the receiver who, as a result of engaging with a fictional narrative like *Anna Karenina*, forms certain beliefs as to what is true in the story. Among those beliefs is the belief that it is true in the story that Anna is a woman with certain qualities who suffers unjustly and eventually commits suicide as a result of her suffering. Neill, like Currie, questions whether this belief, by itself, has the capacity to cause an affective response in the receiver. But, he suggests, the same point might be made about our beliefs that actual people are suffering or have suffered, as in the case of beliefs about the occurrence of a natural disaster such as a hurricane, or about certain historical events. Neither beliefs about fictional suffering nor beliefs about actual suffering are themselves sufficient to elicit an affective response from us, he maintains. Rather, our belief that someone is suffering, either fictionally or actually, affects us through our capacity to adopt the perspective of the suffering party and to appreciate from this perspective the qualities of their situation and their experience. But, in that case, it is not clear why the fictional nature of the suffering of Anna Karenina is an obstacle to our being moved to genuine pity. For what matters is not whether our belief relates to real or fictional suffering, but whether, in adopting the perspective of the suffering party, we can be moved to pity them.

Neill then argues that the affective state to which I am moved in adopting the perspective of Anna Karenina has all of the features that we might take to be characteristic of genuine pity as evoked by real suffering. As Walton and Currie concede in their talk of 'quasi-pity', the reader's feeling for Anna Karenina has all the physiological and phenomenological features of genuine pity – indeed, these features may be more pronounced in our reactions to fictional suffering than to actual, though historically or geographically distant, suffering. Second, so Neill has argued, the belief that the suffering is fictional rather than actual is not a salient difference. The third element that might be thought necessary for genuine pity, however, is at first sight more difficult to accommodate in the case of our feelings for fictional characters. For it can plausibly be claimed that real pity involves not merely belief and affect, but also certain kinds of desires – the desire that the suffering cease or be avoided if possible, and the desire to help the suffering party. But a recognition of the 'ontological gap' between the reader and the characters in the fiction seems inconsistent with the second kind of desire, while to have the former desire seems to require that we wish the *work* to lack the very qualities that move us. Neill argues that both of these objections can be met. A desire to help those whom we pity, while it may be necessary in those cases where we are indeed able to help, is not, he maintains, a necessary condition for genuine pity. For, if the 'ontological gap' is unbridgeable, so too is the historical gap that separates us from those who have suffered in the past, and the geographical gap that may prevent us from intervening in some cases of present suffering. But there is no temptation to deny that we can feel genuine pity for sufferers from whom we are separated in the latter kinds of ways. Fictional characters are like actual people who are very far away and whom we are unable to help: our feelings for fictional characters are no more surprising or problematic than our feelings for these distant and unreachable real individuals. As for our desire that a fictional character should not suffer, Neill offers two responses to the charge that this is inconsistent with our desire that the work not be changed in this way. First, he argues that we can have conflicting desires in respect of the suffering of actual people, as with the grieving parent whom we pity while also accepting that the grief must be suffered through for the process of healing to occur. And, second, he claims that our wishing the suffering of a character to cease does not in fact entail any beliefs about *the work* being different, since our engagement with the work at that time is an imaginative engagement with the content of the story rather than a critical engagement with the work as a literary entity.

However, so Neill further argues, if we defend in this way the claim to genuine emotional status of some of our affective responses to fictions, we must also reject the idea that other affective responses, such as Charles' response to the green slime, are genuine emotions. For we have been able to bracket the issue of whether we believe an episode of suffering to be actual or fictional only because we take the cause of genuine pity to be the adoption of the perspective of the suffering party, and our ability to adopt this perspective doesn't rest upon whether that party is an actual person or a fictional character. In the case of fear for oneself, however, the only perspective that plays a causal role in generating an affective response is *one's own*. But, from my own perspective, I am not threatened by something I take to be a fictional entity, nor do I have the desires – to escape from that entity – that also seem to be an element in genuine fear. So, while there are other affective responses that should be analysed in the same way as pity – fear *for others*, for example – we cannot view Charles' response to the green slime as genuine fear. Charles is either responding to what he believes to be real-life counterparts of the fictional entity, or, more plausibly, experiencing a non-belief-dependent affective state such as shock.

THE 'PARADOX OF TRAGEDY' AND THE 'PARADOX OF HORROR'

The second kind of paradox associated with our affective responses to literary works arises only in respect of certain literary genres – the most obvious being tragedy and horror. It does not depend upon how we resolve the paradox of fiction, in that it can be formulated whether we take our affective responses to fictions to be genuine emotions or only quasi-emotions. David Hume clearly expresses the nature of the paradox as it arises in the case of tragedy: what requires explanation is the 'unaccountable pleasure which the spectators of a well-written tragedy receive from sorrow, terror, anxiety and other passions that are in themselves disagreeable and uneasy'.[16] The analogous puzzle, in the case of horror, is to explain what attracts readers and viewers to literary or cinematic works in the 'horror' genre, where the subject matter seems to arouse disagreeable responses such as disgust and fear. The puzzle, in each case, is to explain why receivers are so attracted to works of art that seem bound to elicit unpleasant emotions, and, if it be answered that the attraction lies in the pleasure that attends engagement with such works, to explain in what that pleasure consists. More schematically, the paradoxes of tragedy and horror can be represented in terms of the following three claims:

1. The attraction, for receivers, of works belonging to the genres of

tragedy and horror is best explained in terms of the pleasure derived from such works. We further assume that, in general, such receivers are 'non-morbid' in the sense that they do not take pleasure in the suffering of others.

2. Given their subject matter, works of tragedy and horror elicit, or are designed to elicit, responses having the affective qualities of pity, fear, and disgust.

3. The affective qualities of pity, fear, and disgust are unpleasant for (non-morbid) people.

This triad of claims is not, as it stands, inconsistent. For one might respond by suggesting sources of pleasure, in the reception of works of tragedy and horror, *other than* the kinds of affective responses most naturally elicited by the subject matter of such works. The pleasure that receivers derive from other sources can then be said to *compensate* for the unpleasantness of these affective responses, the overall experience being pleasurable. 'Compensatory' solutions, as such answers to the puzzle have been termed,[17] can take a number of forms, but will be satisfactory only if they meet two conditions. First, the distinctive pleasure to be derived from works of tragedy and horror must in some way be necessarily linked to the displeasure, so that one could not have the former without the latter. If this condition is not met, the proponent of the compensatory solution will have difficulty explaining the rationality of receivers of works in the tragic and horror genres if, as seems plausible, there are alternative ways of obtaining the distinctive pleasures which *don't* also involve the unpleasantness that attends the reception of such works. Second, the distinctive pleasures ascribed to works in the two genres must have a significance or status beyond being merely enjoyable. Otherwise, even if one cannot have the pleasure without the displeasure, to seek out works of tragedy and horror might seem no more rational than giving oneself a headache because one gets pleasure from the relief provided by taking an aspirin!

Compensatory solutions that meet these two conditions have been offered for both of the paradoxes. A classic solution of this kind to the paradox of tragedy is contained in Aristotle's *Poetics*, at least on some readings. Aristotle defines the tragic work as one that, through its structure and the nature of its plot, is designed to elicit in the receiver the emotions of pity and fear, as a means to bring about the 'proper pleasure' of tragedy by producing what he terms a 'catharsis' of these emotions. Much ink has been spilt in attempts to elucidate just what is meant by 'catharsis' in this context, there being no further explicit clarification of this matter in the *Poetics* and only a couple of other uses of this term, in very different contexts, in Aristotle's other extant writings. Scholars have generally argued for one or other of two alternatives, seeing catharsis as either the *purging* or the *purification* of the emotions in question. There are perhaps reasons to favour the latter interpretation, given Aristotle's more general view of the emotions (in the *Nicomachean Ethics*) as a valuable cognitive resource if properly harmonized with our rational grasp of matters. Catharsis can then be viewed as some kind of transformation of our emotional dispositions to bring them into better alignment with reason. Furthermore, there are problems with the 'purging' view. First, if what is purged is only the 'unpleasant' emotions aroused by the events in the play, we seem to have the 'headache and aspirin' scenario just canvassed. Second, if the purging is taken to be more global, it is difficult to see why Aristotle, given his view of the emotions, would have regarded the experiences produced by tragic art as socially and morally valuable. But the issues are still hotly contested and, rather than trespass further into such a scholarly minefield, we are better advised to look at more forthright presentations of the compensatory strategy.

A compensatory solution to the paradox of tragedy that clearly meets both of our conditions has been developed by Susan Feagin.[18] Feagin makes it clear that the pleasure to be derived from engagement with the tragic work is not superficial, but a deeper kind of satisfaction that she ties to our very nature as moral beings. Furthermore, such pleasure requires, as a precondition, the unpleasant feelings elicited in us by the events represented by the tragedy. In the tragic drama, things end in what we judge to be unmerited unhappiness for the main protagonists, and the subject matter may be unpleasant in other respects – consider, for example, the extreme cruelty of some of the acts performed by the protagonists of a play like *King Lear*. Such events will arouse unpleasant feelings in any normal 'non-morbid' spectator. But, in addition to these feelings directly elicited by the portrayed events, she argues, there is also a 'meta-response' to this direct response – a response directed at ourselves, as individuals who have been affected in a certain way (the 'direct response') by the events of the play. It is the satisfaction that we experience in our meta-response that compensates for the unpleasantness of our direct response, and that explains the attraction of tragedy. The meta-response, she argues, arises from

> our awareness of, and in response to, the fact that we do have unpleasant direct responses to unpleasant events as they occur in the performing and literary arts. We find ourselves to be the kind of people who respond negatively to villainy, treachery, and injustice. This discovery, or reminder, is something which, quite justly, yields satisfaction. In a way, it shows what we care for, and in showing us we care for the welfare of human beings and that we deplore the immoral forces that defeat them, it reminds us of our common humanity. It reduces one's sense of aloneness in the world, and soothes, psychologically, the pain of solipsism.[19]

Furthermore, the direct response that grounds the meta-response in which we take satisfaction is an expression of the feeling that lies at the basis of morality itself, 'sympathy with, and a concern for, the welfare of human beings *qua* human beings'.[20] This, she argues, is why we regard tragic works as greater artistic achievements than works of comedy.

A compensatory solution to the paradox of horror has been developed by Noel Carroll. Like Feagin, he accepts that the feelings aroused in readers or viewers of works belonging to the horror genre are unpleasant. In particular, the creatures that he takes to be central to horror – 'monsters' – disgust us because they are 'impure', where their impurity is a matter of their violating the categorial systems we use to make sense of the world. The fear and disgust aroused by such creatures is to be understood by reference to studies, by cultural anthropologists, of the cross-categorial basis of the 'taboo' reaction. But these unpleasant reactions, he argues, are more than outweighed by the cognitive pleasures we derive from our engagement with horror fictions. In the first place, such fictions are presented to us as narratives, and we take a more general cognitive interest in the unfolding of a narrative. Thus the primary basis of the interest we take in horror fictions, and the central source of the pleasure we derive from such fictions, is 'the disclosure of the existence of the horrific being and of its properties', where this disclosure unfolds through narrative processes of 'discovery, proof and confirmation'.[21] While the pleasure experienced in the stimulation of our curiosity by such narratives might be obtained from fictions in other genres whose reception does not involve such unpleasant feelings as fear and disgust, the cognitive pleasures in question are especially acute when the narrative focuses on monsters. For the latter are 'unknown and impossible beings', and such things provoke our curiosity in virtue of the very features that also generate our fear and distrust. Thus, as with Feagin's defence of tragedy, the claim is that the distinctive satisfaction we derive from horror fiction is possible only if attended by the unpleasant affective responses:

> The disgust that [monsters] evince might be seen as part of the price to be paid for the pleasure of their disclosure. That is, the narrative expectations [*sic*] that the horror genre puts in place is that the being whose existence is in question be something that defies standing cultural categories; thus disgust, so to say, is itself more or less mandated by the kind of curiosity that the horror narrative puts in place. The horror narrative could not deliver a successful affirmative answer to its presiding question unless the disclosure of the monster indeed elicited disgust, or was of the sort that was a highly probable object of disgust.[22]

Compensatory solutions to the paradoxes such as those offered by Feagin and Carroll are ingenious, but face serious difficulties. One problem with Carroll's account of horror fiction is its limited scope, since much of what we would normally view as belonging to the horror genre does not, in any obvious sense, involve 'monsters' as characterized by Carroll. As Berys Gaut points out, such paradigms of contemporary horror as 'slasher movies' and *The Silence of the Lambs* involve only human predators, albeit ones of a psychologically singular nature.[23] To say that the protagonists of such films are 'human monsters' is to give up on a reading of the term 'monster' that can draw upon the tradition in cultural anthropology, and thus to lose the explanation of the disgust and fear aroused by works of horror. Carroll himself offers a different response to this challenge, drawing a distinction between works of horror, to which his analysis applies, and mere works of terror, among which he numbers the sorts of cases cited by Gaut. But this seems both ad hoc and ultimately unsatisfying, since works of terror will still pose the very problem to which we were seeking a solution – namely, to account for the pleasure we take in works that arouse fear in us. Should we not expect that a solution to what we can now term the 'paradox of terror' will also account for our pleasure in works of horror?

A second kind of problem for both Feagin and Carroll is that it is not clear that the compensatory accounts they offer really capture what is pleasurable, for those who seem to enjoy such things, about works of tragedy and horror. Does the pleasure of tragedy really stem from a reinforcement of feelings of humanity and does the pleasure of horror really consist in a curiosity-driven urge to read on? In both cases, the 'proper pleasure' of the genre seems to have been distanced from our immediate engagement with the work, and also from what many might view as a principal reason why they seek out works of that kind. Carroll, responding to this kind of objection, maintains that our fascination with monsters, which is the source of our pleasure in horror fiction, is very closely tied to the very features that engender disgust and fear in the audience, since both are caused by the categorially transgressive nature of monsters. But, even if this is true, it isn't clear that it meets the objection. Gaut, criticizing Carroll, suggests that a horror enthusiast might complain that a given novel or film *wasn't frightening enough*, and this criticism, he argues, is not plausibly re-expressed as a claim about the failure of the fiction to sufficiently stimulate curiosity.

A similar challenge might be made to Feagin's solution to the paradox of tragedy. She carefully distinguishes her account, in terms of a pleasurable meta-response to an unpleasant direct response, from a broadly Aristotelian account which, at least on the 'purgative' reading of catharsis, locates the pleasure of tragedy in some kind of emotional release.[24] But, again, anecdotal evidence concerning those drawn to tragic works suggests that for many the pleasure *does* seem to involve such a release. In the case of more popular works of tragedy, such as the film *Love Story*, the attraction for those who viewed the film seems to be the pleasure of having 'a jolly good cry'. Feagin might argue that this sort of pleasure, derivable from 'low art', is distinct from the true pleasure of high tragic art, which is to be understood in her terms. The weight of the phenomenological evidence here is less clear, and it must be admitted that Gaut's objection more clearly applies to a compensatory theory of horror than to such a theory of tragedy.

If we find this kind of objection to compensatory theories plausible, it suggests that, far from the work of horror being pleasurable *in spite of* its subject matter and the kinds of feelings elicited, it is felt to be pleasurable *because of* those feelings. This further suggests that, rather than offer a compensatory response to the paradox, we should challenge claim (3), that the affective responses to works of horror or works of tragedy are themselves unpleasant. This is the alternative approach that a number of writers have taken to the paradoxes. Hume himself proposes a solution of this kind to the puzzle posed by the 'unaccountable pleasure' that we take in tragic works. Like Carroll, he points to certain kinds of intellectual pleasures aroused by the narrative presentation of tragic events, but, rather than see these pleasures as somehow outweighing the unpleasantness of our affective responses, he maintains that the latter are somehow 'converted' so as to become pleasurable in themselves:

> The force of imagination, the energy of expression, the power of numbers, the charms of imitation, all these are naturally, of themselves, delightful to the mind: and when the object presented lays also hold of some affection, the pleasure rises upon us by the conversion of this subordinate movement into that which is predominant. The passion, though perhaps naturally, and when excited by the simple appearance of a real object, it may be painful, yet is so smoothed and softened, and mollified, when realized by the finer arts that it affords the highest entertainment.[25]

Critics, however, have found this notion of 'conversion', which is not further elucidated by Hume, to be obscure,[26] and, rather than pursue this further, it may be profitable to consider a more radical proposal, by a number of contemporary writers, which challenges the idea that the affective element in such emotions as pity, fear, and disgust is ever unpleasant in itself, even outside of our engagement with fictions. This approach is adopted by Gaut, who sees his account as a clarification of other, similar approaches. The simplest solution to the paradox of horror, Gaut maintains, is what he terms the *enjoyment theory*: 'horror attracts because people can enjoy being scared and disgusted'.[27] Furthermore, he claims, an analogous solution can be given to the paradox of tragedy. Evidence for the enjoyment theory as it applies to horror can be found in the ways in which people describe their motivation for engaging in such pursuits as mountaineering, skydiving, and roller-coaster riding. In each case, so participants maintain, part of the enjoyment resides in the fear elicited by putting oneself into a dangerous situation.

However, as Gaut notes, it is not enough to point to such phenomena if one wishes to resolve the paradoxes. For it can be objected that the phenomena must be misdescribed, since emotions like fear, disgust, and pity are, *by their very nature*, unpleasant. Thus, if there is enjoyment in such dangerous practices as mountaineering and skydiving, it must lie elsewhere, in something that compensates for the unpleasantness of such affective responses to danger or tragedy. To meet such objections, what is required is an explanation of how it is *possible* to enjoy what are traditionally characterized as negative emotions. We can see this as a constraint on any satisfactory solution to the paradoxes that rejects the third of the claims constitutive of the latter, just as, as we saw above, any compensatory solution must satisfy certain conditions.

Gaut considers three ways in which we might explain the possibility of enjoying negative emotions, the first two of which he rejects. First, some authors have claimed that what we normally view as negative emotions can be enjoyable for an individual as long as she has control of the situation.[28] Since, in the case of fictional presentations of tragic or horrific circumstances, I am presumably in control – I can stop reading or leave the cinema – this explains my ability to enjoy the negative emotions elicited by the narrative. But, as Gaut points out, this account still leaves it unexplained how an emotion that, so it can be claimed, is intrinsically unpleasant can be enjoyed, even if we are in control. Furthermore, the grip of fictions upon us may make us feel we are not in control, and many people seem unable to enjoy horror fiction even when it is clear that they know it is merely fiction. A second proposal, which speaks to at least the first of these concerns, holds that, in negative emotions, the negativity resides not in the affective aspects of the emotion, but in its objects.[29] In the case of an emotion like pity or fear, for example, what is unpleasant is the situation that is the intentional object of the emotion, not the affective qualities of the emotion itself. Although this proposal explains how one might enjoy a negative emotion – since, supposedly, the feelings aroused need not themselves be unpleasant – it suffers from two defects, according to Gaut. First, it seems to make the unpleasantness of the affective element in negative emotions purely contingent, in which case, it seems, we could have a culture whose affective responses at the death of close friends were properly classified as grief, even though they generally seem to find these responses enjoyable. Second, on the most plausible view of such matters, to say that a situation is unpleasant is to say that it is disposed to *produce feelings of unpleasantness in us*, so it is not clear that locating the unpleasantness in the intentional objects of emotions really explains how we can enjoy negative emotions.

Gaut's own proposal rests upon adopting a particular kind of cognitivist theory of the emotions, according to which the cognitive element that serves to individuate the different kinds of emotions is a particular *evaluation* of the intentional object of the emotion as desirable or undesirable. Negative emotions are ones that contain, as a necessary component, a negative evaluation of the intentional object, as, for example, dangerous, or shameful, or wrongful. This then resolves the paradox because 'since we can disvalue something without finding it unpleasant, it follows that it is possible to find both negative emotional responses *and* their objects pleasant'.[30] The mountaineer, in feeling fear, must evaluate the situation as dangerous, but may also enjoy the affective qualities of her response to the perceived danger. Gaut further argues that his account can explain why so-called 'negative' emotions must *as a general rule* be experienced as unpleasant, so that the hypothetical culture posited above would not be rightly said to be experiencing grief at the death of their loved ones. There is, he maintains, a link between evaluating something as desirable and finding it pleasant and evaluating something as undesirable and finding it unpleasant. What I evaluate as desirable I will typically be motivated to promote, and what I am motivated to promote I will typically find pleasant. And, *mutatis mutandis*, the same applies for what I evaluate as undesirable and what I find unpleasant. But this allows for *atypical* cases where I can enjoy experiencing a negative emotion, and it is this that explains the pleasures that receivers derive from works of tragedy and horror.

As will by now be clear, whether we are satisfied with a solution to the paradoxes associated with our affective responses to literary works will depend upon how we stand on broader questions in the philosophy of the emotions. Do genuine emotions require sustaining beliefs about their intentional objects, for example, and is the experienced unpleasantness of a negative emotion a necessary feature of that emotion, or can we make sense of the idea that we can sometimes enjoy such emotions? We have seen that philosophers have offered a range of solutions to the various paradoxes, and that, while some of these solutions face serious difficulties, alternative answers to each of the paradoxes remain in the field. Furthermore, it is not clear that a unified answer can be offered to the paradoxes of tragedy and of horror, even though, as we have seen, the paradoxes seem to be formally identical. While it would be satisfying to arrive at a comprehensive solution to the various puzzles presented by our affective responses to literary works, we should remain open to the possibility that the complexity of the phenomena prevent such a solution, and that different kinds of affective response require different explanations.

CHAPTER 8

THE COGNITIVE VALUE OF LITERATURE

LITERARY COGNITIVISM

In David Hare's play *Wetherby*, Miss Jean Travers, an English teacher in a secondary school in the North of England, asks her class, 'Is Shakespeare worth reading although it's only about kings?' A possible answer to this question, of course, is that this is precisely why it is worth reading Shakespeare, or at least the history plays. For, in reading such plays, we may learn about the lives and doings of the depicted monarchs. As we saw in earlier chapters, fictional narratives may contain sentences that express truths about the extra-fictional world, and, if we can identify which sentences these are, then, in reading a work of fiction, we may arrive not only at true beliefs about what is 'true in the story' but also at true beliefs about the extra-fictional world.

But few would be happy with this response to the question posed by Miss Travers to her pupils, for it is clearly insufficient to explain the importance that many accord to literature. If we want to learn about the doings of British monarchs, we are surely better advised to consult works of history rather than works of fiction. For, to the extent that we take the latter to be reliable sources of historical information, it is presumably because we assume that their authors have consulted the former. And, as a consequence, it seems that we will in general need to avail ourselves of historical sources in order to determine which sentences in a fiction can indeed be regarded as conveying true information about the actual world.

Insufficient as such a response may be, it has seemed to some to be on the right track if we want to address the more general concerns underlying Miss Travers' question. What is valuable about reading literature? What explains the resources expended on promoting the reading of literary works, their place in the educational curriculum, and the importance of reading literature in the lives of so many people? What might we hope to gain by reading the works of Shakespeare, Jane Austen, Dostoevsky, Yeats, or Henry James? And can the claim that literature possesses certain kinds of value be supported? For many, the right answer to these questions is some form of what James Young terms 'literary cognitivism'.[1] Literature, so the cognitivist maintains, is valuable because it is a source of *knowledge*, or at least of *warranted belief*, bearing upon the extrafictional world. Critics of literary cognitivism have raised objections similar to those just levelled at our simplistic response to Miss Travers' question. But cognitivism's defenders credit literature with more significant cognitive virtues, viewing it as a source of deeper kinds of knowledge and understanding.

The debate between cognitivists and their opponents is a very long one, and finds one of its earliest incarnations in the works of the Greek philosophers Plato and Aristotle. In *The Republic*, Plato has Socrates, the principal character in his philosophical dialogues, present a scathing indictment of the pretensions of artists and poets to provide genuine knowledge or understanding of the world. All the artist can do, Socrates maintains, is to imitate or reproduce in his works the appearances of things, and the common conceptions of what is true and what is real. To imitate the appearances, one needs no understanding of the reality that underlies those appearances. The carpenter needs to understand various principles of his craft and various purposes of the things he makes in order to make a bed, but the artist who paints a picture of a bed needs no such understanding. Similarly, the poet who writes of personal, political, and historical matters only mirrors back to people, in seductively convincing ways, their own beliefs and ways of conceiving such things. The artist, it is claimed, has no real understanding of the things that he or she represents. Shakespeare, by this reasoning, has no real knowledge of the historical events he portrays, and writes of them in ways that merely reflect contemporary beliefs, but with a literary power that can deceive the audience into thinking that what they are seeing or reading is true. Such arguments lead Socrates to the conclusion that artists should be accorded neither an educational nor a governing role in the well-ordered society, unless closely supervised by those who do possess the relevant knowledge.

Aristotle, in the *Poetics*, defends the cognitivist pretensions of the literary artist. As we saw in the previous chapter, Aristotle may plausibly be read as claiming that tragic works of art make a valuable contribution to the formation of the good citizen by acting in a positive way on the latter's emotional dispositions. But Aristotle also claimed, more forthrightly if somewhat enigmatically, that poetry was 'more philosophical' than history, and therefore, presumably, a source of deeper understanding of the world. Aristotle's point here seems to be that the historian's task is merely to represent to the reader the actual order of historical events, an order that reflects the operation of many conflicting causes and that may therefore appear to the reader to be unpredictable and beyond the human capacity to control effectively. The literary artist, on the other hand, is guided by different principles in the construction of his or her narrative, especially if that narrative is a work of tragedy. For, in order for a tragic narrative to produce the desired effect upon the audience – the catharsis that is the 'proper pleasure' of tragedy – the audience must see the tragic events as unfolding in a 'probable or necessary' fashion, given the initial situation and the characters of the protagonists. Only if the audience views the unfolding of the plot in this way will their emotional reactions to the drama be concordant with a rational appreciation of what is happening, and only in this case can the emotional dispositions of the viewer be harmonized with the demands of reason. Thus, so Aristotle maintains, the composer of the tragic work should prefer probable impossibilities – things that did not happen, for example, but that strike the audience as probable – to improbable possibilities – things that actually happened, for example, but that strike the audience as very unlikely.

The historian, on the other hand, must always strive to include in his narrative only what he believes to have actually occurred, however improbable it might seem. But whether a given sequence of events in a fictional narrative strikes a receiver as probable or improbable will depend upon whether the principles that seem to be operative in, and to account for, this sequence of events are ones that themselves seem plausible. This will depend upon whether the same principles seem to the receiver to make sense of the apparently random unfolding of events in the actual world. Poetry is more philosophical than history, then, because poetry incorporates and makes manifest to the reader general principles that purportedly underlie the unfolding of events, actual as well as fictional. History, by contrast, presents those events as apparently random or unpredictable, and therefore beyond the ability of rational individuals to understand or control.

If this is a plausible reading of what Aristotle is claiming, he can be seen as one of the first to ascribe a particular kind of cognitive value to fictional narratives. It will be helpful here to locate this kind of value within a broader spectrum of cognitive values that might be credited to literary works. There are at least four ways in which fiction has been represented as a source of knowledge or understanding of the real world.[2]

First, as was claimed in our initial response to Miss Travers' question, fictional narratives may be viewed as a source of *factual information* about the world. If authors may incorporate true statements about the real world into their narratives, then readers may come to believe those statements as a result of reading a work. As suggested earlier, an author may incorporate such truths into her narrative in order to 'set' the fiction in a real location, something that may serve her purposes for at least two reasons. First, she can assume shared background beliefs about that setting in narrating her fiction, rather than having to make such details explicit. Second, as in the case of the novel *Riddley Walker*, discussed in Chapter 4, the fictional narrative may acquire added resonance through the receiver's knowledge of what happened in the given setting before or after the time when the fictional events occur. Thus a reader who is ignorant of some of the truths which an author incorporates in her fiction might indeed acquire certain true beliefs about English kings through reading the history plays of Shakespeare, or about the geography of Victorian London through reading the works of Dickens or Conan Doyle, or about bullfighting through reading Hemingway's *The Sun Also Rises*. Dickens' *Bleak House*, for example, contains accurate information about the halts on, and the geographical orientation of, the Victorian coaching routes going north out of London.

Second, as illustrated in our reading of Aristotle, literary fiction may be viewed as providing readers with an *understanding of general principles*. The narrated events may explicitly or implicitly exemplify and make salient to the reader general principles – moral, metaphysical, or psychological, for example – which govern the unfolding of events in the real world. Sometimes such principles are explicitly stated by a narrator or a character – for example, the assertion of the narrator of Tolstoy's *Anna Karenina* that 'Happy families are all alike; every unhappy family is unhappy in its own way.' However, in such cases, we must always be careful to distinguish between principles merely placed by the author in the mouth of the narrator or one of the characters and principles plausibly seen as part of the thematic content of the fiction. It would be wrong, for example, to see, as elements in the thematic content of Shakespeare's *King Lear*, all of the different diagnoses of the human condition placed by the author in the mouths of his diverse characters – Gloucester's morose fatalism, for example, expressed in his conviction that 'as flies to wanton boys are we to the gods: they kill us for their sport', as contrasted with Edgar's cynical opportunism. Or again, various characters in Anthony Burgess's *A Clockwork Orange* offer different analyses of the causes of and remedies for problems of social deviance, analyses which are systematically undermined by the narrative. When it is claimed that an understanding of general principles can be gained by reading fictional narratives, however, the principles are usually taken to be implicit, rather than explicit. It might be argued, for example, that implicit moral insights are to be found in the novels of Henry James,[3] implicit psychological insights in the works of Jane Austen, and implicit insights into the phenomenology of lived experience in the writings of Virginia Woolf.

Third, a number of writers have praised literary fictions as a source of *categorial understanding*. In presenting a fictional world, a narrative may furnish the reader with new categories or kinds, natural or psychological, whose application to the real world illuminates certain matters of fact. For example, a work like *1984* or *The Castle* provides us with a conceptual framework in terms of which to examine critically the ways in which socio-political structures can exercise control over the life of the individual. What we acquire are new ways of *classifying and categorizing* things and situations. Nelson Goodman speaks of fiction as a 'way of worldmaking' which remakes our world by providing us with new classifications like 'quixotic', 'Catch-22', and 'Kafkaesque'.[4] David Novitz suggests that such categorial understanding is best viewed as a kind of *practical knowledge* that readers can obtain from fictions, citing also knowledge of various practical strategies that may be exemplified in the actions or reasoning processes of fictional characters.[5]

Finally, literary fiction has been viewed as a source of what might be termed *affective knowledge* – knowledge of 'what it would be like' to be in a particular set of circumstances. This has been presented as an ethically valuable feature of fictions, in so far as it bears upon our ability to comprehend, and respond appropriately to, morally complex situations that we encounter in the actual world. Effective moral agency, it is claimed, presupposes an ability to grasp how others are affected by our actions and by their circumstances, and, more generally, the ability to understand the moral complexity of a situation – the way in which it affects the welfare or the legitimate expectations of the individuals concerned. Hilary Putnam, for example, suggests that

> if moral reasoning, at the reflective level, is the conscious criticism of ways of life, then the sensitive appreciation in the imagination of predicaments and perplexities must be essential to sensitive moral reasoning. Novels and plays do not set moral knowledge before us, that is true. But they do (frequently) do something for us that must be done for us if we are to gain any moral knowledge.[6]

Apart from the purported moral benefits of affective knowledge, of which we shall have more to say in the following chapter, the capacity of literary fictions to provide such knowledge can be viewed as a cognitive virtue in itself.

THE EPISTEMOLOGICAL CHALLENGE TO LITERARY COGNITIVISM

It might be questioned, however, whether literature can provide *knowledge*, if the latter requires true beliefs to which we are in some way entitled, or whether it can even provide *warranted belief*. In physical science and history, which might stand as paradigm examples of cognitively valuable practices, various assertions are made about the world, upon whose truth or warranted acceptability we can frequently obtain consensus by appeal to shared epistemic norms. We can also engage in reasoned debate, by appeal to such norms, where consensus is not forthcoming. But literary works do not, it would seem, have cognitive value through making explicit assertions about the real world. Even when a literary work contains sentences that express factual truths, the fiction does not work through the assertion of these sentences, but rather by inviting the reader to make-believe what the sentences affirm.

Furthermore, as noted at the beginning of this chapter, it seems that, at least in the case of purported 'factual knowledge' derivable from our reading of fictions, we will need to avail ourselves of other resources in order to verify that certain sentences in a fiction are indeed true of the actual world. For novelists may insert false details into their narratives in order to give them an air of authenticity, and may also, in good faith, insert details concerning which they have false beliefs. Lawrence Durrell's *Alexandria Quartet*, for example, whose descriptions of wartime Alexandria seem strikingly authentic to the reader, is notoriously inaccurate on the historical and geographical details of its setting. And, as we saw in Chapter 4, Arthur Conan Doyle, in 'The Case of the Speckled Band', misrepresents the ability of the Russell's Viper to negotiate bell-ropes. The reader who derives certain beliefs about the Russell's Viper from her reading of the fiction will obtain neither knowledge nor even false but warranted belief. For, recalling Plato's complaint, it would surely be rash to believe, without further evidence, that the snake possessed the described abilities purely on the basis of Conan Doyle's having assumed this in writing his fiction. Why, after all, should we think that Conan Doyle has any knowledge of such matters?

The literary cognitivist, therefore, needs to argue that fictional works do indeed have some kind of cognitive purchase on the real world, and that the cognitive claims of fiction to provide us with knowledge, or at least warranted belief rather than *mere* belief, can be justified. Some critics, however, generalizing from the foregoing objection, argue that the most we can get from reading fiction is *hypotheses* about the general ordering of things in the world or about the phenomenology of a particular kind of situation, or *beliefs* about specific aspects of the world, or *potentially insightful* ways of categorizing things in our experience. The claim, here, is that talk of 'learning' from fiction is justified only to the extent that what we derive from our reading is subject to further testing. Only if those hypotheses, beliefs, and categorizations pass further tests can we talk of cognitive value arising out of our engagement with standard fictional narratives. We find this sentiment expressed even by philosophers who are sympathetic to some of the cognitive claims of fictions. Putnam, for example, while extolling the contribution of literature to moral learning, is quick to stress that this contribution must be an indirect one:

> No matter how profound the psychological insights of a novelist may seem to be, they cannot be called *knowledge* if they have not been tested. To say that the perceptive reader can just *see* that the psychological insights of a novelist are not just plausible, but that they have some kind of universal truth, is to return to the idea of knowledge by intuition of matters of empirical fact . . . If I read Celine's [*sic*] *Journey to the End of Night* I do not *learn* that love does not exist, that all human beings are hateful and hating . . .

What I learn is to see the world as it looks to someone who is sure that hypothesis is correct . . . It is knowledge of a possibility. It is *conceptual* knowledge . . . It cannot be said that after reading [Doris Lessing's *The Golden Notebook*], one has acquired *knowledge* of what it was like to be a communist in the 1940's, unless one has some independent source of knowledge that Doris Lessing's account is factually true. You may feel convinced upon reading *The Golden Notebook*; you may say to yourself, *this is what it must have been like*; but unless you want to substitute subjective plausibility . . . for answering to the objective facts, . . . you have no right to say 'I *know* that this is what it was like'. You do not *know*; and the very next week you may be convinced by an equally plausible novel that it must have all been entirely different from Doris Lessing's description.[7]

Putnam's reservations are developed in a more systematic and forthright manner by Jerome Stolnitz, who has argued for the 'cognitive triviality' of literature.[8] Stolnitz raises a number of distinct challenges to literary cognitivism. First, so he claims, the 'profound truths' supposedly obtainable from reading literary works are, once we succeed in spelling them out, banal. We do not need to immerse ourselves in the novels of Jane Austen to learn that 'stubborn pride and ignorant prejudice keep attractive people apart', for example, and the hope of learning such banalities is not what explains the attractions of reading fictions. Rather it is the intricate details of the narrative from which we are abstracting in formulating such an 'artistic truth' that lure us to read a novel like *Pride and Prejudice*. Furthermore, Stolnitz argues, the *scope* of the supposed insight in a literary fiction is generally unclear. For example, is the moral that might be derived from *Pride and Prejudice* supposed to apply to *all* attractive people or just to some? The 'truth' supposedly extractable from the fiction is unsatisfactory in its imprecision and its banality, and in standing in a tangential relation to what the reader feels is important in the work.

Second, echoing Plato's charge, Stolnitz maintains that there is no proper domain of 'artistic knowledge' comparable to the distinctive cognitive domains of science, history, and even religion: 'none of its truths are peculiar to art',[9] and we assume that those who work in those domains to which these truths 'properly' belong are a much better source of knowledge of the relevant matters. Another problem is that the 'truths' supposedly embedded in different fictions may contradict one another without any established method for resolving the conflict. The view of human nature and human motivation that might be derived from the work of Céline, for example, or from Brecht's *Threepenny Opera*, would seem to be directly contradicted by the characters in Austen's novels, or in the novels of Dickens, even though Austen and Dickens include *some* individuals in their fictions that would not be out of place in the fictional worlds of Céline and Brecht.

Stolnitz's third challenge to literary cognitivism is the familiar charge that the 'truths' supposedly discoverable through the reading of fictions are at best hypotheses, whose cognitive virtues stand in need of empirical testing that is not forthcoming from our engagement with the fiction itself. Art, he claims, never 'confirms' its 'truths'. He grants that there are genuine truths about the world contained in fictions, as in the case of Dickens' portrayal of the Courts of Chancery in *Bleak House*, or Harriet Beecher Stowe's depiction of slavery in *Uncle Tom's Cabin*. In both cases, the authors themselves maintained the truth of their depictions, supporting this claim in other communications outside the fiction itself. But, in such cases, Stolnitz maintains, 'the truth was knowable and known before the fictions appeared'.[10]

In considering Stolnitz's challenges to literary cognitivism, it is important to distinguish a number of different questions.[11] One question – implicated in the 'Platonic' challenge – is whether the creators of fictional narratives have knowledge of the sorts of issues addressed in their narratives. Assuming some kind of positive answer to the first question, a second question is whether the knowledge possessed by the author of a fictional narrative can be communicated to receivers through the act of reading the narrative. And a third question – the 'banality' charge – is whether any knowledge communicable through the reading of fictional narratives is worth having, or worth having given the expenditure of resources required to obtain it from the narrative.

David Novitz and James Young have offered separate defences of literary cognitivism. We may begin with what is perhaps the easiest charge to answer, that of the banality of the supposed truths to be gleaned from the reading of fictional narratives, and of the contradictory nature of such truths when we bring together different literary works. Both Novitz and Young resist the suggestion that the cognitive value of literature resides primarily in certain truths formulable as propositions of the kind proposed by Stolnitz. Novitz, while allowing that literature can serve as a source of both true factual beliefs and general principles applicable to the real world, also stresses the non-propositional nature of the practical and empathic knowledge that can be gained from fictions. On the one hand, what we learn may be an intellectual strategy that leads us to take account of features of real-world situations we might not otherwise have noted. On the other hand, novels and plays may 'enable us to see old and familiar objects in a radically different light. In this way, fiction may help us to notice qualities of, or relations between, objects, persons, and events where these were previously unnoticed.'[12] But, in addition,

> fiction often enables its readers to acquire beliefs about, indeed knowledge of, what it feels like to be in certain complex and demanding situations. Empathic beliefs and knowledge of this sort are derived from, and have to be explained in terms of, our awareness or experience of what is sometimes termed a direct object. A feature of such awareness is that it is irreducibly non-propositional, in the sense that it cannot be captured or adequately conveyed in linguistic descriptions. For instance, no matter how precise and vivid my descriptions are, they will never acquaint you with my feelings as an orphan . . . In these cases we often say . . . that one does not know what it feels like to be bereaved until one has, in one way or another, experienced bereavement.[13]

Novitz's point might be expanded to incorporate the kinds of cognitive values ridiculed by Stolnitz in his suggestion that the 'artistic truth' in *Pride and Prejudice* is contained in the anodyne precept that 'stubborn pride and ignorant prejudice keep attractive people apart'. The appearance of banality, it might be responded, arises only when we succumb to the temptation to try to formulate the cognitive value of such a work in propositional form, the very thing that is impossible in the cases that Novitz describes. What tempts us into offering such banalities is our feeling that the content of the proposition in question somehow serves to individuate the kind of understanding we have gained. But, we might say, it is not that we learn the truth of such a proposition, but that we come to understand more clearly what is *involved* in such a proposition's being true – we deepen our understanding of the truth that it expresses. And this deeper understanding comes from our engagement in precisely those details of the narrative that Stolnitz seeks to set against the supposed 'artistic truth' that can be abstracted from the fiction.

We can combine this idea with Putnam's talk about artistic truth as 'the truth of a possibility' to answer Stolnitz's separate point about the contradictory nature of the 'artistic truths' to be gleaned from different literary works. For if our engagement with a fictional narrative yields a deeper understanding of what it would mean for a proposition to be true, it may also lead us to reject that proposition, and thus the claim to 'artistic truth' of the work that imaginatively explores it as a possible way of seeing the world. Thus, in reading Céline, we not only come to a deeper understanding of a way of perceiving human relationships expressible in terms of a proposition like 'love does not exist and all human beings are hateful and hating'. We also come to see why we should not accept such a vision of humanity, and why, whatever literary qualities may be ascribable to Céline's work, we do not want to ascribe to it cognitive value in virtue of its expressing a *true* vision.

But, in answering these charges, we make more salient Stolnitz's further claim that, even if there may be significant truths about the actual world contained in the thematic meanings of works of fiction, we cannot learn such truths from the fictions themselves, but only from independent sources to which we must appeal to validate or invalidate what we take, as a hypothesis or mere proposal, from the fiction. Novitz argues that we can validate the conceptual and cognitive resources that we derive from literary works, and the beliefs about the non-fictional world that are generated in our reading, by 'projecting' what is gleaned from a literary work onto the world.[14] In so doing, we try to see real people and events in terms of these beliefs and resources in order to determine whether the latter help us to make sense of such things. Literature is rightly held to be of cognitive value when the skills and beliefs derived from our reading of fiction improve our ability to negotiate the real world:

> Readers can only acquire conceptual or cognitive skills from fiction by tentatively projecting the factual beliefs gleaned from the work on to the world about them. They try to see specific objects, events, and relationships in terms of these new beliefs, and they attempt to rethink, perhaps to explain, what was previously baffling or bewildering. If their application of these beliefs is met with obvious rewards, if it helps them to dispel puzzles and doubts, to make sense of or come to terms with enigmas of one sort or

another, they are likely to adopt these ways of thinking and observing.[15]

Literature and science, Novitz maintains, are analogous enterprises in that, in each case, we are offered hypotheses that must be tested against the experienced world before any claims to knowledge can be justified. And works of literature are comparable to works of reference such as encyclopaedias, since in each case our claim to have learned something from a work rests upon beliefs not themselves derivable from our reading of it.

But these arguments seem flawed as a defence of literary cognitivism. First, while the comparison with science might seem to be an answer to the epistemological challenge to literary cognitivism, in fact it concedes the very point at issue. For the cognitive credentials of science rest upon its being a practice that encompasses not merely the formulation of hypotheses but also their comparative assessment in light of experimental testing.[16] Indeed, the vast majority of the hypotheses proposed by scientists prove to be unacceptable as measured by the norms of scientific practice. But Novitz seems to grant that literature merely furnishes us with hypotheses, and is thus a valid source of knowledge only if taken together with an independent practice of subjecting such hypotheses to empirical scrutiny.

Second, in the case of works of reference such as encyclopaedias, the claim to derive knowledge from reading such works indeed rests upon an auxiliary belief – the belief that the work is *reliable*, that, for example, the contributors are experts in their respective fields. But we have no prima facie reason to think that authors of *works of fiction* are, in general, reliable sources of information concerning the things they include in those works – this is where Stolnitz's 'Platonic' objection comes into play. This is why it seems necessary to carry out independent verification of the sentences in works of fiction that seem to furnish us with knowledge of particular matters of fact. This suggests, in fact, a criterion to which we might appeal in determining when we can legitimately claim to be learning about matters of fact in our reading of standard fictional narratives. We should view fictions as a source of knowledge of particular facts only if either (1) (on an internalist conception of knowledge) the facts are true and we have good reason to believe that the particular author is reliable concerning facts of this kind, or (2) (on an externalist conception of knowledge) the facts are true and the author is in fact a reliable source of information about such facts.[17]

We might, then, justly claim to learn particular facts about bull-fighting from reading Hemingway, given his fascination with the practice, while at the same time refraining from making any such claim in reading Durrell on Alexandria or Conan Doyle on snakes. Even so, many cases will be very difficult to adjudicate in these terms. And, significantly, no such cognitive criterion seems remotely plausible if we turn to the other kinds of learning proposed by literary cognitivists – knowledge of general principles, or of classifications that yield a richer understanding of the world. For in neither of these cases would we take the reliability of the source as a criterion for knowledge in scientific or everyday contexts. However successful Einstein may have been as a scientist, we would not claim to obtain knowledge concerning the world from a new untested hypothesis just because it was proposed by Einstein. This indicates, significantly, that the claims to different kinds of cognitive virtues associated with our reading of fictions will require different kinds of defences.

James Young offers a more elaborate and sophisticated defence of literary cognitivism that seeks to contrast, rather than compare, scientific and literary knowledge.[18] He begins with what he terms the 'fictional objects' objection to cognitivism: if fictional characters don't actually exist and fictional events don't actually occur, how can they represent, and therefore tell us about, those things that do exist in the real world? He acknowledges that certain fictional characters do indeed successfully represent real existents. For example, Skimpole, in *Bleak House*, is a somewhat unflattering representation of Dickens' contemporary Leigh Hunt. But this phenomenon is too restricted to provide a more general cognitivist answer to the 'fictional objects' objection. That there is an answer to the objection is suggested by two aspects of our treatment of fictional characters, Young maintains. First, we discriminate between purely fictional characters in terms of how 'realistic' they are, and, second, we often claim to see features either of ourselves or of our acquaintances *in* fictional characters. To explain these aspects of our practice, he suggests, we should see purely fictional characters and situations as representations of *types* of entities. The realism of a character or situation, then, consists in the real existence of people or situations *of that type*. We can find aspects of fictional characters in ourselves and others because real people can also be classified as belonging to different types, including the types represented by fictional characters. While fictional characters represent types, they can do so only if they are 'fully drawn', since only through providing an *individual* instance of the type can the type itself be represented. Representation here is perhaps best thought of in terms of *exemplification*, in that the character exemplifies the type of person or situation that it represents. And the representation of types of situations and characters in fictions can be cognitively valuable because it can lead us to see real people and real situations in significantly new ways.

Cognitive value is ascribable to the representation of types because the latter can change our ways or perceiving and categorizing. This is not a matter of furnishing us with novel propositional truths. Young's broader claim is that this is just one example of the way in which learning from fictions differs from the standard model of learning familiar to us from the sciences, and indeed, from philosophy. Standardly, we represent the world *semantically*, using language to make assertions which represent by being true. We demonstrate the truth of a novel proposition by offering a *rational demonstration* which derives that proposition from other accepted claims by means of argument. By contrast, representation in fiction involves what Young terms *illustrative representation*, where, as noted above, this is often a matter of *exemplifying* some property of the entities represented. Illustrative representations can also serve as demonstrations of a kind – they can furnish us with what Young terms *illustrative demonstrations* by giving us a particular perspective on something – a perspective that allows us to acquire new understanding or knowledge of that thing. Thus, for example, the characters and situations presented in a fiction represent types that can provide us with a new perspective on real people and situations. In seeing those real people and situations as themselves exemplifying the types exemplified by the characters and situations in the fictions, our understanding of those real people and situations can be enhanced.

Young spells out in much greater detail the different forms that illustrative representation and illustrative demonstration can take in fictions. But our concern is with a more fundamental question: how does this account respond to the 'epistemological objection' to cognitivism voiced above? Has Young justified the cognitivist's claim that we can acquire knowledge or warranted belief of some kind from our reading of fictions, or is it still the case that learning from fictions is possible only when we have carried out further empirical tests? This question presents itself, for Young, in the following form. Granted that fictions provide us with novel and potentially interesting *perspectives* on the furniture of the real world, how, other than by subsequent empirical testing, are we to tell whether these perspectives are correct?

Young maintains that the perspectives supplied by fictions are to be assessed as right or wrong according to whether they assist us in acquiring knowledge about, and making sense of, the type of entity on which they are perspectives. We can determine the *rightness* of a perspective if we bring to our engagement with a literary work other knowledge we possess, and apply that perspective in our attempts to acquire further knowledge of the object, and to make sense of other features of our experience. Young illustrates his view by pointing to the ways in which Dickens, in *Bleak House*, provides us with a deeper understanding of the workings of the Court of Chancery by amplifying the characteristics that it actually had:

> His amplification of its characteristics presents the perspective from which it seems that the delays and expense associated with the court are the result of hypocritical greed on the part of lawyers and officers of the court. By itself, this does not provide readers with the knowledge that this perspective is correct and that Chancery was corrupt and ruinous. However, readers are prompted to consider this perspective on the court. They may find that, on reflection, greed is the most likely explanation of such a court's workings. That is, readers are prompted to reinterpret experiences they have had of similar institutions. Having reinterpreted experience using the perspective of the novel, the rightness of the perspective becomes apparent. Notice that the novel's capacity to contribute to knowledge depends on readers' prior knowledge. They need experiences to reinterpret in this case.[19]

While this may remind us of Novitz's talk of 'projecting' literary hypotheses onto the world, it also suggests that the process of 'testing' is more intrinsic to the activity of reading, where, as we read, we bring to bear in novel ways knowledge we already possess. If we want to explore further the possibility of such a defence of literary cognitivism, it will be instructive to consider attempts to resolve an analogous kind of epistemological puzzle that arises in the philosophy of science. How, it might be asked, can we account for the cognitive value ascribed to thought experiments in science? A scientific thought experiment seems to be a kind of fictional narrative in which we imagine carrying out certain operations and propose that those operations would bring about a certain result. But, if we do not actually carry out the operations, what justifies the claim, made by many philosophers of science, that we can obtain genuinely new knowledge of the world by carrying out a thought experiment? In the scientific case, as in the case of literary fictions, a key question is whether we can make sense of the idea that the cognitive rightness of a scientific thought experiment, qua fictional narrative, is somehow given through the experience of entertaining that thought experiment. After briefly sketching how one might give a positive answer to this question in the case of thought experiments in science, we can consider the prospects for offering a parallel answer to the epistemological challenge to literary cognitivism.

FICTIONAL NARRATIVES AND THOUGHT EXPERIMENTS

The epistemological puzzle posed by thought experiments (TEs) in science can be represented as follows. How, if at all, can the following three claims be reconciled:

C1. TEs do not rely on or provide any new empirical data concerning the state of the world. Any empirical data upon which we draw must have been well known and generally accepted before the TE was conceived.
C2. TEs provide us with new information about the physical world.
C3. TEs, while they involve reasoning, cannot be reduced without epistemic loss to inferences of any standard kind (deductive, inductive, or abductive).

We need C3 to get a genuine puzzle because we routinely learn new things about the world by *constructing inferences* based on existing knowledge.

The puzzle admits of broadly 'deflationary' and 'inflationary' responses. A *deflationary* response denies that there is a genuine puzzle, either by denying C2, or by denying C3. (We may take C1 to be true by definition, if 'new empirical data' means new evidence about the world derived directly or indirectly from sense experience.) An *inflationary* response, on the other hand, accepts C2 and C3, thereby takes TEs to have a distinctive epistemological value, and offers an explanation of how TEs are able to possess that value. There are also extreme and moderate versions of each kind of response. An extreme deflationist simply denies C2. A moderate deflationist retains C2 but casts doubt on the epistemic virtues of TEs by denying C3. A moderate inflationist supplements C1 by arguing that prior empirical knowledge can be mobilized in a new way by TEs. And an extreme inflationist argues that TEs involve non-empirical modes of intuition.

While our interest is in a particular kind of moderate inflationary response, we may briefly say something about the other kinds of response and indicate how they view the epistemic value of TEs. For extreme deflationists, scientific TEs are of at best heuristic value, serving as instruments of discovery, but cannot provide justified beliefs about the world unless independently tested.[20] A TE may *suggest* that physical reality has a certain feature, and may even provide the idea for a concrete experiment which may itself justify the belief that such a feature exists. But TEs cannot themselves teach us anything about the world. Either the claims made on the basis of TEs are empirically testable – in which case, knowledge requires that such a test be performed, and the TE is either redundant (if the claim is empirically established) or invalidated (if empirical tests show the claim to be incorrect) – or such claims are not empirically testable, in which case they are without justification. On such a view, scientific TEs are to be assessed in precisely the way that critics such as Stolnitz wish to assess standard fictional narratives outside of science.

The moderate deflationist maintains that, insofar as TEs can tell us about the world, they are epistemically unremarkable.[21] They are merely colourful uses of our standard epistemic resources – ordinary experiences and the inferences that are to be drawn from them. TEs are simply picturesque arguments that reorganize and make explicit what we already know about the physical world. John Norton expresses this view in his 'reconstruction thesis', according to which all TEs can be reconstructed as arguments once we fill in the tacit or explicit assumptions. Belief in the conclusion of a TE is then justified insofar as that conclusion is justified by the reconstructed argument. The principal exponent of extreme inflationism, on the other hand, is James Brown, who offers an account of what he terms 'Platonic' TEs.[22] He maintains that we find such TEs in mathematics, where 'we can sometimes prove things with pictures'. In such cases, he argues, 'we grasp an abstract pattern' via a kind of 'intellectual perception'. TEs in the natural sciences can also function Platonically, according to Brown. Such experiments involve an exercise of intellectual intuition which grasps a law of nature.

In the present context, however, our interest is in one kind of moderate inflationary response to the epistemological puzzle. Such a response stresses the way in which thought experiments allow the scientist to mobilize cognitive resources not available in ordinary scientific reasoning. TEs are epistemically singular, and cannot be reconstructed as deductive or inductive arguments without epistemic loss, because of *the way in which* they mobilize cognitive resources available prior to the formulation of the TE. Ernst Mach, who is widely acknowledged as the progenitor of this approach, argued that we have 'instinctive knowledge', derived from experience but never articulated and perhaps even incapable of being articulated or made explicit, and that this knowledge is activated when we imagine ourselves in a hypothetical experimental situation.

A number of more recent commentators have echoed Mach's strategy,[23] but it has been most fully developed by philosophers who draw on work by cognitive scientists on the construction and manipulation of mental models, and in particular, on the use of mental models in narrative comprehension.[24] TE narratives, it is claimed, are used by the receiver to construct a quasi-spatial 'mental model' of the hypothetical situation. In running the TE, the receiver then operates directly upon the model, deriving the experimental conclusion by manipulating the model rather than operating upon the linguistic representations that make up the narrative used in constructing the model. Crucially, in constructing and manipulating the model, the receiver mobilizes a number of other cognitive resources: her everyday understandings of the world, based on practical experience, and other forms of tacit knowledge, such as individual expertise, practical know-how, an 'embodied familiarity' with the world, and geometrical intuitions. It is in virtue of the role played by these unarticulated (and often unarticulable) cognitive resources in the mental modelling of TEs that TEs yield determinate conclusions and have a bearing on the real world. The 'mental modelling' approach, it is claimed, allows us to solve the original puzzle about TEs. TEs enable us to produce new data by manipulating old data, by providing us with the means to generate a manipulable representation of a problem. In constructing and manipulating this model, we can mobilize various kinds of cognitive resources in ways not possible if we were to work directly on a regimented propositional account of that problem. Because of the role played here by tacit, unarticulated, and often unarticulable forms of knowledge, we cannot reconstruct a TE as an argument without epistemic loss.

Whether or not we think that such a moderate inflationary account is the best story about at least some TEs in science, such an account might be thought to offer a valuable resource if we wish to support Young's response to the epistemological objection to the cognitive claims of fiction. The objection, we may recall, holds that the most we can get from reading standard fictional narratives is *hypotheses* about the general ordering of things in the world, or *beliefs* about specific aspects of the world, or *potentially insightful* ways of categorizing things in our experience. Only if those hypotheses or beliefs pass further tests can they acquire the status of knowledge, it is claimed.

Take, for example, the claim that we learn about the dynamics of complex human relationships through reading Henry James,[25] or about the rhythms of lived experience through reading Virginia Woolf. The challenge is to provide some reason why we should accept such claims, without further empirical test, or why our responses to such works are to be trusted. We might now respond that, as with scientific TEs on the moderate inflationist account, our responses to such fictional narratives mobilize unarticulated cognitive resources based in experience. The fiction is able to elicit such responses because it makes manifest constant patterns underlying the complexity of actual experience – this is reflected in our feeling that the novel has indeed revealed such patterns to us; and this feeling is to be trusted because it reflects the operation of such unarticulated cognitive resources in our reading. This might then be taken to further clarify the intuition, identified earlier, that Young's defence of literary cognitivism differs from Novitz's in that it makes the process of 'empirical testing' of what is exemplified in the fiction *internal* to the process of reading the fiction, rather than something we have to do after we have read the fiction.

But caution is needed in a number of respects if we are to endorse such a defence of literary cognitivism. In the first place, as noted earlier, it is implausible to think that an account that appeals to the mobilization of unarticulated cognitive resources can justify each of the different kinds of claims to knowledge made on behalf of literary cognitivism. In the case of knowledge of particular matters of fact, as we saw, warrant requires that the fictional narrative be, or be rightly believed to be, a reliable source of knowledge of facts of this kind. I cannot, in such cases, put reasonable trust in my personal conviction that what is presented as part of the fiction is factually true of the actual world, since (save in the case where the fiction reminds me of something that I already knew) no amount of unarticulated knowledge can serve to validate such a conviction. The same, I think, applies to claims about affective knowledge derivable from fictions. While we may find ourselves convinced, in reading a fictional narrative, that the narrator has correctly characterized the affective nature of an experienced situation of a kind that we have not actually encountered, this may reflect the narrative skill of the author rather than the correctness of our intuitions. Only if the author is, or is rightly believed to be, a reliable source of knowledge as to the affective nature of such an experienced situation can the claim to affective knowledge from the reading of fiction be supported.

This leaves us with two kinds of claims made on behalf of literary cognitivism that might be supported by appeal to the moderate inflationary account of scientific TEs – claims to learn general principles operative in real events, and claims to acquire illuminating new ways of classifying real entities or events. Even here, the claim that such cognitive benefits can accrue in the act of reading a fictional narrative, without the need to carry out some additional empirical verification, requires that we clarify what is to be included in 'the act of reading'. In the case of fictional narratives presented cinematically, for example, our sense that the author has furnished us with insights into the structures of reality is unlikely to solidify in the very act of watching the film, but only in our subsequent reflections upon it. This can still be cashed out in terms of the bringing of unarticulated cognitive resources to bear upon what is presented in the fiction, rather than in terms of carrying out some kind of empirical enquiry to 'test' the latter's applicability to real entities or events. But it makes the distinction between Young's account and that of Novitz less sharp, and also renders less sharp the distinction between *answering* the epistemological challenge to literary cognitivism and *conceding* that challenge. The same point can also be made for literary fictions, although the extended nature of the process of reading such fictions may often permit the mobilization of the relevant unarticulated cognitive resources during the process of reading itself.

A final worry needs to be addressed.[26] It is undeniable that many 'popular' fictional narratives, such as those to be found in mainstream American war films and romantic comedies, exemplify, in the narrated events, categorizations and explanatory principles that, if applied to real entities and events, would provide a hopelessly simplistic or ideologically distorted classification or explanation of those entities and events. For example, films that present geopolitical events as clashes between forces of good and forces of evil do not furnish us with cognitively useful resources if we are to understand and negotiate the nuanced nature of geopolitical realities. But surely many receivers of such narratives view them as genuine sources of understanding of reality. Is there not, then, a danger in any suggestion that we can trust our sense that a given fictional narrative illuminates reality, and should we not always require that purported 'insights' in fictions be subjected to independent test?

This objection suggests that, to avoid such possible cognitive misuses of fiction, we should resist the literary cognitivist idea that our engagements with fictional narratives can themselves yield knowledge, and grant that all we can get from such engagements are *possible* cognitive benefits that stand in need of independent testing. But the literary cognitivist should resist such a line of argument, and can do so by clarifying what it is that she is claiming. The claim is not that, because our sense that we are learning something about the real world – either about general principles operative therein or about how certain ways of categorizing things bring illumination – draws upon unarticulated cognitive resources, we can trust this sense and rest content, without further exploration, that we are indeed learning what we believe ourselves to be learning. For our sense that we are learning is trustworthy only in proportion to the adequacy of the unarticulated cognitive resources upon which we draw. This is no different from the situation in respect of scientific TEs. If the cogency of the latter sometimes draws upon the receiver's embodied knowledge of how things work in a real experimental context, for example, then only the responses of one who possesses such knowledge can serve to test the TE in question.

So, in the case of fictional narratives, we should admit that there is genuine learning through the reading of such narratives only to the extent that we also allow that the unarticulated knowledge of the world, upon which the reader's intuitions of rightness are based, is itself adequate to validate those intuitions. One who enters the reading or viewing process of a narrative that simplistically represents geopolitical events with a naive or equally simplistic, although unarticulated, general sense of such events will indeed find the narrative to be illuminating, and may indeed trust her sense of being illuminated in her further dealings with reality. But the claim, again, is not that, in the case of the relevant kinds of cognitive resources, a reader's sense of having learned from fiction itself justifies her belief that she has so learned. The claim is only that, when the sense of having learned from a fiction is *in fact* grounded in the right kind of unarticulated knowledge, the reader can indeed be said to have learned what she believes herself to have learned. The claim is, in this respect, an externalist rather than an internalist one, depending upon how the agent in fact stands in relation to the knowledge claim, rather than how she sees herself as standing in relation to it. Learning from fictional narratives in this way requires 'reliability in the reader' rather than 'reliability in the author', we might say.

If qualified in the ways suggested in the preceding paragraphs, it seems possible to answer the epistemological challenge to literary cognitivism by appeal to something like the moderate inflationary account of scientific TEs. But the qualifications are as important as the claim itself, if we are to understand better what is at issue in assessing the cognitive claims of literary fictions.

CHAPTER 9

LITERATURE, MORALITY, AND SOCIETY

We began the previous chapter with the question posed in David Hare's play *Wetherby* by Miss Jean Travers to her students. Generalizing from the specific example that she uses, the question concerns the value that readers may find in reading works of literary fiction. In the previous chapter we focused on answers to that question which point to the purported cognitive virtues of fictions, the different ways in which fictional works can increase our understanding of the real world. But, as we saw, some of the considerations proposed as cognitive virtues of literature also have a strongly practical import. Literary fictions, it can be argued, can not only increase our knowledge and understanding of the real world, but also contribute more directly to our ability to engage with that world, and with other human agents, in ways that contribute to our individual and collective good. Aristotle, we will recall, is perhaps best interpreted as holding that the proper pleasure to be derived from tragedy – the catharsis of the emotions of pity and fear – brings our emotional dispositions into line with the requirements of reason. Since Aristotle believes that this alignment between emotion and reason is central to the achievement of individual virtue, the tragic work is properly seen as contributing to the achievement of such virtue. Hilary Putnam, as we also saw, ascribes a significant moral role to the kinds of 'empathic knowledge' derivable from fictions. Such knowledge, he claims, provides the individual with cognitive resources that can play a crucial part in the making of right moral decisions.

In the first section of this chapter, we shall elaborate further upon these suggestions, and examine different ways in which the reading of works of literary fiction might be held to be morally or ethically valuable. In the middle section of the chapter, we shall turn to the vexed question whether the moral values ascribable to literary works bear on their value *as* literary works. Does a work's moral value enter into its artistic value, and if so, in what ways and to what extent? Finally, we shall turn to some broader questions concerning the relationship between literature and society. To the extent that an author draws upon individuals and circumstances in her society, does she have any moral obligations to those upon whom she draws? And under what circumstances, and to what extent, is society justified in constraining the production and dissemination of literary works?

THE MORAL VALUE OF LITERATURE

Hare's Miss Travers arguably exemplifies one possible answer to her own question, an answer that the film itself can be seen as critically assessing. For what she seems to have drawn from her *own* experience of great literature is a model of narrative structure in terms of which to emplot, and thereby come to terms with, her own experiences. In a series of scenes, including flashbacks to her wartime experiences, we get a sense of how she has employed this narrative structure in coming to terms with what are presented as the defining conditions of her life: the wartime death of her fiancé, her subsequent solitude and acceptance of her social role as the unmarried schoolmistress, and her place in her circle of married friends in the local community. She seems content with her lot, until her world is disrupted by a much younger graduate student who tricks his way into a small dinner party she is holding, has (as we later learn) a brief passionate encounter with her upstairs while the other guests converse below, and then returns to her cottage the next day and proceeds to shoot and kill himself with a revolver while sitting in her kitchen. We learn, from flashbacks and from his former girlfriend, that he was a student of philosophy who was existentially troubled, and, while his suicide is never fully explained, we take it to be a response of some kind to his perception of life. We also learn that, in the brief encounter the night before, he accused Miss Travers of not being able to face up to the horrors of life, and of taking refuge in her literary world. A superficial reading of the film, especially if based merely on the foregoing sketch, might view her ability to draw upon great literature as a source of consolation in dealing with her experiences as a positive thing that enables her to come to terms with her own situation in a way that the troubled young student could not. Literature, so viewed, has a function rather like that ascribed by Peter Winch to systems of mystical belief in non-technological societies.[1] The purpose of such beliefs, Winch argues, is not to enable one to change or transform the world to fit one's purposes. Rather, they provide a framework within which one can give sense to, and

165

thereby come to terms with, those things that one cannot change but must endure.

But such a reading of the film would ignore the many ways in which Hare calls into question the use of the narrative structures of literary fiction to aestheticize one's existential circumstances, thereby using the aesthetic as an anaesthetic. For example, when challenged by one of her pupils, who is considering giving up school in order to get married, to justify her continuing her education, Miss Travers can only say that engagement with the literary and cultural tradition enables one to 'think differently'. But, as the film suggests, such 'thinking differently', while it does indeed allow one to achieve an aesthetic distance from the troubles of life, also tends to act as a substitute for the attempt to transform one's life so as to put such troubles behind one. The danger lies in the satisfaction to be obtained from emplotting one's unhappiness and seeing one's life in narrative terms. There is, then, something to the student's charge that Miss Travers is using the narrative structures derivable from fictions to evade her real circumstances, even if we resist his implicit conclusion that, once one faces up truthfully to one's existential situation, the only honest alternative is suicide.

Wetherby, then, if it can be read, at least in part, in the way I have suggested, exemplifies some of the cognitive values examined in the previous chapter, while questioning at least one kind of broadly ethical value that might be ascribed to works of fiction. For our understanding of the general claim that fictional works are ethically valuable in the way that religious or mystical beliefs have sometimes been said to be – offering us ways of coming to terms with the vicissitudes of life – is deepened through the details of the fictional narrative whose principal character embodies that very claim. And, in this process, the claim itself is called into question. But, even if we are persuaded of the limitations of such a view of the ethical virtues of literature, we need to examine more closely other ways in which our engagements with fictions might be held to have moral or more broadly ethical value.

One possibility is to see the ethical value of fictions as a subspecies of the kind of cognitive value that resides in coming to grasp general principles that are true of the world. We find such a view in Sir Philip Sidney's description of poetry as a 'medicine of cherries'.[2] The idea here is that fictions provide a better medium than philosophical treatises or sermons if we wish to communicate a moral 'message' to a receiver in a way that will transform her moral beliefs and dispositions. The moral 'medicine' is more pleasantly ingested when it is disguised by the 'cherries' of literary language. Sidney's view might seem flawed when applied to 'serious' literature, for it is rarely plausible to ascribe such a simple didactic purpose to the authors of literary works of art, even if writers such as Dickens have a moral or social agenda in mind. For, to recall one of Stolnitz's criticisms of literary cognitivism, it seems to impoverish a work like *Bleak House* if we see it as an attempt to persuade us by covert means to accept a moral critique of the Courts of Chancery. To answer this criticism, as we have seen, we must ascribe to the fiction not merely the role of inculcating some abstract moral principle in the reader, but rather the role of deepening the reader's comprehension of that principle through the details of the narrative.[3]

A different tradition, as we have seen in our discussion of Aristotelian catharsis, locates the ethical value of fiction not in the communication or exemplification of some abstract moral principle, but in the bringing about of some morally beneficial change in the reader's capacities or dispositions. An influential contributor to this tradition is Iris Murdoch. In *The Sovereignty of Good*, she argues that the writing and reading of fictions helps to transform our 'perception' of human affairs and human relationships, enhancing our capacity to perceive a situation in its morally salient respects and thereby to be moved by what we see to act rightly. Murdoch outlines and criticizes what she terms the 'existentialist' view of human nature and the human condition, a view that she takes to underlie the standard conception of morality. On the existentialist view, the self or person is identified with an isolated and impersonal *will*, to be distinguished from the 'historical' or 'empirical' self that is inseparable from a history of experience and the traits that result from that history. The existentialist self confronts a world of objective facts that is devoid of values, and the moral domain is the domain of action, involving exercises of the will in accordance with the dictates of an impersonal reason. Murdoch argues that such a view is empirically false in that it fails to take account of what we have learned from contemporary psychology and psychoanalysis concerning the wellsprings of human action. The self that chooses to act is always the historical, empirical self, and the principal motivation for action is the selfish interest of that self. The proper task of ethics, for Murdoch, is the overcoming of selfishness and the attainment of an accurate and unselfish vision of the world. Morality, then, is primarily a matter of achieving those virtues of character that permit such a 'true' vision of things, and a 'just' and 'loving' perception of moral circumstances that grasps and respects the individuality of others. Once one sees matters truly, action follows directly, for a true vision of matters grasps a situation in terms of 'thick' normative concepts that themselves convey the rightness of a particular course of action.

Literary fiction is presented by Murdoch as one of the most important instruments of 'unselfing', or achieving the kind of unselfish perception that is necessary for right moral action.[4] Literature, and art more generally, provides us with a model of a 'just' perception of things and helps to transform our own perceptual capacities. This is illustrated in a number of ways. First, our response to the aesthetic properties of art, as of nature, is unselfish in the sense of being 'disinterested'. Second, true artists – as opposed to those she terms 'fantasy' artists – themselves require not only talent but also the courage to perceive things unselfishly. Third, the representational works produced by true artists show us how the world appears when viewed unselfishly. Fourth, our more general response to works of literature and works of art in general is itself a model of 'detachment', of how something can be looked at and appreciated without being appropriated by the self. Finally, she maintains, great art shows us the vanity of our selfish pursuits, and illustrates that a realistic vision of the world is all that truly matters.

Martha Nussbaum agrees with Murdoch in linking the moral value of literary works to the idea that moral agency depends upon moral perception. But, unlike Murdoch, she explores this theme by offering a close and detailed reading of the moral 'work' done by particular literary works. A work such as Henry James' *The Golden Bowl*, she argues, is rightly viewed as a serious contribution to moral philosophy which brings out, in a way that philosophical treatments of morality cannot, the significance of moral perception and the place, in such perception, of what she terms 'the moral imagination'. For James, she maintains, moral knowledge 'is not simply intellectual grasp of propositions; it is not even simply intellectual grasp of particular facts; it is perception. It is seeing a complex concrete reality in a highly lucid and richly responsive way; it is taking in what is there, with imagination and feeling.'[5] Moral perception requires that we use our imagination to construct an accurate and refined picture of the others involved in a moral context and of the context itself. This involves sensitivity but also a communicative engagement in which right action depends not merely upon what is done, but upon how it is done and upon the moral imagining that informs it. But to stress the role of moral perception is not to displace moral description of the more standard kind that employs 'standing terms' such as 'moral sacrifice', 'duty', etc. The right response in a situation requires right perception, but right perception is constrained by, and 'perches upon', a grasp of the situation in terms of various kinds of duties and obligations. In the example from *The Golden Bowl* most extensively developed by Nussbaum, where a father and daughter negotiate her maturation from a loving child to a loving wife, it is crucial to the work of moral imagination in finding the right solution to this moral negotiation that the 'moral picture' which each constructs incorporates a recognition of the obligations consequent upon their relationship as father and daughter. But moral pictures are also crucial in that, without them, the path from perceived obligations to right action cannot be forged, since it is only with a right perception of the moral situation that the applicability of more general rules and principles can be determinate.

Nussbaum, like Murdoch, not only sees literature as a source of moral understanding, in its ability to exemplify essential features of moral agency, but also links moral perception to literary experience by reference to the kind of attention that each demands. James' moral ideal, she maintains, requires 'a respect for the irreducibly particular character of a concrete moral context and the agents who are its components; a determination to scrutinize all aspects of this particular with intensely focused perception; a determination to care for it as a whole'.[6] But the same kind of attention is required of the reader of James' fiction: 'If James is right about what moral attention is, then he can fairly claim that a novel such as this one not only shows it better than an abstract treatise, it also elicits it.'[7] Novels, especially the morally centred and psychologically realistic novels of the nineteenth century, provide us with an arena for the sort of engagement required by Nussbaum. The abundance of psychological and situational detail contained in novels such as *The Golden Bowl* would be inappropriate or even impossible within the confines of a philosophical text. In reading such novels we develop our capacities to perceive moral reality sensitively.

For both Murdoch and Nussbaum, a proper understanding of the moral value of literary fiction requires that we reject the standard view of moral agency, as a matter of simply applying general principles to particular cases, and accord to moral perception and moral imagination an essential role in such agency. To assess fully their claims about literature, therefore, we would have to evaluate their picture of moral agency, something that obviously falls outside the remit of a work on the philosophy of literature. Even if we accept this picture of moral agency, however, there are challenges that need to be addressed. First, as Eileen John points out, even if we accept the need for subtlety and imagination in our moral thinking and in our literary thinking, the two need not always go together.[8] A work can be subtle as literature while also being morally unsubtle, and vice versa. Furthermore, the sort of subtlety required of us as good readers need not be the same as that required of us as good moral thinkers. A related question concerns the scope of Nussbaum's analysis.[9] While it may apply very well to the works of Henry James, it is not clear how it would apply to much other literature that we take to be valuable. Nor, indeed, is it obvious that the kind of highly refined moral imagining exemplified in the mental lives of James' characters has any analogue in our ordinary moral deliberations, or even could have, given our imaginative limitations and the less leisured circumstances in which our moral choices are usually made. Nussbaum acknowledges this objection, but suggests that we can view James' characters as 'moral heroes' rather like the 'tragic heroes' of Greek tragedy as conceived by Aristotle. Such heroes surpass us in their characters and capacities, but are models for our emulation rather than representations of the moral agents we find ourselves to be. However, as with any idealized model of a human capacity, there can be a question as to whether the moral life as it confronts us is really illuminated or nurtured by such an idealized model of moral agency.[10] Again, this is not a debate we can hope to settle here.

ETHICAL VALUE AND ARTISTIC VALUE

Thus far, we have been looking at ways in which the reading (or composition) of a literary fiction might be thought to be an ethically valuable activity, such value presumably complementing whatever cognitive virtues we are willing to ascribe to fictions. But a separate issue which we have not yet addressed is whether, supposing that we can rightly ascribe certain kinds of ethical or cognitive value to works of literary fiction, this has any bearing on their value as works of literary *art*. What, in other words, is the relationship between a work's *artistic value* and its ethical or cognitive value? This seems a valid question to ask, given the kinds of distinctions we make in respect of other kinds of human practices taken to be valuable. Watching football, for example, is an activity that many people value for the distinctive kinds of pleasure it involves, and a given match will be found to be more or less valuable by spectators depending upon how far it embodies those features that enhance or diminish that pleasure – fluid movement, goalmouth incidents, ebb and flow of control, the final outcome in the balance until the end, etc. But watching football may also be viewed as valuable insofar as it promotes sociability, involves (for many) healthy outdoor activity in getting to the match, and keeps people off the streets on Saturday afternoons. While these might be seen as valuable aspects of the practice of watching football, they are, we might say, incidental to the practice itself, and do not contribute to the 'intrinsic' value of that practice. We could promote these 'extrinsic' values by encouraging activities other than the watching of football. And the true lover of the game would still watch football matches even if these other values were absent.

In the same way, it might be argued that, whatever cognitive or ethical values can be ascribed to our practices of engaging with literary and non-literary artworks, these values are *extrinsic* to the works themselves, and do not contribute to their value *as art*. The attempt to distinguish artistic value, and the pleasure proper to the appreciation of art, from cognitive and ethical values is associated with the view termed *aestheticism*, often identified with the idea of 'art for art's sake'. A classic formulation of the aestheticist credo in the visual arts is Clive Bell's *Art*, where it is argued that a visual artwork possesses artistic value in proportion to its having 'significant form', something that elicits the 'aesthetic emotion' in properly sensitive receivers. Other values that some may find in looking at visual artworks – for example, cognitive values grounded in the representational content of pictures – have no bearing, for Bell, upon the value of a painting *qua* artwork. In the literary arts, a famous exponent of the aestheticist view was Oscar Wilde, who, speaking through one of his characters, maintained that 'the critic should be able to recognize that the sphere of Art and the sphere of Ethics are absolutely distinct and separate . . . Art is out of reach of morals, for her eyes are fixed upon things beautiful and immortal and ever-changing'.[11]

Wilde's dictum is arguably an expression of the view that Noel Carroll terms 'radical autonomism'.[12] The radical autonomist holds that the artistic value of an artwork cannot depend, even in part, upon its moral value because artworks are not the kinds of things for which moral evaluations can properly be given. In so far as we incorporate moral judgements or the exercise of our moral sensibilities into our reading of literary fictions, we are not engaging with those fictions as works of art. The radical autonomist will therefore dismiss, as conceptually confused, the suggestion, explored in the first section of this chapter, that artworks can be sources of moral value. Carroll argues that radical autonomism must be rejected for at least those artworks that have a narrative framework that must be grasped in order for the work to be properly understood. For, so he maintains, narrative art is always incomplete, and requires that the audience fill in gaps in the story with background knowledge concerning the general nature of the fictional world and the psychology of the characters. This aspect of the understanding of fictional narratives was explored in Chapter 4. But Carroll further argues that the understanding of narrative art also requires certain emotional responses which themselves determine aspects of the fiction. For example, it is through such responses that the reader determines that it is true in the story that the action of one of the characters was unjust or heartless. These responses, he argues, often have a moral dimension. Thus only through the activation of the 'moral powers' of the audience can such narratives be understood.

This kind of 'internal' role for moral judgements in the appreciation of narrative fictions is granted by what Carroll terms the 'moderate autonomist'. What the moderate autonomist will deny, however, is that a judgement as to the moral value of *the work itself*, or of what the work requires of the receiver, has any bearing on its value as *art*. According to the moderate autonomist,

> an artwork may be aesthetically valuable and morally defective, or vice versa. But these different levels of value do not mix, so to speak. An aesthetically defective artwork is not bad because it is morally defective and that provides a large part of the story about why a work can be aesthetically valuable, but evil . . . Moderate autonomism . . . , though it allows that the moral discussion and evaluation of artworks, or at least some artworks, is coherent and appropriate, . . . remains committed to the view that the aesthetic dimension of the artwork is autonomous from other dimensions, such as the moral dimension.[13]

Carroll himself defends the view he terms 'moderate moralism', according to which a moral failing of a work *can* at least under some circumstances constitute an artistic failing, contrary to the claims of the moderate autonomist. Carroll does not defend the *radical moralist* thesis that artistic value *always* contains a moral component, for it is difficult to see how this thesis would be satisfied by non-narrative works in music and by many works in the visual arts. But he thinks the case for moderate moralism can be established if we reflect, once again, on the role played by our moral responses in the understanding of narrative artworks. If features of the story are intended to be manifest to the receiver through the eliciting of a particular moral response, then a failure to elicit that response in the receiver, and thus a failure to make manifest to the receiver crucial elements in the overall design of the narrative, may be seen as an artistic flaw in the work. But, if the response that is called for is one that the receiver is unable to make because such a response is morally unacceptable for her, then the morally defective nature of the work – its requiring a morally unacceptable response – counts as an artistic flaw, contrary to what the moderate autonomist maintains:

> Many artworks, such as narrative artworks, address the moral understanding. When that address is defective, we may say that the work is morally defective. And, furthermore, that moral defect may count as an aesthetic blemish. It will count as an aesthetic defect when it actually deters the response to which the work aspires. And it will also count as a blemish even if it is not detected – so long as it is there to be detected by morally sensitive audiences whose response to the work's agenda will be spoilt by it.[14]

An earlier but less developed version of this argument for moralism can be found in David Hume's 'Of the Standard of Taste', where Hume maintains that 'where vicious manners are described, without being marked with the proper characters of blame and disapprobation; this must be allowed to disfigure the poem, and to be a real deformity. I cannot, nor is it proper I should, enter into such sentiments'.[15]

Both Carroll, explicitly, and Hume, implicitly, assume that it is appropriate, in arguing for moralism, to take the 'morally sensitive reader' as the standard for determining whether a moral flaw in a work is an artistic flaw. In Carroll's case, it is because such a reader would be prevented, by the moral flaw, from responding to the work in a way that is necessary to grasp its full narrative design that the work is artistically flawed. But, Berys Gaut has noted, to appeal here to the judgements of the morally sensitive reader seems to beg the question against the autonomist.[16] For if, as the autonomist claims, moral value is irrelevant to artistic value, then it is unclear why the moral sensibilities of a receiver have any bearing upon her status as a judge of a work's artistic value. Indeed, to develop this point, it seems more appropriate, in light of the discussion of Chapter 5, to consider the responsive capacities of those readers who make up the audience *intended by the author*. Only if *these* readers are prevented from grasping the narrative design of the work by the moral flaw might this be thought to reflect upon the work's artistic value.

Even if the author does intend that readers of his narrative possess a high degree of moral sensitivity, there is a potential problem for Carroll's argument, as Carroll himself acknowledges. For, if a narrative fails to elicit in the reader a response intended by the author, the artistic flaw seems to lie in the author's mistaken belief that a narrative having a given set of properties would elicit a particular kind of response in a reader. We seem to have what Carroll terms a 'tactical error', the selection of the wrong artistic means to secure a given effect. This analysis seems to apply whatever the particular nature of the desired response and whatever the reason for the work's failure to elicit this response. In the cases described by Carroll, the author's 'tactical error' consists in misestimating how a reader with a high moral sensitivity will respond to a given narrative. But this, it might be claimed, doesn't show that the artistic flaw is to be identified with whatever moral failings in the work explain the failure of the intended audience to respond in the desired way.

Carroll insists that the flaw in the cases he describes is not merely tactical, but resides in the moral failings of the work:

> I am not persuaded that this failure is unconnected from the evil involved. For the reason that uptake is psychologically impossible may be because what is represented is evil. That is, the reason the work is aesthetically defective – in the sense of failing to secure psychological uptake – and the reason it is morally defective may be the same.[17]

But this is unconvincing. For consider, by analogy, an author of children's stories who writes a narrative which members of the intended audience – children aged between 4 and 8, for example – are supposed to find frightening. If the children fail to respond in the intended way, this is indeed an artistic flaw in the story, but the flaw does not consist in the story's not being frightening simpliciter – presumably, adults would not be frightened by such a story, nor was it intended that they should be. The error consists in misestimating the psychology of the intended audience – what children of the prescribed ages would *find* frightening. By analogy, in the case under consideration, where the intended audience is people with high moral sensitivity, the author's error, and thus the artistic flaw in the work, consists in misjudging the morally constrained judgements that members of that audience would make in responding to the narrative. Whether or not the moral beliefs exercising such constraints are true or false is irrelevant to the nature of the artistic flaw.

Gaut, who himself favours something like Carroll's 'moderate moralist' position – Gaut terms his own view 'ethicism' – offers a reformulation of the kind of argument for moralism proposed by Carroll. Gaut's reformulation is designed to overcome the kinds of objections to Carroll's argument canvassed above. For Carroll, as we have seen, we establish moderate moralism by pointing to artistic flaws that consist in the inability of the 'morally sensitive' receiver to respond in the manner prescribed by the work. Gaut agrees that works prescribe certain kinds of imaginings, and certain kinds of responses to those imaginings. The Marquis de Sade's *100 Days of Sodom*, for example, prescribes imagining various kinds of extreme sexual torture of innocent persons, and also prescribes that we find the imagined events to be amusing and arousing. But the issue, for Gaut, is not whether the responses are ones that we find ourselves able to make, or ones that a morally sensitive person would find herself able to make. Rather, the issue is whether the responses are *merited* or *warranted* by the subject to which we are invited to respond. A horror movie invites us to imagine certain events and to respond with fear. Such a movie will be flawed if the prescribed response is not *merited* by the imagined events – if the events are not truly frightening – even if many people are in fact frightened by them. Furthermore, this flaw is an artistic flaw insofar as it is internal to the work that it invites us to *see* the subject in a way that is not warranted by the subject. In the de Sade example, the extreme torture of innocents does not merit a response of amused arousal, and, to the extent that the work endorses such a response, this is an artistic flaw in the work, even if readers do respond in the prescribed manner. Furthermore, in such cases, the constraints that must be met for an amused response to be warranted include moral constraints. So it is the ethical failings of the work that are at least in part responsible for its artistic failings.

Gaut's argument indeed meets the specific objections levelled at Carroll, but it is open to related objections. We may note, first, that the argument seems to presuppose that cognitive virtues of a work are among the things that contribute to its artistic value. For the reason why a work's prescribing an unmerited response to a portrayed situation is to be viewed as an artistic failing is not, as with Carroll, that the receiver's failing to respond in the prescribed way will prevent the desired comprehension of the narrative. Rather, it is that the manner of response prescribed by the work presents, as warranted and perhaps enlightening, an unwarranted and possibly false way of viewing the represented subject. It is only insofar as artistic value is taken to include a work's capacity to give us new and valuable ways of seeing things in the real world that the unwarranted nature of the response prescribed by a work can count as an artistic flaw in the work. But, second, at least one of Gaut's critics has suggested that the 'merited response argument' rests upon an equivocation on the notion of a warranted or merited response.[18] By the latter, we may mean a response that is warranted given a particular moral framework. In this sense, the prescribed response to de Sade's *100 Days of Sodom* is clearly unwarranted for nearly all readers. But we may also mean that a response is warranted by the material itself, as when we say that a joke at which we shouldn't (morally) laugh is nonetheless funny. In this sense, the tendency, if such it be, of members of de Sade's intended audience to respond in the prescribed manner is evidence that the response *is* warranted.

Gaut rejects the charge of equivocation, arguing that, in the cases in question, ethical criteria are built into the idea of warrant for the prescribed responses:

> To be amused by sadistic cruelty is to be amused by something that is not, insofar as it is sadistically cruel, amusing . . . So in all cases the point appealed to is that the response prescribed does not correspond to the evaluative properties of the object—it is the cognitive-evaluative aspect of rationality that in each case is impugned by its immorality. That is, . . . these responses are not *warranted* insofar as they are unethical . . . Hence there is no ambiguity or non sequiteur in the argument: rather, there is appeal

to a substantive claim that a range of responses have ethical criteria among their warrant-conditions.[19]

However, we can raise an objection here analogous to the charge of mere 'tactical error' levelled at Carroll. Granted that, taken independently of its presentation in a particular literary work, the sexual torture of innocent persons clearly fails to meet whatever ethical criteria we might build into the warrant-conditions for something to merit the response of amusement, the moderate autonomist may reply that our concern in artistically evaluating a work of literary art is not with its subjects or themes per se, but with the manner in which those subjects or themes have been articulated in the work. Our concern in appreciating a work is indeed, as Gaut maintains, not merely with the subject represented, but with the manner in which that subject has been represented, the manner in which we are invited to see and respond to that subject. But then the question that bears upon the artistic value of a work is whether the prescribed response is merited by the subject *as it is represented in the work*, where this abstracts from the 'cognitive' issue of whether the subject has been *accurately* represented, or whether, were the subject to be accurately represented, such a response would be merited. The issue, in other words, is not whether amusement is a merited response to the sexual torture of innocent persons, but whether it is a merited response given the (surely false) manner in which this subject has been presented in de Sade's work. The work, one might say, invites us to see the subject in a particular way, and then to respond to the subject as represented. We may find the manner in which the subject is represented inaccurate (and thus cognitively flawed) and morally repellent. But, the autonomist will insist, artistic value does not concern itself with these questions, but with what we may term the 'internal' question of warrant.

Of course, we may object that it is difficult to imagine how the sexual torture of innocent people *could* be represented in such a manner as to warrant a response of amusement, and that, if this could be accomplished, it certainly isn't accomplished by de Sade. But the autonomist will insist that, in this case, the artistic flaw ascribable to de Sade's work is a failure to represent successfully the subject in the manner intended. That there are ethical elements in the warrant-conditions for the intended response does not make the artistic flaw an ethical flaw, any more than, in the case of a painter's failure to represent a plate of food as appetising, the artistic flaw is a gastronomic flaw. The autonomy of artistic value, for the autonomist, consists precisely in its concern with relationships internal to what the artist accomplishes, rather than with the bearing of that accomplishment on things external to the work.

This counter to Gaut's 'merited response argument' resembles in some respects the counter presented by Matthew Kieran, who defends a more attenuated form of moralism.[20] Kieran argues that it can be an artistic value in a work that it enables us to see how things would look from what we take to be a morally unacceptable perspective. Thus, to use one of his examples from the visual arts, we may think of Francis Bacon as one of the great modern painters because his paintings enable us to see how the world would look to one who shared Bacon's conception of humanity as no more than 'animated meat, decayed flesh'. While we are not thereby tempted to adopt what we may view as a morally flawed perspective on the world, Bacon's greatness as an artist consists in his ability to make that perspective vivid to us, to represent human beings in such a way that certain responses would be justified. Kieran, who believes that cognitive value is an important part of artistic value, holds that Bacon's work is insightful precisely because the perspective that it makes manifest is one we view as morally defective and which we would not, in the absence of the work, have been able to comprehend. A literary analogue to this example might be Céline's *Journey to the End of Night*, which is, again, widely regarded both as a literary masterpiece and as a work whose moral 'vision' is profoundly wrong.

Kieran does allow, however, that in a limited class of cases a moral flaw in a work may be an artistic failing. This occurs when the moral perspective we are invited to adopt is too distant from our own, such that we are unable to make intelligible the vision proffered by the work. He cites as an example a harsh and explicit fourteenth-century depiction of the crucified Christ in Mary's arms, the *Roettgen Pietà*, which he compares with Michelangelo's first *Pietà*. Both works, he argues, are properly seen as conveying a particular attitude, and soliciting a particular response, towards the crucified Christ, but the attitude and response are very different in the two cases. Because the conception of human nature offered for contemplation in the *Roettgen Pietà* is not, so Kieran maintains, an intelligible option for us, given our broader moral framework, we value it less highly as art in spite of the other artistic values it may realize.

Kieran's more general contention is that, when a work's moral failings affect its intelligibility, this constitutes an artistic failing. Yet it is not clear that this example supports the attenuated moralism that he endorses. For very clearly, the supposed 'unintelligibility' of the conception of human nature expressed in the *Roettgen Pietà* is unintelligibility *to us* – presumably this conception would have been only too intelligible to the intended audience for the piece. But is the failure of a fourteenth-century work to present to us a conception of human nature that we might ourselves consider endorsing a failure in the work, or a fact about our inability fully to appreciate the work? If we take the latter approach, then, if the work has an artistic failing of the sort described, it will reside in its failure to represent the subject in such a way as to warrant the prescribed response in the intended audience. But the autonomist will then insist, as above, that the artistic failure resides in a failure of representation, not in a moral flaw.

Hume, we saw above, held the 'moralist' view that moral blemishes in a work constitute artistic failings. He held, like Carroll, that where a work prescribes a response that is morally defective, this will deter the morally sensitive receiver from responding in the prescribed manner, but he also remarked what he took to be the singular nature of this phenomenon:

> Whatever speculative errors may be found in the polite writings of any age or country, they detract but little from the value of those compositions. There needs but a certain turn of thought or imagination to make us enter into all the opinions, which then prevailed, and relish the sentiments or conclusions derived from them. But a very violent effort is requisite to change our judgment of manners, and excite sentiments of approbation or blame, love or hatred, different from those to which the mind from long custom has been familiarized. And where a man is confident of the rectitude of that moral standard, by which he judges, he is justly jealous of it, and will not pervert the sentiments of his heart for a moment, in complaisance to any writer whatsoever.[21]

This puzzle, usually termed the puzzle of 'imaginative resistance', concerns our imaginative responses to works of fiction. We are willing to make-believe all sorts of things that we take to be false of the actual world, including even things that we might take to be physically and metaphysically impossible (e.g. travel faster than the speed of light, and time travel, respectively). But we seem resistant to the invitation to imagine worlds in which moral truths obtain that are strikingly incompatible with our actual moral beliefs. Kendall Walton proposes, as an example, the one-sentence fiction: 'In killing her baby, Griselda did the right thing; after all, it was a girl.'[22] Rather than take this to be true in the story, we tend to respond by attributing this belief to the narrator or the culture being described in the narrative, holding that it is also true in the story that the belief is false, and that the moral status of the described act in the world of the story is the same as it would be in the actual world.

We have already critically discussed Carroll's claim that, where imaginative resistance occurs, it may constitute both a moral and an artistic flaw in the work. But, even if we reject Carroll's claim, there remains the puzzle as to why 'imaginative resistance' of this sort occurs. A flourishing literature on this topic has sprung up since Walton's paper, much of it in response to a more recent paper by Tamar Gendler.[23] In the present context, it must suffice to provide a brief outline of current debates on the issue. One question is whether the phenomenon is indeed as singular as it is made out to be, or whether there are other fictional invitations to which we manifest a similar resistance. For example, it has been suggested that there is a similar problem if we are asked to imagine that other kinds of normative predicates have very different conditions of application in a fiction – that, for example, things we would take to be grotesque are beautiful, or things we would take to be irrational are rational.[24] Another suggestion that would broaden the scope of the puzzle is that imaginative resistance will arise whenever we are dealing with a predicate whose content is determined by our dispositions to respond in certain ways in the actual world. Stephen Yablo contrasts predicates like 'ticklish', where something is ticklish in a world if it affects us in a certain way in *that* world, with predicates like 'oval', where something is oval if it has the physical properties that affect us in a certain way in the actual world.[25] In the latter kind of case, we will resist any invitation to imagine that something lacking the relevant properties in some fictional world could nonetheless fall under the predicate.

One proposed explanation of 'imaginative resistance' is that it arises when we are asked to imagine something that turns out to be conceptually impossible. Walton, for example, suggests that we take moral properties to supervene on certain kinds of non-moral properties, so that a given moral property can be instantiated only where the relevant kinds of non-moral properties are also exemplified. We are therefore unable to imagine a situation in which the moral properties are instantiated in the absence of the relevant kinds of non-moral properties. However, while this seems to cover some cases of imaginative resistance, it arguably doesn't cover others.[26] An alternative proposal is that we refrain from imagining what is prescribed in the 'Griselda' story because, given the lack of detail in the story, we don't yet understand *how* the moral predicate in question is supposed to apply.[27] But this, it seems, cannot explain why imaginative resistance can still occur even if the detail is filled in, as it would be if we took the 'Griselda' story to be one that is set in our contemporary world.[28] A third suggestion is that we generally acquiesce in the game of make-believe proposed by a fiction because we trust that the narrator, or 'fictional author', of the story is a reliable authority on what is true. But, while the narrator is generally taken to occupy a privileged position in this respect, we do not extend this privilege to the knowledge of moral truths, and perhaps of normative claims more generally.[29]

It is not clear, however, why we shouldn't take the narrator to be equally privileged as to normative facts in 'worlds' distant from our own. Gendler's own solution to the puzzle addresses this question. She argues that our concern about entering imaginatively into certain morally and normatively deviant fictions is generated by our general practice of 'exporting' certain things taken to be true in the story into our understanding of the actual world, if such exportation doesn't generate any contradiction. In the case of prescriptions to imagine deviant moral worlds, she claims, we are concerned that, if we enter into the fiction imaginatively, this will involve 'exporting' the morally deviant 'truths' from the fiction to the real world.

This overview of the literature is obviously too brief to be really informative, but for present purposes we may note that, however one proposes to resolve the puzzle, it doesn't seem to provide further ammunition for the kind of 'moderate moralist' argument developed by Carroll. For, while the phenomenon of imaginative resistance may constrain what authors can realistically hope to achieve in prescribing certain kinds of responses to their fictions, and while we may feel it is an important part of the author's job to be aware of these kinds of constraints, the failure to prescribe a given response due to imaginative resistance is still a *tactical* rather than an ethical flaw in the work.

THE ACCOUNTABILITY OF LITERATURE

The writing and reading of literary works are practices that affect our lives not only in positive but also in negative ways. While some literary works may indeed be cognitively or morally valuable in the ways proposed by literature's defenders, other works, such as Brett Easton Ellis's *American Psycho* and the fictional works of the Marquis de Sade, address issues that many find disturbing, present in a sympathetic or at least an intelligible manner ways of thinking that some regard as dangerously disturbed, and may influence human behaviour in ways that are felt to be socially or morally undesirable. Furthermore, the writer stands in an uneasily ambiguous relation to the culture that both supports her literary activity and often provides her with material that she transmutes into the texts of her fictions. Concerns about the social accountability of the author and the need to constrain her activity for the social good were expressed by Socrates in the *Republic*, and his arguments still resonate in the minds of many people. We customarily hold those who engage in practices that may negatively affect the lives of others morally, and sometimes legally, responsible for their actions. Is it not right, therefore, to hold the practices of literature similarly responsible? We may conclude our philosophical reflections upon literature by briefly examining two ways in which authors and their works might be held morally and socially accountable.

We began this chapter by reflecting upon one possible answer to the question posed by the central character in David Hare's *Wetherby* about the value of reading literature. The proposal was that literature provides us with 'models' that help us to deal with what happens to us in real life – 'models' that enable us to 'emplot' real events in our lives as a way of coming to terms with those events. But we may also raise moral questions concerning the converse relation, where authors use real people or situations as 'models' for their fictional characters. As noted in the previous chapter, Dickens based the character Harold Skimpole, in *Bleak House*, on Leigh Hunt, and presented this character in a rather unfavourable way. But there has been little philosophical reflection upon the obligations that an author incurs when she acts in this way.

Those with an aestheticist perspective on these matters might argue that there are no moral issues here to discuss. William Faulkner, for example, maintained that 'the writer's only responsibility is to his art . . . If a writer has to rob his mother, he will not hesitate; the 'Ode on a Grecian Urn' is worth any number of old ladies'.[30] Felicia Ackerman, in one of the few philosophical treatments of such matters, rejects Faulkner's amoralism concerning authorship, and the related view that, while what authors do may be morally wrong, this is always outweighed by the moral benefits that the mass of people can obtain from their works.[31] According to Ackerman, the writer of fictions is morally constrained in basing her characters on real people because the latter can be *harmed* in various ways by her actions. There are a number of forms such harm can take. Some rest upon the possibility that readers may identify the person S serving as the model for a character. The person may, as a result, be harmed either because readers thereby acquire various true or false beliefs about S that cause him distress, or because the character based upon S is presented in a degrading light. Even if readers are not able to recognize a person S in the character based upon him, S may be harmed in that he feels betrayed by the writer, who may be a friend, acquaintance, colleague, etc. Ackerman considers the suggestion that, as with medical experimentation, we might impose a general requirement for 'informed consent' on the part of those used as models for fictional characters. But she rejects such a suggestion, on the grounds that this would seriously harm the practice of writing fiction, and thus deny us the many benefits that we may gain from the fruits of such practice. Such a requirement is appropriate, however, in cases where there is a pre-existing personal relationship of some kind between S and the author. In such cases, if the author fails to obtain S's informed consent, she may violate prima facie moral duties, such as the duty not to betray a friend or the duty to keep a promise.

Ackerman's account invokes a mixture of consequentialist and deontological considerations, offering a general analysis in terms of the relative harms and benefits of basing a fictional character on a real person, but also pointing to possible violations of prima facie duties. But presumably any appearance of conflict might be resolved by reconstruing talk of harms and benefits in deontological terms – we have, it might be argued, a prima facie duty not to harm others, and our overall obligations are always to be determined by balancing different prima facie duties rather than by balancing consequences. But it is worth noting an alternative way in which this issue might be set up – in terms of a Kantian duty always to treat other people as ends in themselves and not merely as means. It seems that this duty might be violated if an author uses another person as a model for her fiction without considering ways in which that person's capacity for autonomous agency might be compromised by such use. An analogous charge in the case of photography is made by Susan Sontag, who held that the act of photographing someone is always predatory because it involves treating the other as an object. Sontag raises issues similar to those addressed by Ackerman concerning the moral responsibility of the photographer to her subject.[32]

Where a character in a literary fiction is based upon a real person, it seems clear how it is the *person* who is in some sense presented in the fictional work and who might be harmed by being so presented. The aspects of S that serve as a model for a fictional character C are closely tied to our intuitive conception of what individuates us as persons in the actual world – our distinctive personality, character, 'style', or achievements. It is in virtue of sharing these kinds of characteristics, for example, that the character Skimpole, in Dickens' *Bleak House*, was modelled on Leigh Hunt. These aspects are abiding features of a person: they are very much part of one's sense of who one is. But, it might be thought, all that is presented by a photographic image is the transitory *appearance* of a person, not the person herself: our individuality does not reside in how we look at a given moment. Thus the subject of a photograph is not presented in a photograph in the same way that a real person is presented in a fictional character modelled on him: it is merely their appearance at a given moment in time that is there.

But it might also be argued that photographic images present not merely a person's momentary appearance but also the person themselves in a certain light – embody a thought about them in pictorial form – using their appearance, as causally implicated in the forming of the image, as a means of identifying the person in question. Photographic images, then, are analogous to paintings and drawings, or, perhaps, to the work of a caricaturist. The momentary appearance is chosen both to identify the person to the viewer and to represent something about enduring qualities of their personality or character. It is these qualities, ascribed by the photographer to the subject in virtue of the way in which she has manipulated the photographic medium, that are present in the images. And in this case, a real person may be said to 'exist' in the images in a way similar to how a real person may be said to be presented in a fictional character. Thus some of the issues of professional ethics raised by Ackerman seem to arise for photographs also: by representing a person in a certain way, the photographer may harm that person, or breach a friendship, or act in some other morally questionable way.

If the issue of professional ethics in authorship examined by Ackerman has attracted little philosophical attention, this cannot be said for the second issue of literary responsibility to be examined here. Whether or not we take authorial intention to be a constraint on the interpretation of literary works (see Chapter 5), such works, as the linguistic products of their makers, are a form of 'speech' or 'expression'. As such, they have often been subject to control and censorship by those legislators who have seen reason to limit speech and expression. A famous debate over the control of literary 'speech' occurred in the 1930s, when the US government tried to prevent the distribution of James Joyce's *Ulysses* on the grounds that it was 'obscene' given existing statutes against obscenity. It will be instructive to examine the arguments offered on both sides in the legal debate over the banning of *Ulysses*, since they bring out the general structure of much philosophical dispute over censorship.[33]

Justice Hand, setting out the majority verdict against banning *Ulysses*, and Justice Manton, setting out the dissenting minority verdict, are in agreement on a number of things. They both accept that a work is 'obscene' insofar as it tends 'to excite sexual impulses or lustful thoughts'. They agree that literature, and other art forms, are properly held accountable to *some* social standards, and therefore reject the aestheticist idea that art should not be held accountable to societal norms. In holding that the charge of obscenity against a work should be settled by appeal to the social consequences of allowing it to be published, they also reject any attempt to resolve the issue by appeal to more abstract rights or duties, such as the impermissibility, in principle, of imposing social restrictions upon the exercise of speech.[34]

In spite of these agreements, Hand and Manton reach contrary verdicts because they have different views about the nature and value of literary artworks. For Hand, literary works like *Ulysses* are to be judged in terms of both their 'artistic merit' and their 'scientific merit'. The latter is germane, for Hand, because literary art is properly viewed as a potential source of knowledge of the human condition, which entails that literary works are analogous to, and should be judged by the same standards as, works of science. Like the scientist, the literary artist should be hindered as little as possible in her 'research' if we wish to make progress in our overall understanding of the world. This has practical implications if we ask how a work should be tested for obscenity. The test, Hand claims, is not parts of the work taken in isolation, but 'the effect of the book as a whole'. For, if we applied the former test uniformly to works of art and science, we would have to ban many scientific and medical texts as well as many 'classic' literary works. Nor should we ban a literary work simply because it might have a harmful effect on some readers, for this would be 'to destroy much that is precious in order to benefit a few'.

For Manton, on the other hand, literary and other artworks are only intended to amuse, or to provide spiritual refreshment to, the receiver. Art is not properly viewed as a source of knowledge, analogous to science. If some artworks do provide true representations of the world, this is purely incidental and does not yield anything comparable to scientific insight. Thus art is no more than a superior form of entertainment, and should be judged by the same moral standards as other forms of amusement. Again, this has practical implications if we ask how we should test the obscenity of a literary work. The proper test, according to Manton, is the effect of specific passages in a book, taken in isolation. This doesn't commit us to banning scientific and medical texts, since a work like *Ulysses*, unlike scientific works, is a work of fiction 'written for alleged amusement of the reader only'. As with other forms of entertainment, the principal concern for the law must be the effect on the community as a whole, and this requires that we protect the more susceptible even if this deprives the intelligentsia of amusement.

As should be clear, the issue of the social control of literary works cannot be divorced from those questions about the value of art that we have addressed in this and the previous chapter. The kinds of constraints properly placed upon a form of activity cannot be determined without reference to what we take to be the nature and social function of that activity. If, as some argue, our engagement with literary artworks is a source of cognitive and moral value, then we may think it worth the risk of harming or offending a minority if this is the price to be paid for a much greater benefit for the many. Or if we subscribe to the 'aestheticist' view that art, while not properly represented as a source of cognitive or moral value, is a source of a much higher kind of value, we will be even less sensitive to the entreaties of those who seek to hold literature accountable to stricter social standards. To the extent that these broader questions about artistic value remain unresolved, however, so too must the issues addressed in the final section of this chapter. But the very range of issues in the philosophy of literature that are still matters of passionate debate testifies to the robust health and vibrancy of this area of philosophical enquiry.

NOTES

Chapter 1: The nature of literature
1. Eagleton (1983: 1). In addition to Eagleton, another good discussion of the nature of literature can be found in Stecker (1996).
2. Eagleton (1983: 10).
3. Capote (1968: 1).
4. Thompson (1971: 1).
5. Quoted in Eagleton (1983: 2).
6. Hopkins (1953: 29).
7. Thomas (1946: 65).
8. For a bibliography of works by, and also works critical of, the New Critics, see Eagleton (1983: 224–25).
9. Eliot (1954: 56).
10. Palmer (2006). For other contemporary prose poems, see Gonzalez (2003).
11. Foucault (1986).
12. Carroll and Banes (1982: 292).
13. Ibid.
14. Goodman (1968: 252–55) and Goodman (1978: 67–69).

Chapter 2: What is a literary work?
1. Wollheim (1980: 74ff.).
2. Wolterstorff (1975).
3. Goodman and Elgin (1988: ch. 3).
4. Ibid., 58ff.
5. Less clear is the status of an English string like 'water', which may be a verb in one occurrence and a noun in another. Since Goodman and Elgin stress the importance of 'permissible configurations' and the other linguistic entities with which a given entity can be combined, they might count occurrences of the verb and occurrences of the noun as two different texts. In any case, nothing in the present context turns on how we resolve this question.
6. Borges (1970: 66).
7. Ibid., 68.
8. Ibid., 69.

9. Ibid., 70.
10. For example, Tolhurst and Wheeler (1979), Danto (1981), Currie (1991), D. Davies (1991).
11. See Levinson (1980) for a parallel argument against structuralist construals of musical works.
12. Currie (1991).
13. Goodman and Elgin say that this applies even if the first tokening of a text-type is produced by a monkey on a typewriter, or by some other means that doesn't involve the generative activity of a suitably qualified cognitive agent. But this somewhat counter-intuitive claim is not required for their challenge to Currie's argument.
14. Goodman and Elgin (1988: 63).
15. Interestingly, Borges' short story has been read by some in the continental tradition as demonstrating that right interpretations of literary works are *not* contextually constrained, but depend, rather, on how interesting an interpretation is to the community of receivers to whom it is addressed. So, far from being read as an argument for a contextualist view of works – and thus, plausibly, for a contextualist view of right interpretation of works – it can also be read as an argument against contextualist theories of the interpretation of works. These issues are further discussed in Chapter 5 below.
16. Goodman (1978: ch. 2).
17. Textualism and contextualism agree that the artistic vehicle in the case of literary works is a text. But this assumption presents problems if we consider literary works that belong to oral rather than written traditions, and the identity and persistence conditions for such works. It may also present problems if we try to account for various kinds of linguistically based works that make use of the Internet, such as 'hypertexts'. For a critical discussion of the assumption that the vehicles of literary works are texts, see Martel (unpubl.).
18. See Currie (1989) and D. Davies (2004a).

Chapter 3: The nature of fiction
1. See the Introduction to Morrison (1998) for a discussion of the boundaries between fiction and non-fiction.
2. Frye (1967: 71–74).
3. The 'puzzle of imaginative resistance' is one context in which our beliefs about the real truth or falsity of what is 'true in a fiction' might be held to be relevant. The issue here is whether we are able to engage imaginatively with a fiction which requires that we make-believe *moral* claims that we believe to be false. See Chapter 9 for a discussion of this puzzle.
4. Walton (1983). Walton's view of make-believe is more fully developed in Walton (1990).

5. Searle (1974).
6. Currie (1990: ch. 1).
7. Searle's view of speech acts is spelled out in Searle (1969).
8. Searle (1974: 10–13).
9. See Walton (1983).
10. See Currie (1990: 17).
11. Grice's views underwent considerable modification, but Grice (1969) is representative of the elements in Grice's theory upon which Currie draws.
12. Currie (1990: 31).
13. This is not to say that the order of the narrative must inflexibly follow the believed order of the narrated events – flashback and flashforward must obviously be permitted in a non-fictional narrative. What is required is that the author of a non-fictional narrative be constrained by the requirement that the narrated events be *represented as occurring* in the order in which the author believes them to have actually occurred.

Chapter 4: Reading fiction (1): Truth in a story
1. See, for example, Currie (1990: 117–18): 'I have concentrated on story meaning here partly because it is the most tractable element in all that can be called . . . the meaning of a fictional work . . . Story meaning is basic to our understanding of . . . other more, perhaps more glamorous, kinds of meaning. If we have no grip on the story the work has to tell . . . we are likely to go wrong in our probing of its symbolic or metaphorical content.'
2. For such a reading of *Lolita*, see Gaut (forthcoming, ch. 8).
3. See Grice (1975).
4. See Lewis (1978: 37) for this example.
5. Recall, here, the discussion in the previous chapter of fictions whose narratives incorporate events known by the author to have occurred.
6. Lewis develops his theory of counterfactuals in Lewis (1973).
7. Lewis (1978: 42).
8. Lewis restricts his enquiry to worlds in which what is explicitly true in a story S is 'told as known fact', rather than to worlds in which it is *actually true*, in order to exclude cases where, quite accidentally, S is true in the *actual* world.
9. See Lewis (1978: 43) for a discussion of this example.
10. See ibid.
11. See also Currie's 'Gladstone' example (1990: 66).
12. Some, but not all. Neither the 'psychoanalytic theory' example nor Currie's 'Gladstone' example seem to fare any better on the 'readers' belief-world' account than on the 'actual world' account.

13. Lewis (1978: 44–45).
14. Currie (1990: 68ff.).
15. Ibid., 73; emphasis in original.
16. Ibid., 76.
17. Ibid., 74–75.
18. Ibid., 99–100.
19. Ibid., 124.
20. Ibid., 78.
21. Ibid., 79–80.
22. Ibid., 122.
23. For a sophisticated attempt to develop such an account of truth in a story, see Livingston (2005: ch. 7). For criticism of Livingston's proposal as a general account of interpretation, including story meaning, see Chapter 5 of the present volume.
24. Compare this with Currie's proposal, that a given proposition p is true in a story S if it is reasonable for the informed reader to infer that the fictional author of S believes that p. As we shall see in Chapter 5, there are reasons to question whether an account of interpretation in general – including, presumably, interpretation of story meaning – in terms of 'uptake' by the audience should traffic in the ascription of intentions to the author.
25. See Currie (1990: 117–18).
26. One writer who recognizes this point is Peter Lamarque (1996: ch. 4).

Chapter 5: Reading fiction (2): Interpreting literary works
1. Wimsatt and Beardsley (1946).
2. For an argument to this effect, see D. Davies (2004a: ch. 4).
3. Wimsatt and Beardsley (1946: 469).
4. Ibid., 470.
5. Ibid., 477.
6. Ibid., 477–78.
7. Ibid., 478.
8. Ibid., 478.
9. Ibid., 470.
10. Beardsley (1992).
11. Ibid., 33.
12. Brooks (1951: 736), cited in Beardsley (1992: 30).
13. Bateson (1950: 33, 80–81), cited in Beardsley, ibid.
14. Beardsley (1992: 35).
15. Wimsatt and Beardsley (1946: 482).
16. Ibid., 483.
17. Ibid., 484.

18. Ibid., 486–87.
19. Humpty Dumpty appears in ch. 6 of Carroll's *Through the Looking Glass*.
20. Hirsch (1967: 46–47).
21. Iseminger (1992a).
22. Hopkins (1953: 41).
23. Beardsley (1992: 31).
24. Mrs Malaprop is a character in Richard Brinsley Sheridan's play *The Rivals* who frequently misuses words by confusing them with other words that are similar in sound – speaking, for example, of 'a nice derangement of epitaphs' when she wishes to talk about a nice arrangement of epithets – hence the English term 'malapropism' for such a misuse of language.
25. Stecker (2003: 42, 46ff.). Stecker also ascribes this view to Livingston (1998) and Carroll (2000).
26. Stecker (2003: 42).
27. Stecker could avoid this objection if he held, in the spirit of Hirsch and Iseminger, that 'uptake' only determines a *range* of possible meanings, and that the author succeeds as long as her intended meaning falls within that range. But then he faces the Beardsleian objection canvassed above. I am uncertain whether this reading is more faithful to Stecker's own intentions (!), but on either reading, the 'unified view' faces serious difficulties.
28. I base this example on a famous comic sketch from *Monty Python's Flying Circus*.
29. Livingston (2005: chs 6–7).
30. Ibid., 207.
31. Ibid., 199.
32. Livingston does not make it clear whether success requires that the intended reading, once known by the informed reader, (1) makes *best* sense of the work, or (2) makes *good* sense of the work. If he opts for (2), we have a variant on the Hirsch–Iseminger account, where the judgements of the informed reader delimit a range of possible meanings, one of which is 'activated' as the actual meaning if it conforms with the author's semantic intention. Since all variants of this view are open to the same Beardsleian objection rehearsed above, I shall focus on reading (1).
33. Livingston (2005: 8).
34. Ibid., 71.
35. Nathan (1992: 199).
36. See, for example, Levinson (1992). In the case of the interpretation of artistic utterances, Levinson also thinks that, in weighing different interpretations, we try to maximize the artistic value of the utterance.

37. Stecker (2003: 45–46).
38. I say 'usually' here to leave open the possibility that the meanings of some utterances depend upon the meanings of constituents whose interpretive norms *do* accord a determining role to utterer's meaning. Steven Davis, for example, has suggested (personal communication) that this applies to at least some uses of demonstrative expressions.
39. Davidson (1986).
40. For a fuller defence of this claim, see D. Davies (2004a: ch. 3).
41. Wollheim (1980: 205–26).
42. But some use of interpretative intelligence is permitted in literary interpretation. For example, when we are working out story meaning, we 'overlook' what we take to be infelicities or slips of the pen. (See Livingston 2005: ch. 5 for a very interesting discussion of these issues.) But this is only to say that our interpretative norms allow us to take some account of what we take to have been intended, not that the intentions themselves, actual or hypothetical, play the determining role.
43. Some HI theorists (e.g. Levinson 1992) have also claimed that there is indeed such a difference between the ascription of utterance meaning to artworks and to ordinary utterances, but critics have argued that such theorists fail to motivate this distinction.
44. See Steadman (2001).
45. Goodman and Elgin (1988), we may recall, not only take our critical practice as a vindication of the idea that works admit of incompatible right interpretations, but also use this as an argument for a textualist construal of the ontological status of the literary work.
46. Foucault (1986: 118).
47. Ibid., 110.
48. Barthes (1977: 159).
49. Feagin (1982).
50. Ibid., 141.
51. Goldman (1990).
52. Matthews (1997); Dutton (1977).
53. See e.g. Stecker (1994: 198–99).
54. Stecker (1994).
55. Ibid., 193.
56. Stecker (2003: 54).
57. Stecker (1995: 14).
58. Stecker (1994: 194).
59. See Chapter 2 for this distinction.
60. Stecker (1994: 198).
61. Stecker (2003: 66).
62. For further elaboration of these points and for responses to other

arguments offered by Stecker in defence of his 'compatibilism', see D. Davies (2004b).

Chapter 6: The nature of fictional characters

1. Dickens (1971: 49).
2. See Meinong (1960).
3. See Russell (2001).
4. Presumably what is at issue here is the properties that are *true of* the character in the story, once we take account of what is explicitly true in the story and what is either true as unstated background or derivatively true. See Chapter 4.
5. The best-known contemporary exponents of the Meinongian strategy are Terence Parsons (see esp. 1980),and Edward Zalta (1983).
6. This example is taken from Quine's critical account of the Meinongian view (1963: 6).
7. For a compelling presentation of such objections to a Meinongian account of fictional characters, see Thomasson (1999), upon which I draw in the following paragraphs.
8. Thomasson (1999: 56ff.).
9. Or, for the Meinongian, an artist's most engaging discovery.
10. See e.g. Lamarque (2003: 383–86).
11. Thomasson (1999: 104–05).
12. Russell (2001).
13. Huxley (1955: 15).
14. Russell allows that there are some linguistic expressions that can function in the way that names and descriptions are held to function on the 'intuitive picture' that he otherwise rejects. Such expressions – 'logically proper names' – are terms that label things with which we are directly acquainted, such as our own sense-data, where there is no possibility of the expression failing to denote.
15. Kripke (1980).
16. Kripke does allow that, in rare cases, a description can play the reference-fixing role ascribed to descriptions by the descriptions theory. This occurs if a name is introduced as shorthand for a description, as in 'Jack the Ripper', introduced as shorthand for 'the person who committed these murders'. But even in this kind of case, the name designates rigidly, so that there are other possible worlds in which Jack the Ripper commits no murders, and indeed other possible worlds in which someone else commits the murders.
17. Kripke (unpubl.: 6).
18. Ibid., 14.
19. Thomasson refers (1999: 46) to Kripke's unpublished John Locke lectures, 'Reference and Existence', where he seems to endorse

further the idea that fictional names can be seen as referring to fictional characters.
20. Thomasson (1999: 47).
21. Currie (1990: ch. 4, pp. 146ff.).

Chapter 7: Literature and the emotions
1. Walton (1978: 5).
2. I am grateful to Carl Matheson for this example.
3. See, for example, Currie (1990: sect. 5.3).
4. Johnson (1969: 26–28).
5. Radford (1975).
6. Neill (1993: 4).
7. Walton (1978: 5).
8. See, for example, Johnson (1969), Weston (1975), Paskins (1977).
9. See, for example, Novitz (1980); Carroll (1990: 60–88); Lamarque (1996: ch. 7).
10. Lamarque (1996: 126).
11. Carroll (1990: 81).
12. Lamarque (1996: 129).
13. Walton (1978); Currie (1990: ch. 5). Derek Matravers' 'report model' (1998: ch. 3), agrees in essence with this kind of approach, while seeking to remedy certain perceived failings in Walton's account.
14. See Currie (1990: sect. 5.7).
15. Neill (1993).
16. Hume (1993b: 126).
17. See e.g. Levinson (1997: 29). But I am using the term in a broader sense, also to incorporate what Levinson terms 'organicist' solutions, since I think that most of what he classifies as compensatory solutions view the unpleasant experiences as necessary for the distinctive pleasures associated with works of tragedy and horror, and this seems to be what is distinctive of 'organicist' solutions.
18. Feagin (1983).
19. Ibid., 98.
20. Ibid., 99.
21. Carroll (1990: 184).
22. Ibid.
23. Gaut (1993).
24. Feagin (1983: 98).
25. Hume (1993b: 131).
26. See e.g. Feagin (1983: 95).
27. Gaut (1993: 336).
28. See Eaton (1982); Morreall (1985).
29. See Walton (1990: 257) and Neill (1992: 62).

30. Gaut (1993: 341).

Chapter 8: The cognitive value of literature

1. Young (forthcoming). For a more general defence of cognitivism in the arts, see Young (2001).
2. For an overview of these issues, see Novitz (1987: ch. 6).
3. This is argued in Nussbaum (1985). See the discussion of this in Chapter 9.
4. Goodman (1978: esp. ch. 4). See also Goodman (1976).
5. Novitz (1987: 132ff.).
6. Putnam (1978: 87).
7. Ibid., 89–91; italics in original.
8. Stolnitz (1992).
9. Ibid., 198.
10. Ibid., 197.
11. I am grateful to John Hyman for stressing the importance of distinguishing these questions in the present context.
12. Novitz (1987: 120).
13. Ibid.
14. Ibid., 117–20, 130–42.
15. Ibid., 138.
16. This is not to subscribe to a discredited atomistic conception of theory assessment in science, according to which, in Quine's famous metaphor, theories meet the tribunal of experience singly rather than collectively. But it is to insist that, even on the most holistic conception of science, bringing experimental or other empirical evidence to bear in the assessment of theories plays a central role, albeit a role that does not rule unequivocally on the status of a 'tested' theory. I am grateful to Catherine Elgin for pointing out the need to clarify this point.
17. Roughly, and ignoring refinements, the difference between the two conceptions of knowledge is as follows. On an 'internalist' conception, a person S who believes truly that p can correctly be said to *know* that p only if S is in a position to give reasons that justify her belief that p. Knowledge, then, is justified true belief. For the 'externalist', on the other hand, what is required, in addition to true belief, is that S acquires the belief that p by a method that is, in the context, a reliable one – that is, a method that will generally yield true beliefs of that kind in that context. But it is not necessary, for the externalist, that S knows that the method whereby she acquired the belief is reliable, or can explain its reliability.
18. Young (forthcoming).
19. Young (forthcoming).

20. See, for example, Duhem (1914: 200–5).
21. See e.g. Norton (1996).
22. Brown (1991).
23. See, in particular, Gendler (1998).
24. See, in particular, Nersessian (1993) and Miscevic (1992).
25. See the discussion of Nussbaum in Chapter 9.
26. I am grateful to Catherine Elgin for raising this worry.

Chapter 9: Literature, morality, and society
1. Winch (1964).
2. Sidney (1966).
3. For more detailed developments of this theme, see Carroll's claim (1996) that works play a role in 'moral education', and Gaut's defence (Gaut 2007: ch. 7) of the role of fictions in 'vivid imaginings'.
4. Murdoch (1967: 84–90).
5. Nussbaum (1985: 521).
6. Ibid., 526.
7. Ibid., 527.
8. John (1995).
9. See Lamarque and Olsen (1994: 386–97).
10. For a related criticism of 'idealized' models of human rationality, see Cherniak (1986).
11. Wilde (1913: 191).
12. Carroll (1996).
13. Ibid., 231.
14. Ibid., 234.
15. Hume (1993a: 152).
16. Gaut (2007: 228).
17. Carroll (1996: 235).
18. Jacobson (1997).
19. Gaut (2007: 239).
20. Kieran (2005: ch. 4).
21. Hume (1993a: 152).
22. Walton (1994). I am grateful to Yvan Tétrault for assistance in providing this overview of the literature on imaginative resistance.
23. Gendler (2000).
24. Weatherson (2004).
25. Yablo (2002).
26. See Gendler (2000) for this response to Walton. She offers examples to suggest both that there can be cases of imaginative resistance that don't involve conceptual impossibilities, and that there can be fictions involving conceptual impossibilities where we don't experience imaginatgive resistance.

27. Stock (2005).
28. Matravers (2003).
29. Ibid.
30. Quoted in Malcolm Cowley (ed.), *Writers at Work* (New York: Viking Press, 1958), 124. This reference is taken from Ackerman (1991: 144).
31. Ackerman (1991).
32. The issue is raised in Sontag's highly critical discussion of the photographs of Diane Arbus (Sontag 1973). For a critical response to Sontag, see D. Davies (forthcoming).
33. United States Circuit Court (1934).
34. For an 'absolutist' rejection of censorship in these terms, see Dwyer (2001).

BIBLIOGRAPHY

Selected literary works quoted or discussed

Borges, J. L. (1970), 'Pierre Menard, Author of the *Quixote*', tr. J. E. Irby, in *Labyrinths* (Harmondsworth: Penguin), 62–71.

Capote, T. (1968), *In Cold Blood* (New York: Modern Library).

Conan Doyle, A. (1981), 'The Adventure of the Speckled Band', repr. in *The Penguin Complete Sherlock Holmes* (Harmondsworth: Penguin Books; 1st publ. 1800), 257–73.

Deane, S. (1996), *Reading in the Dark* (London: Jonathan Cape).

Dickens, C. (1971), *Bleak House* (Harmondsworth: Penguin Books; 1st publ. 1853).

Eliot, T. S. (1954), 'The Wasteland', in *Selected Poems* (London: Faber and Faber), 49–74.

Gonzalez, R. (ed.) (2003), *No Boundaries: Prose Poems by 24 American Poets* (Tupelo, Miss.: Tupelo Press).

Hare, D. (2002), *Wetherby*, in *Collected Screenplays* (London: Faber and Faber), 1–65.

Hoban, R. (1980), *Riddley Walker* (London: Jonathan Cape).

Hopkins, G. M. (1953), 'The Sea and the Skylark' and 'Henry Purcell', in *Poems and Prose*, ed. W. H. Gardner (Harmondsworth: Penguin Books), 29, 41 (composed 1877, 1879).

Huxley, A. (1955), *Brave New World* (Harmondsworth: Penguin Books; 1st publ. 1932).

Kafka, F. (1961), *Metamorphosis*, tr. W. Muir and E. Muir, in *Metamorphosis and Other Stories* (Harmondsworth: Penguin Books; 1st publ. 1916).

Márquez, G. G. (1970), *One Hundred Years of Solitude*, tr. G. Rabassa (New York: Harper and Row).

Palmer, M. (2006), 'A Mistake', in *CUE: A Journal of Prose Poetry* 3.1, 33; also available at <www.u.arizona.edu/~mschuldt/amistake.html>.

Thomas, D. (1946), 'Fern Hill', in *Deaths and Entrances* (London: J. M. Dent and Sons), 65–66.

Thompson, H. S. (1971), *Fear and Loathing in Las Vegas* (New York: Random House).

Woolf, V. (1964), *Mrs Dalloway* (Harmondsworth: Penguin Books; 1st publ. 1925).

Wordsworth, W. (1939), 'A Slumber Did My Spirit Seal', in *The Poetical Works of Wordsworth*, ed. T. Hutchinson (Oxford: Oxford University Press), 187 (composed 1798).

Selected philosophical and critical works quoted or discussed

Ackerman, F. (1991), 'Imaginary People and Real Toads', *Midwest Studies in Philosophy* 16, 142–51.

Aristotle (1941), *Poetics (De Poetica)*, tr. I. Bywater, in R. McKeon (ed.), *The Basic Works of Aristotle* (New York: Random House), 1455–87.

Barthes, R. (1977), 'The Death of the Author', in *Image-Music-Text*, ed. S. Heath (Glasgow: Fontana-Collins), 142–48.

Bateson, F. W. (1950), *English Poetry: A Critical Introduction* (London: Longmans, Green).

Beardsley, M. C. (1992), 'The Authority of the Text', in Iseminger (1992b), 24–40.

Bell, C. (1914), *Art* (London: Chatto and Windus).

Brooks, C. (1951), 'Irony as a Principle of Structure', in M. D. Zabel (ed.), *Literary Opinion in America*, 2nd edn (New York: Harper), 729–41.

Brown, J. R. (1991), *The Laboratory of the Mind: Thought Experiments in the Natural Sciences* (London: Routledge).

Carroll, N. (1990), *The Philosophy of Horror* (New York: Routledge).

—— (1996), 'Moderate Moralism', *British Journal of Aesthetics* 36, 223–38.

—— (2000), 'Interpretation and Intention', *Metaphilosophy* 31, 75–95.

—— and S. Banes (1982), 'Working and Dancing', *Dance Research Journal* 15.1, 37–41; repr. in D. Goldblatt and L. B. Brown (eds), *Aesthetics: A Reader in the Philosophy of the Arts* (Upper Saddle River, NJ: Prentice Hall, 1997), 290–96.

Cherniak, C. (1986), *Minimal Rationality* (Cambridge Mass.: MIT Press).

Currie, G. (1989), *An Ontology of Art* (New York: St Martin's Press).

—— (1990), *The Nature of Fiction* (Cambridge: Cambridge University Press).

—— (1991), 'Works and Texts', *Mind*, n.s. 100, 325–40.

Danto, A. (1981), *The Transfiguration of the Commonplace* (Cambridge, Mass.: Harvard University Press).

Davidson, D. (1986), 'A Nice Derangement of Epitaphs', in E. Lepore (ed.), *Truth and Interpretation* (Oxford: Blackwell), 433–46.

Davies, D. (1991), 'Works, Texts, and Contexts', *Canadian Journal of Philosophy* 21, 331–46.

—— (1996), 'Fictional Truth and Fictional Authors', *British Journal of Aesthetics* 36, 43–55.

—— (2004a), *Art as Performance* (Oxford: Blackwell).

—— (2004b), 'Review of Robert Stecker, *Interpretation and Construction*', *Journal of Aesthetics and Art Criticism* 62, 291–93.

—— (forthcoming), 'Susan Sontag, Diane Arbus, and the Ethical Dimension of Photography', in G. Hagberg (ed.), *Art and Ethical Criticism* (Oxford: Blackwell).

Davies, S. (1988), 'True Interpretations', *Philosophy and Literature* 12, 290–97.

Duhem, P. (1954), *The Aim and Structure of Physical Theory*, tr. P. Weiner (Princeton, NJ: Princeton University Press; 1st publ. 1914).

Dutton, D. (1977), 'Plausibility and Aesthetic Interpretation', *Canadian Journal of Philosophy* 7, 327–40.

Dwyer, S. (2001), 'Free Speech', *Sats: The Nordic Journal of Philosophy* 2, 1–18.

Eagleton, T. (1983), *Literary Theory: An Introduction* (Oxford: Blackwell).

Eaton, M. (1982), 'A Strange Kind of Sadness', *Journal of Aesthetics and Art Criticism* 41, 51–64.

Feagin, S. (1982), 'Incompatible Interpretations of Artworks', *Philosophy and Literature* 6, 133–46.

—— (1983), 'The Pleasures of Tragedy', *American Philosophical Quarterly* 20, 95–104.

Foucault, M. (1986), 'What is an Author?', in P. Rabinow (ed.), *The Foucault Reader* (New York: Pantheon Books), 101–20.

Frye, N. (1967), *Anatomy of Criticism: Four Essays* (New York: Atheneum).

Gaut, B. (1993), 'The Paradox of Horror', *British Journal of Aesthetics* 33, 333–45.

—— (2007), *Art, Emotion and Ethics* (Oxford: Oxford University Press).

Gendler, T. (1998), 'Galileo and the Indispensability of Thought Experiments', *British Journal for the Philosophy of Science* 49, 397–424.

—— (2000), 'The Puzzle of Imaginative Resistance', *Journal of Philosophy* 97, 55–81.

Goldman, A. H. (1990), 'Interpreting Art and Literature', *Journal of Aesthetics and Art Criticism* 48, 205–14.

Goodman, N. (1968), *Languages of Art* (Indianapolis: Bobbs Merrill).

—— (1978), *Ways of Worldmaking* (Indianapolis: Hackett).

—— and C. Z. Elgin (1988), *Reconceptions in Philosophy and Other Arts and Sciences* (London: Routledge).

Grice, P. (1969), 'Utterer's Meaning and Intentions', *Philosophical Review* 78, 147–77.

—— (1975), 'Logic and Conversation', in P. Cole and J. L. Morgan (eds), *Syntax and Semantics*, Vol. 3 (New York: Academic Press), 41–58.

Hirsch, E. D. (1967), *Validity in Interpretation* (New Haven, Conn.: Yale University Press).

Hume, D. (1993a), 'Of the Standard of Taste', in *Selected Essays*, ed. S. Copley and A. Edgar (Oxford: Oxford University Press), 133–54 (1st publ. 1757).

—— (1993b), 'Of Tragedy', in *Selected Essays*, ed. S. Copley and A. Edgar (Oxford: Oxford University Press), 126–33 (1st publ. 1757).

Iseminger, G. (1992a), 'An Intentional Demonstration?', in Iseminger 1992b, 76–96.

—— (ed.) (1992b), *Intention and Interpretation* (Philadelphia: Temple University Press).

Jacobson, D. (1997), 'In Praise of Immoral Art', *Philosophical Topics* 25, 155–99.

John, E. (1995), 'Subtlety and Moral Vision in Fiction', *Philosophy and Literature* 19, 308–19.

Johnson, S. (1969), *Preface to Shakespeare's Plays* (Menston, England: Scolar's Press, 1969; 1st publ. 1765).

Kieran, M. (2005), *Revealing Art* (London: Routledge).

Kripke, S. (1980), *Naming and Necessity* 2nd revd edn (Cambridge, Mass.: Harvard University Press).

—— (unpubl.), 'Existence: Vacuous Names and Mythical Kinds'.

Lamarque, P. (1996), *Fictional Points of View* (Ithaca, NY: Cornell University Press).

—— (2003), 'Fiction', in J. Levinson (ed.), *Oxford Handbook of Aesthetics* (Oxford: Oxford University Press), 377–91.

—— and S. H. Olsen (1994), *Truth, Fiction, and Literature: A Philosophical Perspective* (Oxford: Oxford University Press).

Levinson, J. (1980), 'What a Musical Work Is', *Journal of Philosophy* 77, 5–28.

—— (1992), 'Intention and Interpretation: A Last Look', in Iseminger (1992b), 221–56.

—— (1997), 'Emotion in Response to Art: A Survey of the Terrain', in M. Hjort and S. Laver (eds), *Emotion and the Arts* (New York: Oxford University Press), 20–34.

Lewis, D. (1973), *Counterfactuals* (Cambridge, Mass.: Harvard University Press).

—— (1978), 'Truth in Fiction', *American Philosophical Quarterly* 15, 37–46.

Livingston, P. (1998), 'Intentionalism in Aesthetics', *New Literary History* 29, 831–46.

—— (2005), *Art and Intention* (Oxford: Oxford University Press).

Martel, M. (unpubl.), *L'œuvre comme interaction: anti-textualisme, action-alisme, et ontologie écologique*, Ph.D. diss., McGill University.

Matravers, D. (1998), *Art and Emotion* (Oxford: Oxford University Press).

—— (2003), 'Fictional Assent and the (So-called) "Puzzle of Imaginative Resistance"', in M. Kieran and D. Lopes (eds), *Imagination, Philosophy, and the Arts* (London: Routledge), 91–106.

Matthews, R. (1977), 'Describing and Interpreting Works of Art', *Journal of Aesthetics and Art Criticism* 36, 5–14.

Meinong, A. (1960), 'Theory of Objects', in R. Chisholm (ed.), *Realism and the Background of Phenomenology* (Glencoe, Ill.: Free Press; 1st publ. 1904), 76–117.

Miscevic, N. (1992), 'Mental Models and Thought Experiments', *International Studies in the Philosophy of Science* 6, 215–26.

Morreall, J. (1985), 'Enjoying Negative Emotions in Fictions', *Philosophy and Literature* 9, 95–102.

Morrison, B. (1998), *Too True* (London: Granta).

Murdoch, I. (1967), *The Sovereignty of Good* (Cambridge: Cambridge University Press).

Nathan, D. (1992), 'Irony, Metaphor, and the Problem of Intention', in Iseminger (1992b), 183–202.

Neill, A. (1992), 'On a Paradox of the Heart', *Philosophical Studies* 65, 53–65.

—— (1993), 'Fictions and the Emotions', *American Philosophical Quarterly* 30, 1–11.

Nersessian, N. (1993), 'In the Theoretician's Laboratory: Thought Experimenting as Mental Modelling', in D. Hull, M. Forbes and K. Okruhlik (eds), *PSA 1992*, vol. 2 (East Lansing, Mich.: Philosophy of Science Association), 291–301.

Norton, J. (1996), 'Are Thought Experiments Just What You Always Thought?', *Canadian Journal of Philosophy* 26, 333–66.

Novitz, D. (1980), 'Fiction, Imagination, and Emotion', *Journal of Aesthetics and Art Criticism* 38, 279–88.

—— (1987), *Knowledge, Fiction, and Imagination* (Philadelphia: Temple University Press).

Nussbaum, M. (1985), 'Finely Aware and Richly Responsible: Moral Attention and the Moral Task of Literature', *Journal of Philosophy* 82, 516–29.

Parsons, T. (1980), *Nonexistent Objects* (New Haven, Conn.: Yale University Press).

Paskins, B. (1977), 'On Being Moved by Anna Karenina and *Anna Karenina*', *Philosophy* 52, 344–47.

Plato (1941), *The Republic of Plato*, tr. F. M. Cornford (Oxford: Oxford University Press).

Putnam, H. (1978), 'Literature, Science, and Reflection', in *Meaning and the Moral Sciences* (Boston, Mass.: Routledge and Kegan Paul), 83–94.

Quine, W. v. O. (1963), 'On What There Is', in *From a Logical Point of View* (New York: Harper), 1–19.

Radford, C. (1975), 'How Can We Be Moved by the Fate of Anna Karenina? (I)', *Proceedings of the Aristotelian Society* suppl. vol. 49, 67–80.

Russell, B. (2001), 'On Denoting', repr. in A. P. Martinich (ed.), *The Philosophy of Language*, 4th edn (New York: Oxford University Press).

Searle, J. (1969), *Speech Acts* (Cambridge, Mass.: Cambridge University Press).

—— (1974), 'The Logical Status of Fictional Discourse', *New Literary History* 6, 319–32.

Sidney, Sir Philip (1966), *A Defence of Poetry* (London: Oxford University Press; 1st publ. 1595).

Sontag, S. (1973), *On Photography* (New York: Farrar, Straus and Giroux).

Steadman, P. (2001), *Vermeer's Camera* (Oxford: Oxford University Press).

Stecker, R. (1994), 'Art Interpretation', *Journal of Aesthetics and Art Criticism* 52, 193–206.

—— (1995), 'Relativism About Interpretation', *Journal of Aesthetics and Art Criticism* 53, 14–18.

—— (1996), 'What is Literature?', *Revue internationale de philosophie* 198, 681–94.

—— (2003), *Interpretation and Construction* (Oxford: Blackwell).

Stock, K. (2005), 'Resisting Imaginative Resistance', *Philosophical Quarterly* 55, 607–24.

Stolnitz, J. (1992), 'On the Cognitive Triviality of Art', *British Journal of Aesthetics* 32, 191–200.

Thomasson, A. (1999), *Fiction and Metaphysics* (Cambridge: Cambridge University Press).

Tolhurst, W., and S. Wheeler (1979), 'On Textual Individuation', *Philosophical Studies* 35, 187–97.

United States Circuit Court (1934), *United States v. One Book Entitled Ulysses by James Joyce*, 459 and Circuit Court of Appeals, 7 Aug. 1934, printed in 72 *Federal Reporter* 2nd ser., 705–11.

Walton, K. (1978), 'Fearing Fictions', *Journal of Philosophy* 75, 5–27.

—— (1983), 'Fiction, Fiction-making and Styles of Fictionality', *Philosophy and Literature* 7, 78–88.

—— (1990), *Mimesis as Make Believe* (Cambridge, Mass.: Harvard University Press).

—— (1994), 'Morals in Fiction and Fictional Morality', *Proceedings of the Aristotelian Society*, suppl. vol. 68, 27–50.

Weatherson, B. (2004), 'Morality, Fiction, and Possibility', Philosophers' Imprint 4.3 (<www.philosophersimprint.org/004003>), 1–27.

Weston, M. (1975), 'How Can We Be Moved by the Fate of Anna Karenina? (II)', *Proceedings of the Aristotelian Society*, suppl. vol. 49, 81–93.

Wilde, O. (1913), 'The Critic as Artist', *Intentions* 8th edn (London: Methuen; 1st publ. 1891), 93–128.

Wimsatt, W. K., and M. C. Beardsley (1946), 'The Intentional Fallacy', *Sewanee Review* 54, 468–88.

BIBLIOGRAPHY

Winch, P. (1964), 'Understanding a Primitive Society', *American Philosophical Quarterly* 1, 307–24.

Wolfe, T. (1973), *The New Journalism* (New York: Harper & Row).

Wollheim, R. (1980), *Art and Its Objects* (Cambridge: Cambridge University Press).

Wolterstorff, N. (1975), 'Toward an Ontology of Artworks', *Nous* 9, 115–42.

Yablo, S. (2002), 'Coulda, Woulda, Shoulda', in T. Gendler and J. Hawthorne (eds), *Conceivability and Possibility* (Oxford: Oxford University Press), 441–92.

Young, J. (2001), *Art and Knowledge* (London: Routledge).

—— (forthcoming), 'Literature, Representation, and Knowledge', in D. Davies and C. Matheson (eds), *Contemporary Readings in the Philosophy of Literature* (Peterborough Ont.: Broadview).

Zalta, E. (1983), *Abstract Objects* (Dordrecht: D. Reidel).

INDEX

CPSIA information can be obtained
at www.ICGtesting.com
Printed in the USA
LVHW082056220720
661297LV00008B/175